Additional Praise for *Create Your Own ETF Hedge Fund*

"If you're thinking about building a portfolio of ETFs, David Fry's expertise can help!"
—Charles E. Kirk, *The Kirk Report*

"I had the good fortune of working with David Fry when I was a rookie at PaineWebber in the late 1970s. Of all the people whom I have met in the securities industry, Dave may be the most diligent about putting his clients' interests first and managing the inevitable conflicts of interest that arise. Dave's greatest talent, though, is his ability to analyze and distill complex financial concepts and explain them in language that a reasonably intelligent layperson can understand."
—William W. Bowden, municipal bond trader and salesman

"David Fry is one of the most popular contributors to SeekingAlpha.com. His annotated charts and accompanying commentary provide an actionable and compelling commentary on the market."
—David Jackson, founder, Seeking Alpha

"In *Create Your Own ETF Hedge Fund*, Dave Fry channels his vast industry experience and keen insight into a practical and useful guide that will help investors effectively use ETFs as building blocks for their investment portfolios. Fry's description of how the markets developed along with the evolution of the participants and their incentives provides the context to further understand the relative effectiveness of ETFs, why ETFs have experienced such accelerated growth, and positive long-term prospects for the ETF industry and the investors who use them."
—Kevin Rich, CEO, DB Commodity Services LLC,
a wholly owned subsidiary of Deutsche Bank AG

"David's immense experience and expertise shine through in this highly enjoyable and invaluable insight into the evolution and use of ETFs, a necessary tool in the expanding universe of global investment."
—Terry Alexander, Head of Country Risk,
Business Monitor International

Create Your Own ETF Hedge Fund

Founded in 1807, John Wiley & Sons is the oldest independent publishing company in the United States. With offices in North America, Europe, Australia and Asia, Wiley is globally committed to developing and marketing print and electronic products and services for our customers' professional and personal knowledge and understanding.

The Wiley Finance series contains books written specifically for finance and investment professionals as well as sophisticated individual investors and their financial advisors. Book topics range from portfolio management to e-commerce, risk management, financial engineering, valuation and financial instrument analysis, as well as much more.

For a list of available titles, please visit our Web site at www.WileyFinance.com.

Create Your Own ETF Hedge Fund

A Do-It-Yourself ETF Strategy for Private Wealth Management

DAVID FRY

WILEY

John Wiley & Sons, Inc.

Published by John Wiley & Sons, Inc., Hoboken, New Jersey.
Published simultaneously in Canada.

Wiley Bicentennial logo: Richard J. Pacifico

For general information on our other products and services or for technical support, please contact our Customer Care Department within the United States at (800) 762-2974, outside the United States at (317) 572-3993 or fax (317) 572-4002.

Wiley also publishes its books in a variety of electronic formats. Some content that appears in print may not be available in electronic formats. For more information about Wiley products, visit our Web site at www.wiley.com.

Library of Congress Cataloging-in-Publication Data:

Fry, David, 1945–
  Create your own ETF hedge found: a do-it-yourself ETF strategy for private wealth management / David Fry.
      p.cm. — (Wiley finance series)
  Includes index.
  ISBN 978-0-470-13895-3 (cloth)
 1. Exchange traded funds.   2. Hedge funds.   3. Portfolio management.   I. Title.
  HG6043.F79 2008
  332.63′ 27—dc22
                                                                    2007029953

Printed in the United States of America.

10   9   8   7   6   5   4   3   2   1

For "FF"

Contents

CHAPTER 3
The Rise of Hedge Funds

CHAPTER 4
A Convergence Story

Acknowledgments

The author would like to thank the following people and organizations:

Tiburon Strategic Advisors
FPA Journal & Millicent Holmes
StockCharts.com
PowerShares
Hedge Fund Alert
Greg Newton, Naked Shorts
HedgeCo.net
Hedge Fund Research, Inc.
Stocks & Commodities Magazine
Richard Dennis
DB Commodity Services
Investment News
BusinessWeek
Nate Most
Index Universe
Investopedia.com
Investment Company Institute
Stephen Winks, SrConsultant.com
NYSE
AMEX
FTSE
Bloomberg.com
Forex-Markets.com
Financial Times
Morningstar
SSgA Funds
Barclays Global Investors
Mark Hoyer
Marissa Fry
Francia Fry
Seeking Alpha
Pritchett Cartoons
Shadow Government Statistics

Kitco.com
AMG Data Services
Charles Kirk [The Kirk Report]
Barron's
Investors Business Daily
the *Wall Street Journal*
The Economist
John W. Henry [John W. Henry & Company]
Ben Murillo Jr.
Robin Kameda
Patricia Reilly
Sidney Eng
Donald Putnam [Grail Partners, LLC]
The Hennessee Group

About the Author

Dave Fry has devoted more than 35 years to the business of trading and portfolio management. His registration as an arbitrator with both the National Association of Securities Dealers [NASD] and the National Futures Association [NFA] attests to his extensive experience and spotless compliance record.

Dave founded the ETF Digest in 2001 and was among the very first to see the need for a publication that provided individual investors with information and advice on ETF investing.

By 2002 ETF Digest trading programs were making triple-digit gains, despite the sharp overall market decline at that time, and Dave's newsletter began attracting favorable coverage in *Barron's* with three positive reviews in 2002, 2004, and 2007.

Dave is a frequent commentator on ETFs and other issues important to individual investors, and his perspectives are featured in financial news sources such as the *Wall Street Journal*, MarketWatch, *Investors Business Daily*, Smart Money, Dow Jones Newswire, *National Business Review*, MSN Money, Yahoo! Finance, Bankrate.com, Emerging Markets Monitor, IndexUniverse.com, and ETF Investor.

As the scope of ETF investing has expanded dramatically over the past few years, Dave has maintained a vital position as an investor advocate. He speaks out in favor of new ETFs to cover important market sectors and has seen new ETFs issued as a result. He is also very active in pointing out problems in the ETF marketplace to sponsors, issuers, brokers, and the media. Dave is committed to remaining at the forefront as this major investment trend continues to grow.

Some of the highlights of Dave's career before he launched ETF Digest include the following:

- In 1999, he founded TechInvest Inc. and began sharing his expertise through the Internet in his TechTrend Advisor newsletter.
- From 1997–1999, he was Managing Director, Proprietary Investments, at JWH Investment Management [JWHIMI], an affiliated company of John W. Henry & Company. In that capacity, Dave was responsible for the management of private investments as well as some corporate accounts.

- For a period of 10 years prior to joining JWHIMI, David owned and operated an NASD broker/dealer, Fry & Co., and an SEC registered investment advisory firm, Asia-Pacific Investment Management Inc. He was also a registered Commodity Pool Operator, Commodity Trading Advisor, and Introducing Broker.
- Prior to operating his own investment firms, Dave was a Vice President, Investments, at Shearson Lehman Bros. and held a similar position at Paine Webber.

During his tenure with registered firms he maintained the following licenses: Municipal Bond Principal [Series 53], Options Principal [Series 4], General Securities Principal [Series 24], General Securities [Series 7], Commodity [Series 3], State Securities License [Series 63], and State Insurance License [Life].

Introduction

To modify the message of a popular book, the investment world is *really* flat these days. Money flow to both traditional and far-flung overseas markets is increasing dramatically, major U.S. stock exchanges are merging with their overseas counterparts, electronic trading platforms are becoming more ubiquitous, and Wall Street firms are positioning themselves to take advantage of what soon will become a 24-hour trading world. As contemporary investors, you're either with the major trend of the twenty-first century both as to global exposure and hedge fund style, or as hip urbanites say, "You're so last century."

Here are the new facts and trends individual investors should know:

- The flow of *new* investment funds favors exchange traded funds [ETFs] more than common mutual funds or any other product except hedge funds.
- The number of ETFs in 2005 numbered 201 with assets of $296 billion.
- At the close of 2006 there were 359 issues with $417 billion in assets—a growth rate of nearly 80 percent year-over-year.
- And guess what? There are nearly 350 new ETFs in registration with the Securities and Exchange Commission [SEC] that if issued would double the issues outstanding in 2007.
- The number of new ETF issues is constrained only by the imagination of new product engineers on Wall Street.

ETFs are still tiny when compared to conventional mutual funds where according to the Investment Company Institute assets at the end of 2006 were $7.9 trillion excluding money market accounts, an increase of roughly $1 trillion from 2005. However, these figures include asset growth while fresh contributions including money market accounts averaged $140 billion—almost at the same rate as ETF growth.

Meanwhile according to consulting firm the Hennessee Group, hedge funds expanded from around 8,000 at the end of 2005 to 8,900 by the end of 2006. Further, assets under management grew from roughly $1 trillion to $1.3 trillion by the end of 2006. The source of all these funds comes from a variety of institutional and high net worth individuals. And many of these funds utilize ETFs as a major part of their focus.

All this activity isn't lost on conventional mutual fund issuers. A convergence story is developing whereby mutual funds will start issuing hedge fund-like funds using ETFs as basic components. Incorporating these strategies will allow mutual funds to charge and maintain higher fees. Doing so will alleviate some of the drain conventional mutual funds are losing to low-cost ETFs.

As someone who's spent more than three decades either managing investments or advising clients one thing remains clear to me: Things change. If you're an advisor utilizing antiquated financial plans from the past century, you're behind the curve. To retain your clients, keep them satisfied, and grow your business, you'll need to adopt a newer approach. In so doing you'll be perceived as contemporary knowledgeable, and on the cutting edge of investment trends.

Further, the business model for financial advisors is ever changing. Commissions have yielded to discount firms and in-house "wrap fee" accounts, discount firms are facing competition from commission-free regimes, and recurring fee-based models built on high mutual fund fees are being threatened by low-cost ETFs that pay no fees to advisors. Finally, younger investors are more in tune with the online world and will opt for the more hip route rather than seeking an advisor.

What's an advisor to do? If you can't beat 'em, join 'em. Use ETFs in a portfolio structure that incorporates simple hedge fund strategies, charge a realistic fee for doing so and grow your business. That may include trendier mutual fund issues that will incorporate hedge fund-like strategies.

Individual investors who want to change or break away from their conventional relationships and plans find it difficult. For retail investors most Wall Street firms are designed like a typical casino—easy to find your way in, hard to find your way out. Most investors feel trapped and handcuffed to outdated, inflexible, and costly financial plans as assets are distributed over a wide variety of high-fee mutual funds. And most of these funds contain costly redemption fees, making the exit even more difficult.

This book is designed to help you by:

- Demystifying hedge funds.
- Explaining why they're so popular.
- Outlining basic portfolio strategies in a clear and easy to understand language.
- Outlining the number and type of current, new, and proposed ETFs that provide you the tools you need to put some oomph into your investment returns.

And, most importantly, give you sample portfolios to help you get started.

Even with the simple strategies outlined in this book, individual investors may still want help either because the information is still overwhelming, they don't have time, or they like their current advisor. There are tools available to help both individuals and advisors alike such as investment newsletters that can assist both in portfolio construction, research, and timing. If you're an individual investor not interested in the do it yourself [DIY] thing, find an investment advisor who understands the concepts outlined in this book and is willing to implement them for a reasonable fee.

Most investors are intrigued by the buzz about popular hedge funds and feel like they're on the outside looking in. High investment level thresholds, usually greater than $1,000,000 are off-putting or beyond the reach of most investors. So hedge funds have remained the playground of the superrich.

Again, a wide variety of ETFs from those linked to basic equity market indexes, currency, commodity, Emerging Market, fixed income, and so forth, combined with severely discounted [or even new commission-free accounts] have given typical investors the tools they need to get in the game. And this is true without having to pay the enormous fixed and incentive fee laden funds customarily the province of hedge funds.

There are at least 20 different hedge fund strategies and structures. Average investors wouldn't be interested in 99 percent of them from Distressed Securities to Convertible Arbitrage. These strategies exist to fit complex and arcane overall institutional portfolio needs beyond the interest of retail investors. No, this book primarily focuses on the most common and popular Global Macro Long/Short and Aggressive Growth themes where portfolios are constructed to take advantage of both bullish and bearish conditions across the globe. Although available for those wishing to use it, the use of leverage is not required, only a desire and willingness to put a plan of action together and, if necessary, find the help you need to put it to work.

What is commonplace on the investment scene is that popular hedge fund investment strategies and new products like ETFs become overdone as their attraction increases. For example, as the summer of 2007 ended hedge fund strategies revolving around "private equity" peaked as a so-called credit crunch developed making new buyouts almost impossible to finance. Further, strategies utilizing leveraged mortgage-backed securities and exotic derivatives like CDOs [Collateralized Debt Obligations] caused heavy investor losses. As July 2007 data revealed nervous investors withdrew assets [$32 billion] from hedge funds for the first time since 2000 according to TrimTabs BarclayHedge Fund report. It would come as no surprise if this trend continued.

The tsunami of ETF issuance seems overdone to most and it probably is. But from our perspective the more ETFs the better since among the many being issued will be some needed that can complete an all-ETF hedge fund. We strive to identify only those ETFs from the hundreds issued that are the most useful.

This book will help you develop a strategy that suits your goals and personality. Better still, we outline real portfolio construction techniques that are easy to explain and implement.

Contemporary Investment Conditions

Hobson's Choice

For the Model T, you may have any color as long as it's black.
                                        —Henry Ford

"**H**obson's choice" originated from English liveryman Thomas Hobson, who kept at least 40 horses for hire but never let a customer choose his own horse in the stable. He offered only the horse nearest the door or no horse at all.

No choice at all has been the theme for many retail investors when securing investment choices from most FAs [financial advisors, consultants, and brokers]. In 2004 a distressed friend told me of a difficult situation she was experiencing with her FA, also a family friend of hers, making solutions even more awkward. She is a well-educated, intelligent, professional person and has maintained a long-term relationship with her FA who was associated with a well-known national firm. She had a variety of small accounts, which the advisor loaded up with high fee mutual funds that pay a share of the recurring annual fees back to the firm and advisor.

She had become increasingly dissatisfied with the low returns, so she asked the FA if she could consolidate her accounts and invest in exchange-traded funds [ETFs] or index funds instead since she had read and heard so many positive things about them. Rather than accommodate her, the advisor just told her no, that it wouldn't be appropriate for her and to stick with what she had. Further she was told that what positive attributes she had heard about ETFs and index funds was nonsense, that if she went down that road, the commissions to make these changes would be too high both in redemption penalties and transaction commissions. Frustrated and very reluctantly, she did as she was told but her relationship with her family friend and FA was forever changed.

So, you might ask, how did she allow her FA to set up the accounts in this manner? Didn't she know about the penalties for early redemption? The facts are straightforward but this type of situation occurs more often than most expect and with the same unpleasant results. A typical problem might start with a client calling their FA saying, "I have some funds to invest. What do you recommend?" The FA will give what they consider a good recommendation and then most busy clients accept the advice and give the go-ahead. Both are too impatient. The FA wants the client to buy their recommendation and if avoidable not be bothered explaining alternative choices. The client isn't interested in listening to lengthy and complex alternatives, either. The clients don't ask a lot of questions since they're busy and just want to get this task scratched from the "to do" list and get on with their work. It's just human nature, but down the road problems often surface. Whose fault? Both are to blame.

CURRENT SITUATION: THE CAPTIVE CLIENT

Most firms have set up their investment plans like Las Vegas would design a typical casino—easy to find your way in but almost impossible to find your way out. If you get dissatisfied with what you own, or you didn't ask all the right questions up front, you will find just impractical or costly surprises to make needed or desirable changes. And in the end, like my friend, you will just find frustration and feelings of helplessness.

Many individual investors have their financial savings locked up in retirement accounts that offer them only one choice: to keep adding money every year to the the plan some sponsor, employer, advisor, or broker has set up for them. And, unfortunately from the market top of 2000 through 2006, most conventional mutual fund averages have underperformed both conventional index funds and ETFs. As outlined in Chapter 2 some mutual funds have barely broken even over that period. I can't tell you how many times some acquaintances have said, "Well, my account is finally back to the previous high after five years."

As noted in *Financial Services Review*, Summer 2006 edition by John Haslem, H. Kent Baker, and David M. Smith, "The bulk of the evidence, however, suggests that actively managed funds, on average, underperform benchmark portfolios with equivalent risk by a statistically and economically significant margin [Jensen, 1968; Malkiel, 1995; Gruber, 1996; Carhart, 1997]. That is, after accounting for expenses and transactions costs, active managers typically destroy value." A sobering thought.

HOW THE INVESTMENT BUSINESS CHANGED

How did the lack of investment choice get this way? In May 1975 the U.S. Congress ended the NYSE's fixed-commission schedule that Wall Street firms charged and the era of discount commissions was introduced. Most retail brokers didn't think much of the change since it primarily affected institutional business, at least initially. So brokers continued to charge relatively high retail commissions until Charles Schwab & Co., which entered the markets around the same time, really started to gain traction with retail investors in the early 1980s. Schwab was joined by others and by the mid- to late 1980s there were several well-established discount firms dealing with both institutional and retail investors.

Most brokers scoffed at the upstart discounters. In fact, many major Wall Street firms told their landlords that if they rented to one of those firms, they would terminate their lease for cause. I did my share of scoffing, too; I was living off those high commissions myself. As a matter of fact, I prided myself on being ahead of industry trends then since I was one of the first brokers in the firm to make a living by gathering client assets for outside money managers. Managers paid me commissions from the accounts at the full retail rate, thank you very much, and both the client and I were seemingly content.

Then sometime in 1987, the firm I was then associated with, Shearson Lehman Bros., presented a tape from Fidelity Investments that its high-end brokers were asked to watch. Both firms had exchanged tapes regarding their respective vision of the financial services future. [We didn't get to see our firm's tape, which with hindsight would've been as, or more, interesting.] At that time Fidelity was the leading sponsor of mutual funds and had started a complementary discount brokerage firm. The CEO of Fidelity made a convincing case that the discount commission and mutual fund business were going to continue to grow due to expanding retirement accounts and favorable Baby Boomer demographics challenging the conventional Wall Street models—including mine!

After initially dismissing these themes out of pride, I started to notice a short time later that the money managers hired for my clients were starting to agitate for lower commission rates. Excuse me? Every broker in this position would naturally resist at first. But the money manager stated it was his fiduciary duty to seek the best transaction prices and his peers were doing the same. You certainly can't go to your clients and complain that you want to make more of their money when better executions were available. So, you went along. Commissions started to drop in short order from an average of 1 percent per transaction to just pennies.

What to do? Since most FAs were paying nearly 60 percent of what was left of the commission revenue to their firm, perhaps it would be better to alter that relationship by starting my own firm. I rented some cheap office space, went through the expensive and exhausting registration and licensing requirements, and after all was done changed the split, increasing our take before expenses to 85 percent. We also registered with the Securities and Exchange Commission [SEC] as investment advisors so that we could share some of the managers fee income the money manager was charging. This was an awkward period since the money manager also wasn't interested in sharing but eventually saw my worth as a member of the team. Now we were on the same side working in the client's best interests.

But our commission revenues suffered as customers who didn't qualify for privately managed accounts, or who wanted to do their own thing, including some of our best trading oriented clients, started to take a portion of their business to places like Schwab. A good client who might usually buy 1,000 shares of stock from us was suddenly just buying a few hundred shares and taking the balance to the discount firm. And that's if we were lucky!

It got worse. Our in-house research analyst wrote a report recommending a stock. I mailed the report to a client who called to chat about it subsequently. He placed no order. Then about a year later the analyst put out a sell recommendation on the stock. The stock dropped and I received a call from the client who seemed interested as to what happened to the stock. The client was upset that the stock had dropped and became even more furious when told that we had put a sell recommendation on it previously. Believing that the client hadn't bought the stock, or so we thought, he hadn't received the sell recommendation. No, he obviously had purchased it from a discount firm. So he was taking our research that we were paying a high cost analyst to research and prepare a report only to take his business to a discount firm. This is something that happens every day now, and is a big part of the reason that investment banks have cut back on their research efforts.

Needless to say, we had to find a way to compete and raise a lot more money. One way was to hire more brokers and grow the company. So we proceeded to grow following that path over the next 10 years. But in a highly regulated environment where the largest firms dominate and have more influence over the rules, they can make things rough for the smaller firms. After all, they have the economies of scale to deal with all the regulatory requirements including filings, audits, examinations, additional registrations, reporting requirements, and endless red tape. You start a small broker/dealer and investment advisory firm to manage your clients' investments, and end up spending more time on regulatory matters, benefiting the big firms by driving smaller competitors out of business. Anyway, I did something about it and sold the company.

Now I'm back to doing what I value most, studying the markets and writing about it them our newsletter, but that's another story.

THE AGE OF THE DIY INVESTOR

Many retail investors don't realize they can pursue other alternatives on their own without complicating their lives too much. If you have a computer, an Internet connection, and enough money—and it doesn't have to be a huge amount, although more is always better—you can do everything yourself.

The success of the discount brokerage firms has made investing online a low cost and convenient way to deal with investments for those willing to take the time to do so.

During the 1990s when the bull market was roaring day trading became a popular activity even for the most unsophisticated investor. Armed with

"Online Trading Makes Broker Obsolete."
Source: Courtesy Pritchett Cartoons.

high-speed computers and handheld quote devices, individuals were having a great time. Some quit their jobs and started trading full-time for a living. Small unlicensed shops sprang up sponsored obliquely by newbie online firms where individuals could open accounts and learn rudimentary trading skills. It all worked well until the bear market arrived in 2000. By the time it was all over in early 2003, most of these boutiques were closed and the full-time traders were back looking for conventional employment.

As we learn in Chapter 2 online investing reached a peak in 2000, fell substantially with the bear market, but is now back to the heights of 2000. Many online brokers consolidated during the bear market as day traders and others left the scene for greener pastures or more stable forms of investing. After all, the quick money crowd who were day trading later found flipping real estate a new and more lucrative activity at least until that, too, ended in late 2005.

As firms consolidated, their services expanded to include more online investing help while at the same time a commission price war ensued. Of course all this accrued to the benefit of customers. Commissions for transactions have been reduced to single digits for most online firms. In late 2006, Zecco.com, a new online brokerage firm, introduced the "zero commission" structure. That's right "zero." That action was quickly matched by Bank of America Securities for accounts with $25,000 minimum balances. And in February 2007, Wells Fargo also introduced a zero commission structure for 100 transactions per year for accounts also with $25,000 minimum balances. The services aren't as free as they look, though. These accounts pay very low interest rates, and some have questioned execution quality. No doubt, however, this commission model will pressure the traditional online brokers, much as the online brokers in their day pressured traditional brokers' revenues.

New services offered by online firms allow you to more easily monitor your portfolio checking on performance, asset allocation, dividends, and taxes with an open architecture to make further customization constrained only by your own imagination. Low cost and even free IRA accounts are standard fare as are many other services online investors would expect only from conventional wire-house firms.

The big wire-houses have fought with the "wrap" account concept that offered free trading, with some limits [200 trades a year at Merrill Lynch], all-inclusive fee for high net worth clients. The fee charges are on a sliding scale with lower fees maybe less than 1 percent per annum for balances greater than $1 million. The initiative goes some way toward meeting the challenge, but has run into regulatory problems as some firms moved large, but largely inactive accounts, into this structure, essentially charging customers huge sums for what are basically custodial services.

Customers with other managed assets, such as hedge funds and privatized partnerships, can be "stuck" if they don't want to deal with the complexity of different accounts at different institutions, but the writing is on the wall for this business. After all 1 percent on $1 million is $10,000. That's a foolish amount for investors to pay and eventually they'll get hip to it.

Younger investors who are starting to earn and save funds in their retirement accounts are more likely to want to do their own thing online in the most contemporary manner but they'll want more help and tools. Further they will gravitate toward ETFs since they are easy to use with many different issues and sectors to choose from.

DIY investors will find many resources to help them structure and employ various strategies including guidance with some handholding from online investment newsletters and other conventional news sources. Younger investors may find most current FAs to be a little too old school for their tastes. Further all the scandals over the past decade that have rocked the mutual fund and brokerage community have been off-putting.

IF YOU CAN'T BEAT 'EM, JOIN 'EM

Just as when I first saw that Fidelity tape, for the contemporary advisor things are beginning to change again. And the changes are coming fast and furious—more quickly than can be written about. The ETF boom taking off in earnest in early 2004 has overwhelmed the financial markets with a wide array of low-cost products and choices. Their popularity is challenging conventional business models for FAs as retail investors want to participate in the most contemporary investment models and schemes.

Today's modern broker is not the same skilled and educated financial expert common several decades ago. When just a teenager in Chicago, I asked my father what all the men did for work who were walking home from the train station early in the afternoon while everyone else was working later hours. He said they were probably working at the commodity exchanges downtown. I was intrigued by them and their profession. They toted their ubiquitous *Wall Street Journal* [WSJ] under their arm, had an enigmatic aura about them and what they did for a living. I tried to read the *WSJ* once back then, but I may as well have been reading a detailed medical journal. I wanted to learn more since this looked like an intriguing profession. Besides, from a youthful perspective, these guys got off work early!

But seriously, when first entering the business I worked for a "wire-house," which is an old expression that defined firms headquartered in New York that had remote offices scattered about the country connected by a teletype or wire. These firms pushed product just like firms today do mutual funds and other managed money products. The difference was that back in the mid-1970s firms pushed stocks and bonds primarily. Perhaps they took down positions of stock in inventory, marked them up, and dispatched them over the wire to the brokers to pitch to their clients with a detailed story. A broker in those days needed to know a lot about stocks and bonds beyond the scripted story. Many experienced brokerage clients and prospects would have good questions and you had to have good answers.

Since I started in the business as a bond salesman if I wanted to expand my business to stocks it was better to find others more knowledgeable about the subject than me to do it. That's how I gravitated to the now popular "managed-money" format.

Not meant as a putdown but today's FA just carries the *WSJ* around for show. That doesn't mean they're unskilled but they don't know as much about stocks, bonds, or other complex financial instruments as did their predecessors. They don't come to the business educated in finance and accounting. Studying and understanding corporate financial reports including balance sheets, earnings statements, and strategy are skills of a former age. Today's FAs are trained to pass the various licensing tests, taught asset gathering techniques, and provided computer generated financial plans designed to sell products. The latter advisors allocate assets to a range of high-fee mutual funds or even individual money managers, getting you to fund them and to continue doing so with perhaps occasional reallocations.

Changing from a commission to a fee-based business model was the major brokerage firm's strategy to compete with the discount firms. Most wire-house firms liked the idea of gathering assets or building "evergreen income" [industry jargon for developing recurring fee income structures] approaches for many reasons. First, it was easy to supply the brokers with product like mutual funds. Second, many believed there would be less compliance issues from trading abuses of ["churning" primarily] common stocks, options, and commodity trading—but as we shall see later they were mistaken on that count.

For clients with small accounts the FA's fee business tools of choice were mutual funds. Firms made deals with mutual fund families, provided FAs with computer driven financial plans that spit out canned presentations for clients with certain profiles including risk tolerance, age, goals and objectives, and so forth. The broker/FA would enter the data and out would pop a series of recommendations. The FA would then present the preferred models to the client and let them make choices.

Clients with larger assets would be offered an SMA [separately managed account]. This would consist of the obligatory computer driven financial plan but in lieu of mutual funds would incorporate firm approved outside money managers to allocate the assets as if they were mutual funds.

It all sounds convenient and compelling for all parties involved. Naturally there were flaws. Many computer driven financial plans are based on previous performance data that may contain 5 to 10 years of data. If the previous study period benefited a certain style over another it doesn't necessarily follow that the future period will replicate the past. It's a major "garbage in, garbage out" pitfall for most computer driven models. And since most modern FAs have more of this kind of experience and knowledge than from basic investing skills, trouble can often be the result.

For SMA accounts the FA's firm locates suitable money managers through their own internal due diligence process and cuts marketing deals with them. It doesn't necessarily follow that firms on the approved list are the best money managers in each style category since the best probably don't need to share fee revenue with anyone. Naturally, this is a significant conflict of interest that needs more disclosure than the industry currently provides. It's logical to assume that firms sometimes feature only money managers who are the most fee lucrative to them versus the best for the client. This is a conflict simmering beneath the surface and not often discussed.

BAD APPLES AND UNETHICAL PRACTICES

As in any other profession there are some bad apples. Before the industry changed from a commission to a fee-based model most of the abuses revolved around "churning" where brokers whipped their client's portfolio assets around more for the commissions than for the client's well-being. The practice was the subject of many complaints and litigation.

Broker and FA abuses typically involve mutual fund switching, purposeful multiple allocations to avoid commission breakpoints, and other nondisclosure issues.

Many mutual funds are offered in four series: A, B, C, and H shares. Series A shares are termed front-end loaded, generating the highest *initial* sales commission that may exceed 5 percent of assets, meaning less money at work for you. Series B are back-end loaded and spread a lower fee out many years with a penalty if you wish to redeem before a certain date. Series C are level-load funds where a lower fee is charged every year without redemption penalties. H shares are no-load offerings that allow FAs the ability to add a recurring management fee of their own on top of existing management fees charged by the fund.

A common unethical practice is having clients switch frequently from one high front-end loaded Class A series fund to another to earn excessive commissions, also considered churning.

Breakpoints are threshold levels where sales loads or broker commissions are reduced. When breakpoints are used, commissions can be reduced from around 5 percent to maybe 2 percent or less making them cheaper to own over the long term, although FAs just receive that commission once. Some abuses occur when sales are made just beneath the breakpoint. Further, most mutual funds are sponsored by firms that offer a "family of funds" with perhaps similar or very different objectives. Another serious abusive practice is for the FA to recommend several different A funds from different fund families depriving you of cost-saving breakpoint opportunities from within a fund family.

It's the FA's duty to inform you of alternative opportunities and to wisely recommend distribution of your assets in a cost-effective manner. Further, it is their supervisor's duty to monitor the FA's activities since they personally initial and inspect every transaction ticket.

Class B, or 12b-1 funds have become the most popular offerings for career FAs. They like them because B shares provide them with a potentially higher recurring income over the long term from annual fee splits with the mutual fund company than if they sold the initially more costly Class A share series. Selfishly or nefariously FAs also like them because sometimes costly redemption fees keep investors captive to the fund since clients are less likely to leave. As noted previously, within the business model this is known in the trade as building "evergreen income" for the FA. It is their primary career focus.

It is in this latter area where more unchallenged abuses occur. My friend who wanted to alter her accounts found the redemption fee an undisclosed surprise. Many FAs don't really explain this negative feature to their clients upfront or clients don't understand that the financial plan, based on old historical assumptions, won't work. Only then do they discover or remember the redemption fee drawback. If the mutual fund performs poorly and the investor wants to make a change, they still must pay the redemption fee on top of enduring poor results.

FAs also like investment plans that require you to add more funds every year, [IRAs and other contribution plans] because even if these plans make no money, the FAs can continue to collect their fees.

Based on fines levied by regulators, management at the top of each firm has also been complicit in unethical and undisclosed conflicts of interest. In the recent past management had created selling agreements favoring one mutual fund family versus another not owing to anything other than more lucrative agreements with the fund. For example, mutual funds might request brokerage firms to grant them special "shelf space" [like merchandise at the supermarket] in exchange for certain favors. Such have included brokerage transaction kickbacks created by the fund that benefit the brokerage firm. Management might also create and implement sales contests and other promotional schemes to promote certain funds, which had been another undisclosed conflict of interest. Further abuses include offering incentives such as special bonuses, sports and theater tickets, golf outings, expensive trips, and other benefits.

According to a February 19, 2007 article from *Investment News*, "Many brokerage firms are disclosing the existence of 'shelf space' agreements but are not disclosing the details of those agreements." So severe are some conditions that the article notes:

> *Smith Barney and UBS Financial Services Inc. of New York and Morgan Stanley say that funds that don't pay to be in their top tier of providers aren't allowed to send wholesalers to their branch offices. In its own disclosure documents, Merrill Lynch & Co. Inc. of New York says funds that do 'not enter into [shelf-space] arrangements ... are generally not offered to clients.' " And in a concluding comment from an anonymous Smith Barney broker the article continues, "I'm not sure [Smith Barney] is really searching for the best funds or it's just a matter of who's paying."*

These types of schemes aren't just confined to typical Wall Street wire-house firms. MetLife Inc. was sued in January 2007 for allegedly providing secret incentives to its advisors to meet quotas for sales of its proprietary mutual funds and life policies. As noted in a March 5, 2007 article also from *Investment News*, "Advisers often wind up selling the proprietary products, because they flock like moths to a flame to products paying greater compensation," noted attorney Andrew Stoltmann a securities attorney and partner with Stoltmann Law Offices PC in Chicago.

HIGH PRESSURE ENVIRONMENT

Working as an FA isn't all peaches and cream. There's a lot of pressure on FAs to perform and meet production mandates. This pressure can often tempt FAs to make poor or unethical judgments. For the underachievers, and you know who you are, things can get pretty ugly.

In an October 16, 2006 *Investment News* article it was noted that James Gorman, President, Global Wealth Management Group, Morgan Stanley called for "brutal treatment of the lower half of the brokerage force, because—like it or not—a company is defined by its bottom half." In the same article it was noted that Gorman was also chairman of the Securities Industry Association [which has since merged with the Bond Market Asssociation to form the Securities Industry & Financial Markets

Association]. "I'm sure what he said wasn't cleared by SIA, but when the chairman of an organization makes a statement, it's difficult for the organization to back away from it, especially at a function where he's the keynote [speaker]," noted Ross Albert, partner with Morris Manning & Martin LLP of Atlanta.

And lastly, within the same article, Steve Winks, principal of SR Consultant.com of Richmond, Virginia, states, "Nobody wants to acknowledge the reality of the brokerage industry, which is that most novice brokers receive cursory training and then spend five years working phone books in an attempt to survive."

No, it can become an ugly picture and only reinforces my previous more negative description of the modern FA.

THE REGULATORS CRACKDOWN

The frenetic growth of both mutual funds and the brokers selling them could only mean there would probably be trouble ahead. Pushing more lucrative commission laden mutual funds at the expense of others and receiving commission kickbacks started to give the industry a black eye and hurt them in the wallet.

- In 2003 Morgan Stanley was fined $50 million for pushing their own and other more costly mutual funds at the expense of more cost-effective offerings.
- In late December 2004 Edward D. Jones was fined $75 million for failing to disclose conflicts of interest with certain mutual funds. According to the National Association of Securities Dealers [NASD] December 22 NASD order, "Edward Jones told the public and its clients that it was promoting the sale of the Preferred Families [the name the firm gave to mutual funds it preferred its brokers to sell] mutual funds because of the fund's long-term investment objectives and performance. At the same time, Edward Jones failed to disclose that it received tens of millions of dollars from the Preferred Families each year, on top of commission and other fees, for selling their mutual funds. Edward Jones also failed to disclose that such payments were a material factor, among others, in becoming and remaining an Edward Jones Preferred Family member."
- In January 2005, the NASD fined American Funds Distributors for $100 million in undisclosed commission kickbacks to 50 different brokerage firms selling or pushing their products.
- In February 2005 the NASD fined Quick & Reilly [now a part of Bank of America Securities] and Piper Jaffrey nearly $1 million for directed commissions back to firms promoting their mutual funds.

- In the spring of 2005 the NASD leveled $21 million in fines against American Express Financial Advisors, Chase Investment Services, and Smith Barney for pushing mutual funds that carry higher fees such as Class B funds without telling customers that Class A funds would be cheaper over the long term and could be purchased at a discount [breakpoints].
- June 2005, 14 different brokerage firms involved with AIG mutual funds were fined $34 million for pushing higher cost funds without offering competing funds that were more cost-effective.

The litany of fines continues to this day. In February 2007, the NASD fined Fidelity Investments $3.75 million for among other reasons poor record and that Fidelity Distributors, the chief underwriter for Fidelity Mutual Funds, failed to "supervise certain registered individuals for compliance with Fidelity's ethics and conflicts of interest policies." The latter finding revolved around gifts to Justin Timberlake and Christina Aguilera concerts, chartered flights, tickets and lodging at expensive hotels, and "twenty bottles of wine." So, the beat goes on and one must wonder, "What is it about the rules they don't get?"

The previous is just a portion of the fines levied against both brokerage firms and mutual fund companies. These fines expose the level of corruption that can occur within the industry at all levels. And this doesn't include abuses and fines from the so-called "mutual fund timing scandal," which thus far has netted an additional $2 billion in fines and counting, discussed in the next section.

The compliance and legal benefits imagined by the bigwigs running wire-house switching from high commissions to a fee-based business didn't exactly pan out as planned. This was because the fee business came with its own set of compliance issues that were largely ignored in the rush to cash in on the stock boom.

At the extreme, and without naming names [you know who they are], what can you say about some firms who set up FAs in claptrap one person offices, put them through a crash license testing course, arm them with the most high cost mutual funds, and have them out on the street in rapid fire succession schlepping mutual funds door-to-door like encyclopedia salespeople? Without a proper education and training what kind of ethical behavior can you expect?

We all know about how many real estate salespersons suddenly appear with licenses when that market is hot. Or suddenly everyone you know is a mortgage broker. The same thing occurred with the proliferation of new stockbrokers as financial markets experienced a bull market from the 1980s until the bubble burst in 2000. And new mutual fund families stepped in to grow with them aided by demographics from the new investor class, the Baby Boomers, and the advent of IRAs and other tax deferred savings vehicles. Funds grew from around 1,000 in 1982 to more than 8,600 by the end of 2006 and according to the Investment Company Institute [ICI] assets grew to nearly $10 trillion.

Not to be left out were banks and insurance companies. When the Glass-Steagall Act, which prohibited banks from owning brokerage firms, was allowed to meet its demise in the mid-1990s, banks quickly stepped in to establish mutual fund sales desks within each branch. Trust officers and even bank tellers were getting licensed to push new mutual fund products. Some large CPA firms got themselves licensed as broker/dealers along with some of their accountants. The thinking was, Who was in a better position than your accountant to make investment recommendations? In short, everyone wanted to cash in on the boom times. Now some of these firms are abandoning their brokerage operations given their obvious conflicts of interest with clients.

Now seriously, what can all these folks suddenly know about the investment world in such short order? Not much. So when I say the average FA is not the *WSJ* toting financial expert of decades ago, you can easily grasp the point. That's why the industry suffered so many abuses caused by an uneducated sales force and management just there to "make hay while the sun shines" if you'll pardon the old proverb.

Don't get me wrong; mutual funds have their place and we'll explore in later chapters what should be a more contemporary use of them.

THE MOTHER OF ALL MUTUAL FUND SCANDALS

One thing is clear: The mutual fund industry operates on a double standard. Certain companies and individuals have been given the opportunity to manipulate the system. They make illegal after-hours trades and improperly exploit market swings in ways that harm long-term investors.
— New York Attorney General Eliot Spitzer,
September 3, 2003

Aside from the litany of abuses already listed, the most publicized scandal was the so-called "market timing" affair that rocked the mutual fund industry further from 2002 to 2005. As was mentioned previously the consequences have been more than $2 billion in fines meted out to a variety of well-known brokerage firms, mutual funds, and hedge funds.

Not many people realize that using mutual funds for "market-timing" strategies had been a long-standing practice among a small group of specialized asset managers, and a larger group of registered investment advisors handling client accounts. The constant skirmishing between these traders and mutual funds was a major contributing factor in the emergence of now well-known companies like Rydex and ProFunds who developed special derivatives-based mutual funds that were intended to offer daily liquidity. The ProFunds affiliate, ProShares, brought these products to the ETF market in mid-2006.

What was different about the latest market-timing scandal was the scale of corruption uncovered. It started small with the initial disclosure that hedge fund Canary Capital Partners had entered into schemes with a variety of mutual funds and brokers that included Bank of America, Bank One, and both Janus and Strong funds. It was just the tip of the iceberg for as the investigation continued, more and more similar circumstances of abuse surfaced: "Every time we turn over a rock in the mutual fund business, we find vermin crawling beneath it," Spitzer said.

There were two elements to the scandal: Late Trading and Market Timing.

1. In the instance of Late Trading, net asset values [NAV] are established for mutual funds at 4 P.M. or the close of trading each day. Orders placed before are given that NAV valuation and execution price. Any orders placed thereafter are given the next day's closing NAV. With late trading, some funds allowed firms like Canary to take post 4 P.M. market moving news and receive transactions based on that day's closing NAV. Canary and others' purchases diluted the holding of long-term investors in the fund when buying the shares and then flipping them out a day or two later.

2. Market Timing on the other hand is not illegal as long as the rules of the mutual fund company permit it. In some cases, however, the fund's prospectus noted that firms who engaged in active buying and selling of funds would be barred from further transactions. However, some funds looked the other way and didn't prohibit the activity, instead agreeing to allow the trading in return for so-called "sticky" assets placed in other funds. In other cases, hedge funds evaded the funds' "timing police" by opening multiple accounts and otherwise working the system for their own benefit. The creativity was, in some ways, admirable: One hedge fund offered its employees dinner at the most expensive restaurants in New York in return for undergoing health checks for variable annuity insurance policies; the manager then used those polices to make the the market-timing trades.

The scandal took down some of the biggest names in the business. Richard Strong, founder of the Strong mutual fund family, was banned from the business, along with the Pilgrim Baxter founders. Dozens of executives lost their jobs in the fallout, which involved congressional hearings and SEC investigation that continues four years later and provided further evidence that money mnagers don't always have their clients best interests in mind.

BUT WAIT, THERE'S MORE POTENTIAL SCANDAL AHEAD

Are Wall Street trading scandals a thing of the past? Not a chance. With so much information and money changing hands every day there's bound to be abuse. It's naive to think otherwise. In fact, according to a February 2007 report from *Fortune* magazine, "the SEC is investigating whether major brokerage firms were tipping off hedge funds to the trades brokers handle for big clients like mutual funds." This activity is called front-running and is illegal since it relies on inside information to succeed. As Doug Atkin, the former CEO of Instinet who now runs the research boutique Majestic Research says, "Privileged information is the real currency that runs Wall Street." Amen.

Scandals like this usually start with a few drips and end with a torrent of fines, more black eyes for firms, and a continual shattering of the ethic of fair dealings.

Doesn't it make sense then that individual investors want more not less control over their investments?

CLIENT RUMBLINGS AND GRUMBLINGS

All this cumulative malfeasance coupled with the bear markets of 2000 to 2003 wasn't lost on many individual investors. They wanted change but again were locked in by costly redemption fees and uncooperative FAs.

Indeed, according to a survey conducted by Charles Schwab in their Advisor Outlook Study reported in *Investment News*, March 12, 2007, "Accounts that clients transfer from wirehouse brokers have investment guideline statements that consistently are misaligned with client financial goals. Fully 75% of these accounts arrive with poorly structured portfolios, according to 1,400 registered investment advisers—managing a combined $347 billion in assets."

Most whiz-bang financial plans offered to investors don't include ETFs since they're set up to deliver returns directly to the investor, not to provide recurring fee income to advisors. This is because ETFs are tied to established indexes where management skills are less [they just have to hold the same assets in the same proportion as the linked index] and they don't have special share classes that pay commissions, making for lower costs. It's understandable that the purveyors of high cost mutual funds would fight this trend since their income is under assault. FAs and conventional mutual funds have been busy putting down ETFs for one reason or another. Mutual fund research firms like Morningstar have made their living on that industry and are trying to add ETF research, but they seem stuck in the mode of offering criticism for criticism's sake, overlooking the benefits to individual investors of entirely new investment offerings. Gold's a good example of a place where investors can now make their investment decisions without having to worry about having a futures trading account, or trying to guess which mutual fund offering with some mix of mining stocks and the commodity has a better handle on what's going on. And, of course, with huge volumes of fee ETF-related information available on the Internet, Morningstar and its kind can't make the same kind of money as they did in mutual funds promoting the sector.

At the same time, many retail investors are intrigued by the enormous growth in hedge funds [which we describe and discuss in Chapter 3]. They and ETFs are the subject of cocktail party conversation whenever investing and the stock market become the topic. If you tell your friends you are a hedge fund investor, they would be more than a little impressed. But your FA doesn't offer these funds to you unless you have at least $1 million to invest and then their firm might insist you have several different funds for diversification. That is a steep threshold for the average retail client.

One of the main attractions of hedge funds is their fee structure may be better for investors: Fund managers collect lucrative fees if the fund actually makes money for all parties versus adding money to losing mutual funds and paying fees for the privilege.

So it's not hard to see why so many are losing confidence in following their FA's plan. They tell their clients that they have very few investment choices and retail investors are being led to believe that they have little ability to take action when needed.

Over the years, individuals have been clinging to what appear as outmoded schemes laden with conflicts of interest that primarily benefit the FA and their firm, while placing them in a deceptively limited, even debilitated, position.

I STILL WANT SOMEONE ELSE TO DO IT

Like my professional friend many people are too busy to take the time to deal with their personal finances directly. They want a professional to help them and to take care of things on a daily basis. But just remember one thing: just as we don't have many "full serve" gas stations anymore, the quality of investment advice has diminished making it more necessary to take greater interest in your investments. As opposed to the go-go days of the 1990s, you will more than ever need to be an active steward over your assets. There's just no getting away from it.

While we discuss this more in later chapters it's important to note that recent studies completed by our friends at Tiburon Strategic Advisors point out that after the bear market of 2000 to 2003 investors who previously were or thought they wanted to be DIY investors no longer want to go it alone. But their research also reveals something even more important: Individuals want more control over their investments, but they also want some help.

This might include using a FA to implement various strategies that you jointly develop and clearly understand. The FA you choose should not be based on family or social connections. Rather you should find an individual FA who is learned and skilled in contemporary investment themes and portfolio structure. Stay away from the "product pushers" with the dated computer based financial plans filled with antiquated high cost funds.

That FA may be independent or, if not, use soundly based strategies and themes that may even be unique from what the FA's firm pushes. This can be tricky since you must discover if the FA is knowledgeable, has done their homework, is ethical, and puts your interests above just moving product out the door.

But if you want to invest like the superrich and still have an FA represent you, taking the time for some thorough due diligence will be a critical component for your success.

Finally, if you're just lazy, you can't be complaining about poor performance results later because you'll have only yourself to blame.

REPORTS OF MY DEATH HAVE BEEN GREATLY EXAGGERATED

After the bear market and later revealed scandals the mutual fund and large Wall Street firms along with their associated FAs are still going strong. To count them out would be foolish. *Never underestimate the marketing power of these combined forces.*

The central idea as indicated previously was to convert the commission business to a fee-based mode. That meant converting the business style and methods of current FAs from someone who schlepped stocks and bonds for a living to one now offering financial planning solutions for a fee. Some more ambitious and thoughtful FAs also became Certified Financial Planners [CFPs] in addition to carrying the normal licensing and registrations. Doing so greatly expanded their professional capabilities, knowledge, and credibility.

In fact, according to a 2006 poll by National Financial [a part of Fidelity Investments] of registered representatives, 23 percent of broker sentiment index would prefer to be paid based exclusively on asset based fees.

Their firms started to package mutual fund "wrap account" products combined with computer driven financial plans and models. This initially became the overriding marketing thrust of wire-house firms. When dealing with clients with more assets the separately managed account was packaged with approved outside money managers splitting recurring management fees with the firm and the FAs.

It wasn't much different from what I was doing previously in a slightly different way. The major difference is that their firms were behind them 100 percent and were much better organized to find and deliver product than someone on their own.

Brokerage firms created the financial plans and computer programs, signed marketing and fee-sharing relationships with mutual fund families, and left it to FAs to "just add money" from their clients and prospects. Sounds simple enough and with a bull market providing wind to the FAs' backs it only got easier. The only rub was that so many others were getting into the act. But with the rapidly expanding wealth of the Baby Boomers in the 1980s through today, the supply of clients seemed endless.

Also let's not forget the expansion of all manner of retirement account assets whether they were from smaller IRAs, 401[k] plans to large pools of corporate pension plans, wire-house firms had plans and products to suit most clients.

The mutual fund industry is huge with more than $10 trillion in assets by the end of 2006. According to Tiburon Strategic Advisors,

> *19.5% of all US consumers financial assets were invested in mutual funds. [And away from wire-house firms] "independent FAs primarily utilize mutual funds, with fee-only financial advisors having 61% of client assets invested in no-load mutual funds inside fee-accounts, and independent reps having 39% of client assets invested in commissionable mutual funds and another 16% invested in no-load mutual funds inside fee-accounts.*

And firms have been successful at incorporating this format. In 2006 per the Investment Company Institute, mutual fund assets average recurring fees paid to FAs firms was nearly $2 billion.

The other area enjoying great growth continues to be separately managed accounts [SMAs] for investors with larger accounts with assets in excess of $250,000 to $500,000. For these investors firms developed "approved lists" of outside money managers who FAs and clients could choose to manage their money. Fee income was shared by the manager and the firm with the FA getting a cut. Clients liked the customized service and prestige of having their own outside manager versus mutual funds. These had some snob appeal but their performance wasn't necessarily superior to accounts featuring mutual funds only. Independent money managers with either modest or short track records needed the marketing leverage that larger firms provided and were all too willing to share fees. It makes sense that money managers with outstanding performance records didn't need to share their fees as money would find them like a heat seeking missile. Further the best managers would more likely gravitate to becoming hedge fund managers where fees are even higher and fee-sharing is not a subject for discussion. While wire-houses dominate separately managed accounts with more $1.5 trillion in assets, also included are bank trust accounts with assets now more than $1 trillion and of course money managers. See RIA p. 23. $.5 trillion marketing directly to clients. Therefore, according to Morningstar this is now a $3 trillion business.

FUTURE AREA OF GROWTH: UNIFIED ACCOUNTS

The unified account is coming to a brokerage office near you soon—in fact some are already appearing at a variety of firms.

Simply stated a unified account features multimanager and sector strategy where different client assets are housed in one account. This makes sense for both firms and clients. Currently with separately managed accounts brokerage statements to clients were scattered and not consolidated. The unified account puts multi-manager accounts into statements clients can read and understand.

One of the biggest areas of client complaint beyond portfolio performance continues to be hard to read and understand brokerage statements. Clients have been complaining about this for decades. They would say, "Why is it so difficult to just tell me what I own, what it cost, and what its worth?" "Why can't you put all these disparate assets together in a simple snapshot?" "Why do you overwhelm us with so much useless mail?" And so forth.

Consolidating and providing clients with meaningful and easy to understand statements was the biggest challenge I had when using multiasset class investments for clients in the 1980s and 1990s. It was made worse since we had a penchant for incorporating alternative investments with clients who were willing to use them. Why worse? Futures and commodity accounts were overseen or regulated by entirely different organizations: the Commodity Futures Trading Corporation [CFTC] and National Futures Association [NFA]. These were the facsimile organizations to futures and commodities as the SEC and NASD were to securities. But because they were different they required a completely different set of account documentation and client reports.

Clients always wanted and demanded to know how their "entire" portfolio was doing rather than viewing it piecemeal. What to do? We took the risk and made the investment of crafting our own consolidated statements. Why risk? Because many abuses and criminal activity were associated with FAs creating their own phony client reports to either mislead investors and/or steal from them. So with great scrutiny we started to create complicated statements while I was still at Shearson Lehman Bros. in the early 1980s.

I remember buying the first PC that was in the office and hiring with my own funds an accounting student from the local university to perform the research and produce reports. I created a draft of how a client report should appear and we set about our task. This was easier said than done. First, we were all new to operating PCs and at the time, we used Lotus since Excel wasn't even available. Everything had to be done by hand and our university student struggled with all manner of issues from first just learning how to use the computer to dealing with complex industry standard rate of return formulas. Other brokers milled about our office wondering what we were doing and why. Since it was a proving ground operation so to speak we didn't say much until it was complete and approved by the powers that be in Albany.

After many months of effort we rolled out the first statement and sent it off for compliance approval. That approval never arrived since even New York legal and compliance officials couldn't figure out what to do with our efforts and results. This was another reason to strike out on my own since the reports were costly to produce [remember in 1982 PCs were expensive not to mention the help] but their production was much needed.

But essentially what we were doing is what's being done now for unified accounts: providing clients with a comprehensive analysis of how their total portfolio is doing including its disparate elements.

Around that time there was also a movement to start pension consulting practices within wire-house firms. An acquaintance had pioneered one in Honolulu and he was doing what we were doing except that he was dealing with large unions, foundations, corporations, and government. His services were valued by trustees and investment committees who had fiduciary responsibilities over large sums. They needed a consultant to provide cover for their oversight. He did an excellent job of sensing their needs intuitively and started crafting reports similar to what we were trying. In those days it was common practice for consultants such as these to be paid via commission business from the accounts. The investment committees liked it since they didn't have to pay a consulting fee out of assets thinking, "We have to pay the commissions to someone anyway." The consultant would bring the committee a group of money managers including several from each style sector and allow the committee to vote or select the managers they wanted. Further they allocated amounts to different sectors and styles per a plan crafted by the consultant and approved by the committee.

However, it didn't take long for committees to realize that there were potential conflicts of interest since the consultant might bring managers only to the group that was willing to pay the consultant commissions or those willing to pay the highest commissions.

Even though commissions were falling during this period, when you're dealing with $100 million accounts even reduced commissions would add up to substantial sums. Eventually committee trustees became aware of the potential for conflicts to arise. Committee members felt that by paying a flat consulting fee and no commission from the account, the potential for abuse would fall and only the best managers would be brought to their attention. However abuses could and would still occur as managers could pay a stream of commissions to the consultant from other accounts, which were an undisclosed activity. When discovered many trustees sought to eliminate the potential by requiring third party money managers not to pay any commissions to the broker from any source. And so it went.

The important thing is that these consultants were able to craft their own unified account structures that are now making their way to brokerage firms.

THE FUTURE FOR FINANCIAL ADVISORS NEVER BRIGHTER—MAYBE

The savings rate in the United States has never been lower at a mere .2 percent of income. But Baby Boomers pending retirement will cause investment assets for them to rise since pension and 401[k] monies will be rolled over into IRA accounts. In fact, according to Tiburon research, "investable assets will rise from approximately $17 trillion to almost $30 trillion by 2010, creating a tremendous opportunity for financial advisors."

FAs who are successful at raising funds are living a good life today. It's been reported that the "average" production for industry leader

Merrill Lynch FAs was $750,000 in 2005. With their take at around 40 percent that means they're making a tidy $300,000 per year. Not bad, is it?

However, there is an important caveat. Many third party managers and some considered "in-house" are cutting fees. Some are cutting fees completely to FAs and their firms. For example, on January 29, 2007 Eaton Vance with $133 billion in assets announced it is no longer paying brokers at Merrill Lynch [ML]. Merrill Lynch also in early 2007 announced a sharp reduction in the fees it charges for fixed-income investment management meaning the FA's share would be reduced proportionately. So despite all the future potential, FAs will have to work harder collecting more assets for each dollar they earn. And ML is moving to a portfolio-based package for their SMA accounts where money-managers' fees might be drastically reduced by 40 percent according to *Investment News*, February 6, 2006.

In fact, according to an *Investment News* article of October 16, 2006, wealth managers are also being forced to restructure fees. "The most pressing concerns in the rarified circles of firms catering to high and ultrahigh-net-worth clients are fee transparency and the sustainability of percentage of assets under management as the industry's pre-eminent prices model." That's a pretty shocking admission. From the same article CEO Chris Snyder, Private Client Resources LLC said: "Pricing is hugely in turmoil. Banks are reasonably frightened, and it seems clear that the pricing paradigm needs to change."

Companies like Fidelity are rolling out interactive tools that allow DIY investors to create their own retirement plans that circumvent brokers and advisors. These tools allow willing investors the help they need to go it alone more easily.

These types of pressures will continue whether driven by customers from the bottom up or from the top down. FAs can count on being under growing fee pressure from all quarters for a long time.

These types of pressures may force many current FAs to reconsider their current FA status with a major firm and move to become an independent registered investment advisor [RIA]. In fact from the previously mentioned National Financial poll, fully 60 percent of current FAs would leave their firm to better control their ability to determine how they are paid.

The drive to compete and create more efficient cost structures move from one delivery cost to the next. First commissions and now fees. As we learn later ETFs are also a force in driving down product fees.

TWO BODY BLOWS TO WALL STREET FEES

Financial planners have long chafed at the notion that brokers not registered as investment advisors could charge a fee. The planner's organization alleged that brokers couldn't have it both ways and should either be charging a commission as brokers or register as investment advisors. And in a major court decision by the U.S. Court of Appeals for the District of Columbia Circuit, on March 30, 2007 the court agreed overturning the controversial broker–dealer rule. The SEC has elected not to appeal the decision.

Naturally, this decision has created chaos within existing product structures for major Wall Street firms. The consequence is that assets in fee-based brokerage accounts must be moved to either an advisory account or a traditional commission account. This will be no easy feat since it's estimated that there exists some $300 billion in roughly one million fee-based accounts.

The SEC has asked the courts for a four month extension and the sentiment is that it will be granted to allow the firms to transition accounts. In the meantime many firms are not accepting new accounts' popular existing products. Morgan Stanley stopped offering its fee-based Choice account to new clients on May 19, 2007. The same is true for other industry firms from Merrill Lynch to Smith Barney. According to *Investment News*, Merrill Lynch, Morgan Stanley, UBS, Smith Barney, and Charles Schwab together account for 75 percent of fee-based brokerage accounts. They are rapidly putting together "alternative advisory accounts." By the time you read this, these accounts should be available.

But the financial planners aren't done yet. They're also complaining that the planning tools used by Wall Street firms to allocate assets to portfolios are also a violation of rules that encroach on their legal turf. They may make this a litigious issue as well.

The next body blow may be that according to industry sources, the SEC is considering a ban on B or 12b-1 shares. These are the funds that possess costly redemption fees that serve to trap investors. The elimination of these products would hurt the evergreen income strategies enjoyed by many brokers where recurring fees are their bread and butter.

In all this it's important to remember that Wall Street is a powerful political force. They won't sit idly by while their business is threatened. Accommodations will be made but the game is changing hopefully to the benefit of individual investors. The bottom line is that by 2008 the structure and variety of product offerings from many firms will change.

CONCLUSION

While most individuals are not able to invest in hedge funds due to high minimum account sizes, ETFs are soon going to make individually constructed hedge funds possible. There are new types of ETFs that have been issued over the past year and more entering the registration process. These new securities will allow retail investors with $50,000 to $100,000 portfolios to take market positions just as easily as hedge fund investors. With proper online brokerage accounts or teamed with knowledgeable FAs small investors will be willing to step up to contemporary account structures and cutting-edge portfolio strategies and management.

DIY investors and forward-thinking FAs can take control and exercise much more choice. With the many structural changes taking place on Wall Street investors and FAs will find new tools and freedom to follow the best investment path. If they do a little research and consult unconflicted sources of portfolio advice, like unaffiliated newsletters, they will find that a broad range of low-cost investment alternatives are within their reach—such as ETFs, index funds, and, eventually, an ability to create their own individual hedge fund. Investing in the market does not have to be like a visit to Hobson's stable.

CHAPTER 2

ETFs—The New Investment of Choice

ETFs are a very disruptive technology to the mutual fund world.
—Donald Putnam, Managing Director, Grail Partners LLC

It never fails to happen that after an orgy of bull market investing the inevitable bear market follows. In the aftermath problems and abuses shunted aside are revealed. It's like that in all business ventures it seems, as when good conditions end previously ignored problems that stick out like a sore thumb. Such occurred after the bull market bubble popped in 2000 and a nearly three–year bear market ensued.

As we described in the previous chapter the litany of negative news visited upon the mutual fund industry shocked and rocked the investment world. The subsequent trauma inflicted on Wall Street was looked upon with revulsion by even the most casual investor. And, of course, when your own mutual fund account is down, it's not surprising to find investors scrambling about looking for alternative investment vehicles.

The logical choice for mainstream investors was and continues to be ETFs [exchange traded funds]. Why? Because these securities contained many positive attributes that conventional open-end mutual funds lacked including those that gave rise to many of the recent scandals.

- ETFs carry very low management fees commonly ranging from .10 percent to .40 percent versus 1.00 percent to 2.00 percent for many actively managed mutual funds. While some ETFs are more expensive, they tend to offer specialized investment options and ideas that are not available in, or are considerably more expensive than, conventional mutual funds.

- They are more easily bought and sold than most mutual funds since they trade like stocks. Therefore there can't be end-of-day late trading or other market timing shenanigans common to previous mutual fund scandals.
- Other than normal and hopefully heavily discounted commissions, there are no expensive or cumbersome redemption fees.
- ETFs are linked to indexes that they are supposed to and generally do track. That makes them transparent and not so easily subject to manipulation.
- A wide variety of index-linked ETFs now exist that provide enough choice to achieve more than adequate diversification opportunities.

Subsequent to the mutual fund scandal revelations of 2002–2003 ETFs became the most dominant preferred new investment vehicle available to retail investors. DIY investors gravitated to them immediately while Hobson's choice victims could only watch with envy unless they took decisive action.

DIY INVESTORS TAKE CHARGE

In 1998, Launny Steffans of Merrill Lynch said, "The do-it-yourself model of investing, centered on Internet trading, should be regarded as a serious threat to American lives." He also said, "Let me say clearly; online trading itself is not bad. In fact, it a refreshing wind in our industry and one that we welcome and embrace."

The first Steffans' quote was a knee-jerk condescending reaction to the popularity of do-it-yourself [DIY] investing. Naturally it also revealed an attitude that this investment phenomenon was a serious threat to Merrill Lynch's existing business model. According to Tiburon Strategic Advisors, "Online brokerage firms in the late 1990s were predominantly taking accounts away from the traditional playing field, with only 10 percent of accounts from new investors."

The second quote reflected the quick realization that ML had to join the party and they immediately launched ML Direct, their online trading platform.

Further in 1995, IBM's CEO Lou Gerstner, a Shearson Lehman Bros veteran, had predicted the entire industry would move to the Web by 1997. And the major wire-house firms did launch web sites that got them digitally connected with their clients. But their efforts were mostly symbolic initially since their sales force was understandably nervous about the obvious threat from discount commissions and the online trading boom.

As pointed out in the previous chapter, prior to discount commissions and later the Internet revolution, retail investors were captives of the major wire-house firms. Many investors remain with these firms, in thrall of their powerful marketing capabilities and thinking that the shift in focus from commission to fee-based worked to their advantage. Retail investors who feel they need help retain their relationship with their FAs and firm since they're either overwhelmed by the DIY process, are too busy and want or need someone to help them, trust their FA, are lazy or just don't want to offend their FA golfing buddy by doing their own thing.

With the advent of the discount commission and sophisticated online trading platforms, DIY investors emerged as a significant new force in the market. Online trading activity rapidly expanded through the boom dot.com era then deteriorated after the bust. After all the average transaction cost of a discount firm in 1998 ranged from a low of $8 to a high of $30 compared to the full service firm's $300–$500 per trade. Prior to the bear market it was estimated by eMarketer Senior Analyst David Hallerman that the number of online retail accounts would grow from 17.4 million at the end of 2001 to more than 30 million by the end of 2004. He went on to say:

> *Because of market conditions many experts were expecting people to abandon online investing in droves. It's true that some day traders are leaving, but many more long-range investors are coming online to take their place. These users aren't going to come and go with market fluctuations. They are aging and have more money available for investment. They are coming online because they want greater control of their investments and the direction of their retirement plans. In addition, they are more comfortable with all forms of internet commerce. These factors will contribute to increased stability and continued growth in the online investing sector.*

Mr. Hallerman never imagined the depth of the bear market after 2001 as investors abandoned stocks in favor of greener pastures like real estate. Although now fully recovered, the decline in trading volume made online brokerage consolidation inevitable, and that process continues today [although it is being somewhat undermined by the emergence of new firms].

Nevertheless, even with a horrific bear market, the actual number of online investment accounts is unknown. Even though account growth within the United States remained static or declined, this was offset by increasing online trading occurring by international retail investors. Over the past few years, investors in Europe and Asia especially have demanded more discount commission structures and online services. Intuitively, this can only continue.

And, sure enough, in an April 2006 report "Back to the Future" from industry research boutique Tiburon Strategic Advisors opined, "Online financial services in 2006 are undergoing a renaissance." They add, "The number of households trading online is expected to double by 2010, from six million today to twelve million by 2010." Now when you discuss households you need to multiply the figure by perhaps a factor of three considering multiple accounts from within each household. If that were true, then we could speculate there may be 18 million active accounts currently or as many as existed at the bubble peak. Further, the same Tiburon report pointed out, "Amazingly, the average number of daily trades in 2006 in the online brokerage industry has actually eclipsed the peak of 2000, 1.26 million per day versus 1.20 million." "Amazingly" is an apt description since 2000 statistics were riddled with many now extinct day traders.

The bear market of 2000 through early 2003 slowed down Mr. Hallerman's estimate of 30 million online accounts by 2004. If you accept Tiburon's projections of 2010 featuring 12 million households multiplied by a factor of three, then you exceed 36 million online accounts, a goal only delayed by the bear market.

WHAT TOOK ETFs SO LONG TO CATCH ON?

Nate Most, ETF creator and pioneer, passed away in early 2005 at the age of ninety, but he told me over lunch in 2004 how thrilled he was at how his baby had grown. He was a true gentleman and someone who cared deeply about the business. Nate labored for many years at the American Stock Exchange where he was charged with among other things coming up with some ideas to raise revenues for the exchange. He hit on the ETF and in 1993 the Standard & Poor's Depository Receipt, known as the SPDR [SPY] was launched.

Index investing had become more and more popular since many studies had been reflecting that indexes were outperforming active management for some time. That gave rise to index funds like those offered by index fund leader Vanguard Funds. Nate's preliminary research indicated that indexes were the best tool to link a product that could trade all day on the exchange. He sought out Jack Bogle, who was then head of Vanguard Funds. After meeting with Bogle shortly before the market crash in 1987, Nate set about researching more and refining more about the product he envisioned. For his part Bogle didn't like the idea of investors moving in and out of funds intraday. The practice of pricing only open-end mutual funds at the end of each trading day restricted trading and kept investors more focused on long-term investing. Of course, Bogle never considered the possibility of the subsequent trading scandals caused directly by the abuses of end-of-day pricing.

In his research Nate wanted to prevent premiums and discounts from occurring making index tracking efficient. His solution was the "creation unit" [typically 50,000 to 100,000 shares] whereby institutions could sell to individual investors pieces of the unit and would also act as an arbitrage mechanism that kept ETF prices closely matched to indexes.

Nate felt the ETF product best served the interests of the end user investor. Meanwhile, Jack Bogle remained dead-set against ETFs since he never believes in selling—only buying. The fact that you can trade ETFs intraday gives investors the opportunity to hurt only themselves and their long-term performance, in his rather paternalistic opinion. But Bogle is now retired and his former firm Vanguard is now launching ETF products almost as quickly as other sponsors. And they're no doubt doing so since as Nate told me, "That's where the money is."

And due to the various mutual fund scandals fund sponsors are increasing their redemption fees for conventional mutual funds to limit or restrict investor trading of the shares. Doing this only increases the flow of money from more active or aware investors to ETFs.

INDEXING VERSUS ACTIVE MANAGEMENT

The argument over index investing versus active management continues and with each passing study indexes continue to be the more effective strategy in cost and performance.

According to a recent and very thoroughly researched study by Millicent Holmes published in the January 2007 edition of *Journal of Financial Planning*, passive index management beat most categories of active management.

CASE STUDY: Improved Study Finds Index Management Usually Outperforms Active Management*

EXECUTIVE SUMMARY

- This study seeks to improve in several ways upon previous studies examining the relative performance of index management versus active management. It concludes that index management outperforms active management in most asset classes.
- To make comparisons between index management and active management as accurate as possible, the study segregated funds by style and then compared funds of the same style. This "apples to apples" comparison is the most accurate methodology. Many other studies suffer from some level of benchmark mis-specification or "size bias," as they compare all actively managed funds, which include Large-, Mid-, Small-, and Micro-cap funds to a Large-Cap Blend index, the S&P 500.
- Many studies on indexing versus active management have used only gross returns, which tend to overstate active manager fund performance. By contrast, this study examines fund performance net of management fees, expenses, and the impact of taxes.
- Also, these studies typically have used commercial mutual fund databases as their investment universe. Unfortunately, all commercial databases suffer from survivor bias, overstating the returns for the universe of active managers that have survived to the present date. This study uses "survivor-biased minimized" data to help solve this difficulty.
- In general, index management outperformed active management in the Large-Cap Blend, Value, and Growth asset classes. The results in Mid-Cap were mixed, with active Mid-Cap Value outperforming index management for most periods. Active management also outperformed in active Small-Cap Blend and international Mid/Small-Cap Blend.
- Surprisingly, indexing outperformed active management in the active Small-Cap Value and Growth asset classes, precisely the asset classes in which one would expect active management to outperform index management.

Millicent Holmes is director of research at Brownson, Rehmus & Foxworth Inc., a firm in Chicago, Illinois, that offers comprehensive wealth management, including investment consulting and multi-family office services. Her past experience includes working with fund of hedge fund managers, developing alternative investment products for international institutional investors in the United States and abroad, and trading options from the floors of the Chicago Board of Trade and Chicago Mercantile Exchange.

The debate between active management and index management has raged for many years. While many studies have been conducted to solve the question of whether index management outperforms active management, we have found that several of these studies contain basic flaws. Chief among them is benchmark mis-specification, where these past

---

*Reprinted with permission by the Financial Planning Association, Journal of Financial Planning, January 2007, Millicent Holmes, "Improved Study Finds Index Management Usually Outperforms Active Management." For more information on the Financial Planning Association, please visit www.fpanet.org or call 1-800-322-4237.

studies did not make accurate asset class or style comparisons; rather, they tended to compare *all* actively managed funds—which include large-, mid-, small- and micro-cap funds—with one large-cap blend index, the S&P 500. Another flaw involved the comparison of actively managed funds with indices rather than with index funds. This is an important distinction, since many index funds have not successfully replicate[d] their indices. An additional flaw involved the use of gross returns, which tended to overstate active manager fund performance. Finally, the most prevalent flaw has been survivor bias. Many studies on indexing versus active management used commercial mutual fund databases as their investment universe. Unfortunately, all commercial mutual fund databases suffer from survivor bias, meaning they exclude the track records of funds that have ceased doing business, overstating the returns of the universe of active managers that remain.

Our study attempts to rectify the flaws in previous studies by making accurate asset class and style comparisons, accounting for management fees, expenses, and taxes, as well as incorporating mutual fund data that minimizes survivor bias. Through examination of current and survivor-bias-minimized fund data as well as other academic studies on this issue, we found that index management outperformed active management in most asset classes. Our results confirm the findings in other previous studies in the Large-Cap Blend, Value, and Growth asset classes, where index management outperformed active management. But surprisingly, our results differ from other studies in the Small-Cap Growth, Small-Cap Value, and International Large-Cap Blend asset classes where index management outperformed active management.

METHODOLOGY

Most investors do not directly invest in indices, they invest in index funds. Therefore, we focused this study on the comparison between active fund management and index fund management. In so doing, we compared the performance of the universe of actively managed funds relative to their counterpart index funds in the ten years from 1995 to 2004, using the data and fund classifications of the Morningstar database. The Morningstar database, which includes over 23,000 funds, is the largest fund data set in the industry. In addition to Morningstar, we also used survivor-bias minimized data from the Lipper database.

To make the comparison as accurate as possible, funds were segregated by style and then comparisons were made between funds of the same style. For example, we compared Large-Cap Blend index funds with Large-Cap Blend actively managed funds. To further ensure a close comparison, the Morningstar fund category and equity style box must be in the same asset class for a fund to be included in the domestic Large-, Mid- or Small-Cap asset classes. For example, a fund whose Morningstar category was Small-Cap, but whose equity style box indicated that it had grown to Mid-Cap, would not be included in either the small- or mid-cap asset classes, but excluded from the study altogether. We segregated international funds using Morningstar's classification between International Large-Cap and International Mid/Small-Cap. For the International category, we excluded individual country, region, and sector funds. Each fund in the International category must have regional allocations that were between 20–80 percent Europe and 5–50 percent Japan. Tax-managed funds were included in the index fund universe, not the actively managed fund universe.

NET OF FEES AND TAXES

Many past studies on indexing versus active management have not included investment management fees or the impact of taxes. By contrast, this study examines fund performance net of management fees and expenses. Additionally, we use the most conservative method to measure the impact of taxes—return after-tax on distribution and sale—which reflects the effect of both taxable distributions by a fund to its shareholders and any taxable gain or loss realized by the shareholders upon the sale of fund shares.

SURVIVOR BIAS

As noted earlier, our comparison of active versus index funds in the U.S. Large-Cap, Mid-Cap, Small-Cap, International Large-Cap, and International Mid/Small-Cap asset classes were taken from the Morningstar Database. Unfortunately, all commercial mutual fund databases, including Morningstar, suffer from survivor bias, meaning they exclude the track records of funds that have ceased doing business. Many of these databases also accept return histories after the fact, known as back-filling or instant history bias.

Excluding the track records of funds that have ceased doing business tends to inflate the returns of the universe of active managers that remain. Brown and Goetzmann (1995); Carhart (1997); and Carhart, Carpenter, Lynch, and Musto (2001) demonstrated that funds tended to disappear from mutual fund databases following sustained periods of poor performance. Thus, using data free of survivor bias lowers the returns of active manager universes to a level that more accurately reflects their true performance.

Several studies have provided estimates of survivor bias, including Grinblatt and Titman (1989); Malkiel (1994); Brown and Goetzmann (1995); Elton, Gruber, and Blake (1996); Swenson (2000); and Carhart, Carpenter, Lynch, and Musto (2001). Their estimates of survivor-bias range from .10 percent to as high as 2.2 percent a year. The academic studies on survivor bias serve to enhance the reasons for using data free of survivor bias. But it appears specious to use the bias estimates from these studies for comparisons that do not cover the same period or use the same methodology.

To directly examine survivor-bias-free data, we sought a database that was free from this bias and found that it had issues as well. The CRSP (Center for Research in Security Prices) Survivor-Bias Free U.S. Mutual Fund Database uses the method of segregating funds via prospectus objective: "Growth," "Growth and Income," "Aggressive Growth," and so forth. Unfortunately, these prospectus objectives are not specific enough to provide accurate comparisons, given that the "Growth" objective could include both Large-Cap and Mid-Cap funds. Additionally, Elton, Gruber, and Blake (2001) found that the CRSP database has an omission bias that has the same effect as survivor bias. Elton et al. found that "although all mutual funds are listed in CRSP, return data is missing for many and the characteristics of these funds differ from the populations."

To attempt to solve the survivor-bias issue, we used "survivor-bias minimized" data sets from the Lipper database. This data was compiled by segregating funds by asset class and investment style and then calculating equally weighted averages of these monthly fund returns. These average returns were linked geometrically. This Lipper data is net of fees. All funds that existed for the entire month were included in each monthly return, but any fund that closed or merged during that month would not be part of the performance calculation for that period. For example, the Small-Cap Blend return for January 2004 is the return for all Small-Cap Blend funds included in the Lipper category for that month.

Unfortunately, similar to the CRSP database, this "survivor-bias minimized" data do not separate index funds from actively managed funds. But the current breakdown within each category indicates that the average Small-Cap series has only 10 percent index or index-based funds, while the average International series has only 5 percent index or index-based funds. Thus, these "survivor-bias minimized" data series can be classified as largely active manager data sets.

We find that survivor bias is not an issue in performance comparisons between active and index management in the Large-Cap Blend, Value, or Growth asset classes. As indexing largely outperforms active management in these asset classes, using survivor-bias-minimized data would only serve to strengthen this conclusion. But we find that survivor-bias-minimized data has a particular impact on performance comparisons between active and index management in the Small-Cap and International asset classes. [See Table 2.1.]

TABLE 2.1   Summary of Index Management versus Active Management

Index Management Outperforms Active Management	Active Management Outperforms Index Management
U.S. Large-Cap Blend	U.S. Mid-Cap Value
U.S. Large-Cap Value	
U.S. Large-Cap Growth	U.S. Small-Cap Blend
U.S. Mid-Cap Blend	International Mid/Small-Cap Blend
U.S. Mid-Cap Growth	
U.S. Small-Cap Value	
U.S. Small Cap Growth	
International Large-Cap Blend	

STUDY FINDINGS

We find that index management outperforms active management in the Large-Cap Blend, Value, and Growth asset classes on a pre-tax and an after-tax basis (See Tables 2.2 and 2.3). For example, the pre-tax 10-year average for Large-Cap Blend Index was 11.6 percent, versus 10.4 percent for Large-Cap Blend Active. While the conclusion in the Large-Cap asset classes does not preclude the existence of successful Large-Cap active managers, these results provide guidance that this is a less productive area to search for active management.

The results in Mid-Cap were mixed. In the Mid-Cap Blend and Growth asset classes, index management outperformed active management on a pre-tax and after-tax basis. For

TABLE 2.2 Results of Study on Index Management versus Active Management (Pre-Tax Performance Comparison, as of December 2004)

US LARGE-CAP

	1995	1996	1997	1998	1999	2000	2001	2002	2003	2004	10 Yr.
Large-Cap Blend Index	36.7%	22.6%	32.7%	28.0%	20.3%	−9.1%	−12.1%	−22.2%	27.6%	10.2%	11.6%
Large-Cap Blend Active	32.3%	21.3%	27.6%	22.5%	21.4%	−4.8%	−12.6%	−22.6%	25.8%	9.5%	10.4%
Large-Cap Value Index	37.0%	21.5%	30.9%	15.0%	18.2%	8.1%	−6.7%	−17.9%	28.4%	13.2%	13.5%
Large-Cap Value Active	33.2%	20.8%	28.1%	12.8%	4.9%	8.0%	−4.6%	−18.7%	27.7%	13.3%	11.5%
Large-Cap Growth Index	38.1%	23.7%	28.1%	28.1%	28.0%	−22.7%	−21.4%	−28.7%	32.9%	6.3%	8.2%
Large-Cap Growth Active	32.6%	19.4%	27.6%	32.4%	35.8%	−28.2	−23.9%	−27.8%	28.1%	6.6%	6.9%

US MID-CAP

	1995	1996	1997	1998	1999	2000	2001	2002	2003	2004	10 Yr.
Mid-Cap Blend Index	30.0%	18.6%	31.5%	18.3%	17.4%	15.4%	−2.1%	−16.4%	38.7%	18.1%	15.9%
Mid-Cap Blend Active	32.0%	21.3%	27.8%	9.4%	23.1%	11.2%	0.3%	−16.6%	34.5%	16.0%	14.9%
Mid-Cap Blend Surv. Bias Min.	29.2%	18.2%	22.0%	8.9%	38.7%	9.8%	−6.2%	−18.6%	36.6%	15.4%	13.9%

	1995	1996	1997	1998	1999	2000	2001	2002	2003	2004	6 Yr.
Mid-Cap Value Index	—	—	—	—	5.2%	11.0%	3.5%	−18.6%	37.8%	20.8%	8.6%
Mid-Cap Value Active	—	—	—	—	6.5%	26.2%	5.4%	−12.2%	37.3%	19.1%	12.6%
Mid-Cap Value Survivor Bias Min.	—	—	—	—	7.7%	14.3%	7.0%	−13.5%	38.5%	19.1%	11.1%

	1995	1996	1997	1998	1999	2000	2001	2002	2003	2004	4 Yr.
Mid-Cap Growth Index	—	—	—	—	—	—	−8.2%	−23.0%	33.0%	13.9%	1.7%
Mid-Cap Growth Active	—	—	—	—	—	—	−20.1%	28.4%	36.4%	12.8%	−3.1%
Mid-Cap Growth Surv. Bias Min.	—	—	—	—	—	—	−21.7%	−28.6%	35.6%	12.3%	−3.9%

US SMALL-CAP

	1995	1996	1997	1998	1999	2000	2001	2002	2003	2004	
											4 Yr.
Small-Cap Blend Index	—	—	—	—	—	—	-8.2%	-23.0%	33.0%	13.9%	1.7%
Small-Cap Blend Active	—	—	—	—	—	—	-20.1%	-28.4%	36.4%	12.8%	-3.1%
Small-Cap Blend Surv. Bias Min.	—	—	—	—	—	—	-21.7%	-28.6%	35.6%	12.3%	-3.9%
	1995	**1996**	**1997**	**1998**	**1999**	**2000**	**2001**	**2002**	**2003**	**2004**	**10 Yr.**
Small-Cap Blend Index	29.2%	17.7%	23.4%	-3.3%	15.0%	5.7%	4.3%	-17.2%	43.2%	19.9%	12.6%
Small-Cap Blend Active	27.2%	21.7%	26.2%	-4.4%	15.9%	15.4%	11.7%	-15.8%	40.6%	18.6%	14.6%
Small-Cap Blend Surv. Bias Min.	31.2%	19.5%	26.9%	-1.4%	26.3%	6.0%	6.4%	-18.5%	44.1%	18.5%	14.5%
	1995	**1996**	**1997**	**1998**	**1999**	**2000**	**2001**	**2002**	**2003**	**2004**	**10 Yr.**
Small-Cap Value Index	29.1%	22.2%	30.8%	-7.2%	9.1%	16.0%	16.3%	-13.0%	42.9%	21.8%	15.6%
Small-Cap Value Active	24.5%	22.0%	29.5%	-5.2%	6.3%	15.7%	14.6%	-9.5%	45.6	20.0%	15.3%
Small-Cap Value Survivor Bias Min.	23.1%	22.5%	29.2%	-7.5%	5.4%	17.8%	16.2%	-11.4%	42.0%	21.0%	14.8%
	1995	**1996**	**1997**	**1998**	**1999**	**2000**	**2001**	**2002**	**2003**	**2004**	**6 Yr.**
Small-Cap Growth Index	—	—	—	—	19.8%	1.6%	-3.2%	-19.4%	42.0%	17.6	8.0%
Small-Cap Growth Active	—	—	—	—	69.4%	-6.5%	-10.8%	-30.5%	44.2%	10.2%	7.7%
Small-Cap Growth Survivor Bias Min.	—	—	—	—	57.7%	-7.8%	-11.5%	-29.6%	44.4%	10.7%	6.4%

INTERNATIONAL

	1995	**1996**	**1997**	**1998**	**1999**	**2000**	**2001**	**2002**	**2003**	**2004**	**10 Yr.**
Large-Cap Blend Index	10.5%	9.8%	6.2%	20.3%	27.1%	-14.7%	-21.5%	-17.2%	37.1%	19.2%	6.0%
Large-Cap Blend Active	10.2%	11.8%	5.9%	15.0%	41.1%	-16.2%	-22.0%	-16.6%	33.5%	16.9%	6.1%
Large-Cap Blend Survivor Bias Min.	10.6%	12.9%	6.5%	14.1%	39.4%	-16.4%	-21.9%	-17.5%	30.8%	16.7%	5.7%
	1995	**1996**	**1997**	**1998**	**1999**	**2000**	**2001**	**2002**	**2003**	**2004**	**8 Yr.**
Mid/Small-Cap Blend Index	—	—	-23.7%	8.2%	21.9%	-5.4%	-10.5%	1.9%	58.8%	30.9%	7.7%
Mid/Small-Cap -Cap Blend Active	—	—	-8.8%	8.9%	93.4%	-13.2%	-14.4%	-6.2%	50.4%	26.4%	12.4%
Mid/Small-Cap Bld Survivor Bias Min.	—	—	0.8%	13.9%	66.8%	-13.4%	-21.0%	-12.5%	53.4%	24.9%	10.3%

TABLE 2.3 Results of Study on Index Management versus Active Management (After-Tax on Distribution and Sale, As of December 2004)

US LARGE-CAP

	1 Year	3 Years	5 Years	10 Years
Large-Cap Blend Index	6.06%	2.11%	−2.50%	9.79%
Large-Cap Blend Active	4.94%	1.33%	−2.15%	7.84%
	1 Year	**3 Years**	**5 Years**	**10 Years**
Large-Cap Value Index	8.25%	4.47%	1.24%	9.68%
Large-Cap Value Active	7.46%	4.03%	2.73%	8.54%
	1 Year	**3 Years**	**5 Years**	**10 Years**
Large-Cap Growth Index	3.42%	−0.08%	−6.95%	7.02%
Large-Cap Growth Active	3.01%	−1.10%	−6.94%	4.22%

US MID-CAP

	1 Year	3 Years	5 Years	10 Years
Mid-Cap Blend Index	11.80%	9.21%	3.48%	11.12%
Mid-Cap Blend Active	9.69%	7.22%	4.55%	10.27%
	1 Year	**3 Years**	**5 Years**	**10 Years**
Mid-Cap Value Index	13.86%	8.50%	4.85%	—
Mid-Cap Value Active	11.85%	9.41%	10.37%	—
	1 Year	**3 Years**	**5 Years**	**10 Years**
Mid-Cap Growth Index	8.21%	4.38%	—	—
Mid-Cap Growth Active	7.04%	2.06%	—	—

US SMALL-CAP

	1 Year	3 Years	5 Years	10 Years
Small-Cap Blend Index	12.88%	10.54%	7.12%	9.13%
Small-Cap Blend Active	12.08%	9.52%	7.97%	10.59%
	1 Year	**3 Years**	**5 Years**	**10 Years**
Small-Cap Value Index	14.18%	12.98%	13.70%	15.20%
Small-Cap Value Active	13.10%	12.82%	12.36%	10.72%
	1 Year	**3 Years**	**5 Years**	**10 Years**
Small-Cap Growth Index	11.88%	8.10%	5.99%	—
Small-Cap Growth Active	5.63%	2.07%	−2.62%	—

INTERNATIONAL

	1 Year	3 Years	5 Years	10 Years
Intl Large-Cap Blend Index	11.81%	8.41%	−2.40%	5.13%
Intl Large-Cap Blend Active	9.76%	7.10%	−3.22%	4.60%
	1 Year	**3 Years**	**5 Years**	**10 Years**
Intl Mid/Small-Cap Blend Index	20.56%	24.30%	10.20%	—
Intl Mid/Small-Cap Blend Active*	15.95%	17.38%	4.26%	—

*After-tax return International Mid/Small-Cap Blend do not include 1999, which would have changed the results of this analysis.
Sample Estimate Error with 95% Confidence.
Data Source: Morningstar.

example, the pre-tax 10-year average for Mid-Cap Blend index management was 15.9 percent, versus 14.9 percent for active management and 13.9 percent for the survivor-bias-minimized average of Mid-Cap Blend active management. On an after-tax basis, Mid-Cap Blend index management's performance was 11.12 percent over the 10-year period, versus 10.27 percent for Mid-Cap Blend active management. (After-tax survivor bias minimized data was not available.)

In Mid-Cap Value, active management outperformed index management over the last five years and three years but not over the last one-year period. It should be noted, however, that the Mid-Cap results could be affected by the small sample sizes in these asset classes.

In the Small-Cap Blend asset class, active management continued to outperform index management, even when using survivor-bias-minimized data. But as markets have become progressively more efficient, this outperformance trend may be nearing an end. For example, while Small-Cap Blend active management outperformed index management on an after-tax basis over the last five and ten years, it underperformed over the last one-year and three-year periods. Surprisingly, indexing outperformed active management in the Small-Cap Value and Growth asset classes, precisely the asset classes that one would expect active management to outperform index management.

We have observed an evolution in the relationship between indexing and active management in the International Large-Cap Asset class over the last four years. In 2002, we conducted an unpublished study on indexing versus active management that indicated that in the International Large-Cap Blend asset class, active management outperformed index management. But as with Mid-Cap Value and Small-Cap Blend, there were indications that this margin of outperformance was narrowing. Based on the findings of this more recent study, it would appear that indexing has taken a small lead over active management in the International Large-Cap Blend asset class.

The improvement of indexing relative to active management in the International Large-Cap asset class is likely due to the progression of information efficiencies on a global basis. Information efficiencies appear to affect Large-Cap International stocks the same way they affect Large-Cap U.S. stocks. (Just as there are hundreds of analysts that evaluate IBM or Microsoft, there are a similar number of analysts that evaluate British Petroleum or Sony.)

Active management has outperformed index management in the International Mid/Small-Cap Blend asset class. However, our data show signs that this trend may be nearing an end. In the International Mid/Small-Cap Blend asset class, active management has outperformed index management over the longer-term eight-year period, but during more recent periods, indexing has outperformed active management.

Generally, we observed that while taxes had a greater adverse impact on active management than index management, the use of after-tax returns did not change the conclusion in any asset class. For example, if index management outperformed active management on a pre-tax basis, it also outperformed on an after-tax basis.

Over the years, we have observed that financial markets have become progressively more efficient. This increased efficiency can potentially explain the above-noted pattern of improvement in the near term performance of index management relative to active management in the Mid-Cap, Small-Cap, and International asset classes.

The sample sizes of several of these index universes were small. For example, the International Mid/Small-Cap Blend index universe consisted of only one fund. These small sample sizes can potentially affect the results of this analysis. While this situation would usually cause concern, these small index fund universes typically consist of Vanguard or DFA funds, which are known to have successfully tracked their respective indices. (More detail on sample sizes and dispersion is included in the appendix.)

STYLE BOX COMPARISON

As index funds can periodically be unsuccessful in replicating their respective indices, we also compared the active manager universe to the Standard & Poor's Blend and S&P/Barra Growth and Value indices. (As the Standard & Poor's indices require companies to have at least four quarters of profitability prior to inclusion, these indices appear to present an appropriate comparison against actively managed funds.) The conclusion: over the last 10 years, the S&P indices outperformed the majority of actively managed funds in all U.S. asset classes. While this outcome is daunting, we observed somewhat better relative performance by active managers during the bear market from 2000 through 2002. For example, while the S&P Small Cap 600 Value Index outperformed 80 percent of the active small-cap value managers over the longer 10-year period, this index outperformed only 28 percent of the active managers during the bear market from 2000 to 2002. (See Tables 2.4, 2.5, and 2.6.)

TABLE 2.4 Percentage of Funds Outperformed by the S&P Style Indexes
(10 Years ended 12/31/2004)

	Value	Blend	Growth
Large	S&P 500/Barra Value Index	S&P 500 Index	S&P 500/Barra Growth Index
	12.24%	12.07%	11.44%
	66%	88%	92%
Mid	S&P Mid-Cap 400/Barra Value Index	S&P Mid-Cap 400 Index	S&P Mid-Cap 400/Barra Growth Index
	16.80%	16.10%	15.24%
	86%	84%	98%
Small	S&P Small-Cap 600/Barra Value Index	S&P Small-Cap 600 Index	S&P Small-Cap 600/Barra Growth Index
	16.06%	14.29%	11.56%
	80%	62%	69%

Data are not adjusted for survivor bias.
Sources: Lipper Inc, Standard & Poor's, The Vanguard Group.

TABLE 2.5 Percentage of Funds Outperformed by the S&P (Style Indexes during a Bear Market, 3 Years Ended 12/31/2002)

	Value	Blend	Growth
Large	S&P 500/Barra Value Index −18.90% 32%	S&P 500 Index −22.24% 59%	S&P 500/Barra Growth Index −27.65% 78%
Mid	S&P Mid-Cap 400/Barra Value Index −13.00% 66%	S&P Mid-Cap 400 Index −16.91% 61%	S&P Mid-Cap 400/Barra Growth Index −27.48% 86%
Small	S&P Small-Cap 600/Barra Value Index −10.30% 28%	S&P Small-Cap 600 Index −15.57% 54%	S&P Small-Cap 600 /Barra Growth Index −28.37% 95%

Data are not adjusted for survivor bias.
Sources: Lipper Inc., Standard & Poors, The Vanguard Group.

SUMMARY

Through examination of current and survivor-bias-minimized fund data, as well as other academic studies on this issue, we find that index management outperformed active management in most asset classes.

Surprisingly, index management outperformed active management in the Small-Cap Value and Small-Cap Growth asset classes—precisely the asset classes where one would expect active management to outperform.

In the areas where active management outperformed index management, there were signs that this trend may be nearing an end. For example, active management in Mid-Cap Value and Small-Cap Blend outperformed index management over longer periods of five and ten years, but underperformed index management in near-term one-year or three-year periods.

As index funds can periodically be unsuccessful in replicating their respective indices, we also compared the active manager universe to the Standard & Poor's Blend and S&P/Barra Growth and Value indices. The S&P indices outperformed the majority of actively managed funds in all U.S. asset classes, including Mid-Cap Value and Small-Cap Blend.

Finally, we reviewed academic studies that examined the "persistence" of investment manager performance. Often, persistence studies examine active manager's ability to generate consistent (or persistent) performance. While most of these studies found some evidence of persistence, it is important to note that several of these studies found that the persistence phenomenon was mainly due to the persistent underperformance of the lowest returning funds.

TABLE 2.6 Studies on Performance Persistence

Authors	Year Published	Funds Covered*	Dates	Evaluation Periods	Persistence Observed	Notes
Sharpe	1966	34	1954–1963	1 Year	None	
Jensen	1968	115	1945–1964	1 Year	None	
Carlson	1970	82	1948–1967	5 & 10 Years	Partial	Yes, persistence in 5-year risk-adjusted performance. None in 10-year adjusted performance.
Grinblatt & Titman	1989	157	1974–1984	5 Years	Partial	Explained by expenses.
Grinblatt & Titman	1992	279	1974–1984	5 Years	Yes	Persistence for next 5 years, consistent with managers' ability to earn abnormal returns.
Brown, Goeztmann, Ibbotson & Ross	1992	153	1976–1987	3 Years	Yes	Persistence for next 2 of 3-year periods.
Hendricks, Patel & Zeckhauser	1993	165	1974–1988	Quarterly	Yes	Persistence for next 2 to 8 quarters.
Grinblatt & Titman	1993	All US	1976–1985	Quarterly	Yes	Persistence for next 3-year periods.
Goetzmann & Ibottson	1994	728	1976–1988	3 Years	Yes	
Kahn & Rudd	1995	300 Equity & Fixed	1983–1990	N/A	Partial	None for Equity. Yes for Fixed Income.
Brown & Goetzman	1995	829	1976–1988	1 Year	Yes	1-year persistence mainly due to behavior of worst performing funds. Also persistence strongly dependent on time period of study.
Malkiel	1995	724	1971–1990	1 Year	Partial	Stronger in 70s than 80s.
Elton, Gruber, & Blake	1996	188	1977–1993	N/A	Yes	Observed persistence for both 1 and 3-year risk-adjusted performance.
Gruber	1996	270	1984–1994	N/A	Yes	

Author	Year	Sample	Period	Horizon	Persistence	Findings
Carhart	1997	All US	1962–1993	N/A	Yes	1-year persistence seen in a few of the top and many of the bottom performing funds.
Sauer	1997	All US	1976–1992	N/A	Partial	Persistence by style not observed.
Phelps & Detzel	1997	87	1983–1994	1 Year 2 Year 3 Year	No	Persistence not seen once returns are adjusted for risk.
Wermers	1997	All US	1975–1994	N/A	Yes	Once performance was advertised performance deteriorated.
Jain & Wu	2000	294 Advertised Funds	1994–1996	N/A	No	
Davis	2001	All US	1962–1998	1 Year	Negligible	Some persistence seen in best-performing growth funds and worst-performing value and small-cap funds.
Wermers	2001	All US	1974–1994	1 Year 3 Year	Yes	One year showed performance persistence. Three year shows manager skills.
Carhart, Carpenter, Lynch, and Musto	2001	All US	1962–1995	1 Year 5 Year 3-Year 4-Factor Alphas	Yes	Persistence seen in all periods even after effects of survivor bias.
Bollen & Busse	2002	230	1985–1995	Quarterly	Yes	Finds persistence beyond expenses and momentum of stocks.
Ibbotson & Patel	2002	All US	1978–1999	1 Year	Yes	Sees persistence after adjusting for style. Limiting "winners" to top 10% = more repeat winners.

*"All US" indicates that author constructed a survivor-bias-free database.

A portion of the table was excerpted from "A Review of Research on the Past Performance of Managed Funds," a report compiled by the Funds Management Research Centre and [FMRC], September 2002. The Australian Securities and Investment Commission [ASIC] commissioned the report. Authors: Professor David Allen [Edith Cowan University], Professor Tim Brailsford [University of Queensland], Professor Emeritus Ron Bird [University of Technology, Sydney], and Professor Robert Faff [Monash University].

PRACTICAL APPLICATIONS FOR FINANCIAL PLANNERS

Given that index management has outperformed active management in most U.S. asset classes, financial planners can use index funds to improve their clients' pre-tax and after-tax performance, in addition to lowering portfolio expenses. (Please see Table 2.7, which contains the average expense ratios for the U.S. Large-Cap, Mid-Cap, Small-Cap, International Large-Cap and International Mid/Small-Cap asset classes.) For example, while the average expense ratio in the actively managed Large-Cap Blend asset class is 1.35 percent, diversified index funds managed by high-quality organizations can be accessed with expense ratios as little as .09 percent. Financial planners with clients in higher marginal tax brackets may also find that tax-managed index funds or separate accounts are attractive alternatives. While tax-managed index funds and separate accounts typically possess higher investment minimums (for example, $10,000–$1 million) as well as modestly higher expense ratios than typical index funds, many of these vehicles have successfully avoided capital gains distributions through active tax-loss harvesting.

TABLE 2.7 Average Net Expense Ratios for U.S. and International Asset Classes (Funds with minimum investment levels less than $1 million)

	Active Mgmt Category Average	Index Mgmt. Category Average	Index Mgmt. Lowest 10th Percentile
US LARGE-CAP			
US Large-Cap Blend	1.35%	0.58%	0.09%
US Large-Cap Value	1.35%	0.61%	0.10%
US Large-Cap Growth	1.50%	0.82%	0.136%
US MID-CAP			
US Mid-Cap Blend	1.54%	0.68%	0.10%
US Mid-Cap Value	1.43%	0.35%	0.25%
US Mid-Cap Growth	1.56%	0.80%	0.25%
US SMALL-CAP			
US Small-Cap Blend	1.50%	0.79%	0.15%
US Small-Cap Value	1.75%	0.82%	0.175%
US Small-Cap Growth	1.65%	0.81%	0.175%
INTERNATIONAL			
Intl Large-Cap Blend	1.65%	0.92%	0.145%
Intl Mid/Small-Cap Blend	1.72%	0.64%	0.64% [I Fund]

ETFs AND INDEXING

ETFs and index investing combine the right product with the best strategy. Let's examine the popular and original ETF SPDR [SPY] versus the Vanguard S&P 500 Index fund. The only difference is in fees where SPY charges .10 percent per year while Vanguard charges .18 percent. Advantage SPY.

The only knock on SPY is for investors making frequent contributions since commissions can be costly perhaps even defeating the advantage and hurt overall performance. That's definitely true if you're paying high commissions. But again, in late 2006 and early 2007 commission free trading was introduced. First, a new firm Zecco.com launched its stunning new zero commission schedule, which was quickly matched with some differences by Bank of America Securities and later Wells Fargo. Who else will follow suit is difficult to tell. The drawback for the zero commission offerings is that yields on money market funds are lower. But if you're an active trader or just making monthly contributions, the free commission ends the Vanguard advantage and they know it, which is another reason they're now in the ETF business as well.

Despite Bogle's mantra about investing for the long-term most investors want the flexibility to invest or sell their assets when and at what price. Perhaps buying early in a trading day produces a better price than waiting until the end of the day for a price. This is a feature I personally value. The transparency of a major ETF like SPY allows you to select the price rather than having a mutual fund do it for you at prices beyond your control.

THE ETF TSUNAMI

Aside from the popular NASDAQ 100 ETF, QQQQ and the S&P 500 ETF, prior to the mutual fund scandals, ETFs were a quiet backwater of the investment sector. After the scandals reached their zenith and record fines were handed out DIY investors in particular scoured the ETF sector for more choices. And ETF issuers were only too happy to accommodate them with more and more new issues.

ETF asset growth has been dramatic.

- In 2001 $85 billion in ETFs existed globally with $75 billion listed in the United States.
- By 2003 ETF assets totaled $150 billion.
- By the end of 2006 assets reached $422 billion and growing.

- At the beginning of 2007, there were more than 350 issues listed in the United States with another 350 plus in registration with the SEC.
- Morgan Stanley predicts that by 2010 ETF assets could reach $2 trillion.

Current Choices

With more than 500 ETFs now listed [as of August 2007], it's hard to think of any investment strategy that can't be implemented with an ETF, or a portfolio of ETFs. From broad market categories to specifically targeted sectors there's either enough for some or for others too many to choose from. From the original broad market SPDR [SPY] to the narrowest sectors like nanotechnology [PXN] the array of selections is enough to make an investor's head spin. For the average investor this makes finding the right mix of products to suit their objectives more challenging.

Has the growth been too fast? Many think so and in some media outlets no ETF discussion starts without the "too many, too fast" mantra. Other critics are just overwhelmed by the menu, and some are just plain conflicted and can't be expected to comment impartially.

There are many repetitive ETF sector issues basically covering the same territory with some issuers of a slightly different twist. However, one thing to remember is that many investors, particularly institutional investors, are creatures of habit. For example, if these investors are accustomed to trading a subsector such as Semiconductors within the broader technology sector, they'd probably gravitate to Semiconductor Holders [SMH]. SMH isn't even an ETF but a trust structured like an ETF. There's an index that it follows, but as a trust it cannot add new issues to the group. This makes rebalancing and adding new issues impossible. Yet despite these odd differences, SMH remains the Semiconductor vehicle of choice, which is reflected in high daily volume and liquidity characteristics. Other ETFs that are highly correlated to SMH in the same sector include iShares GS Semiconductor ETF [IGW] or SPDR Semiconductor ETF [XSD]. Both have less liquidity, and investors stubbornly cling to SMH.

The same conditions exist with other sectors where sponsors have launched competing index-based ETFs ranging from energy, biotechnology, consumer discretionary, utilities and so on. Not only these specific types of sectors exist but sponsors have also even gone to issuing style- based themes including "value" and "growth."

It's always important to remember that while Wall Street's new product engineers are busy at work their motivations are driven by their firm's unique business plans. Some firms are organizing ETFs just to position themselves in the sector while others are doing so with the hope of being bought out by another firm wanting in.

I interviewed one sponsor and the discussions turned to what we at the ETF Digest felt were needed—new ETF issues. After listening politely to our suggestions he observed, "We're not in the business to fill needs but to build a business." That statement should tell you all you need to know and, sure enough, later that firm was purchased by another.

But all this doesn't mean we're unhappy with the frenetic growth of new ETFs. Much to the contrary, within all the rubble or tailings from these issues are some needed gems—commodity, currency, leveraged, international, and inverse issues come to mind. So, as far as we're concerned, the more the merrier.

However, we're rapidly approaching a point where with just a few exceptions all the ETFs one needs for diversified portfolio construction are at hand.In fact in this tsunami of new issues, some pundits are discussing how some less popular, obscure in focus, or merely repetitive ETFs may well disappear in a few years. That's quite possible, and already happened several years ago when the FITRs family of fixed income ETFs, beaten to market by iShares, folded after barely being in the market. Guessing which ones are going to drop first is fun, but essentially a pointless game because the leading candidates are in full view at the bottom of the assets and volume lists.

Like any explosive Wall Street product growth phenomena, ETFs will get overdone. It may be that ultimately one issue may fall by the wayside just because of redundancies and a lack of assets for the sponsor reducing fee income and making the business profitable. Consolidations as some less profitable ETFs get folded in with others or just dropped. These are just other reasons individual investors need to be vigilant about the issues they choose and seek some guidance before taking the plunge. The downside or difficulty for investors is an inability to pore through all the choices and make productive and effective choices. Knowledgeable FAs, newsletters, and specialty web sites resources exist to assist in that regard with the latter outlined in subsequent chapters.

NEW QUANTITATIVE INDEXES

Trying to find their own niche ETF sponsor PowerShares developed proprietary "dynamic" indexes. Rather than offering repetitive index-based ETF products they consciously tried to distinguish themselves from the pack. They launched what they boldly called "intelligent" indexes. They chose to name all sequential offerings based on this model, "Intellidex" methodologies or PowerShares XTF. As they describe on their web site:

PowerShares XTF [indexes] are based on Dynamic Indexes that use rules-based quantitative analysis. This Intellidex methodology chooses stocks for their capital appreciation potential, evaluating and selecting stocks based on multiple valuation criteria. Power-Shares XTF replicate a rules-based Intellidix, thereby overriding the emotional conflicts that may interfere with sound investment decisions. This eliminates the subjective nature of securities research, which can also cloud the quality of recommendations, stock selection, and portfolio management. Actively-managed money can suffer from common shortcomings such as Style Drift, Manager Turnover, Window Dressing, and Investor/Manager Goal Misalignment. These are rarely concerns when investing in PowerShares XTF because of their purely objective, rules-based, transparent, and emotion-free management structure. (www.powershares.com)

Wow! What does all this mumbo-jumbo mean? "Quantitative investment analysis [defined per "12Manage.com"] is the process of determining the value of investments, mostly securities, by examining a corporation's financial, numerical, and measurable data and projections such as its:

- Revenues/sales.
- Profits/earnings.
- Margins.
- Market share.
- The value of its assets.
- The cost of capital.

Often ratios are used for this purpose."

This all sounds pretty impressive but let's deconstruct this approach further. Constructing indexes based on this methodology, obviously customized for proprietary Intellidex purposes, does alter typical index construction. Remember typical index construction just evaluates its constituent members by market capitalization and weights them within the index accordingly rebalancing on a schedule quarterly, semiannually, or annually.

With new PowerShares products, the Intellidex Indexes have been back-tested as to efficacy. However, back-testing can often suffer from the dangers of "data mining" or "curve-fitting," two citizens well-represented in the densely populated computational classification of "Garbage in, Garbage out."

Data mining as defined by Answers.com is

the identification or extraction of relationships and patterns from data using computational algorithms to reduce, model, understand, or analyze data. The automated process of turning raw data into

useful information by which intelligent computer systems sift and
sort through data, with little or no help from humans, to look for
patterns or to predict trends.

Christian Schaer, head of Risk & IT, Agora Capital Services SA, defines
"curve-fitting or data mining as the art of drawing conclusions based on past
information. When applied to an investment scheme or trading strategy,
history shows that [too] often such conclusions do not hold true once they
are implemented."

So, there's a fine line between optimizing and curve-fitting. For new
schemes such as those utilized by PowerShares and their Intellidex Indexes
it's probably the wiser course to wait and see how these indexes perform
compared to conventional indexes over different market cycles. This could
take years, but for investors who have a prove it attitude, that may be
the most prudent choice. It's important to note that the first handful of
these PowerShares products now have 3-year-plus track records and the
news is good: They've outperformed their benchmarks by enough to earn
a Morningstar 5-star ETF rating. But they also were launched close to the
market bottom of 2000–2002.

On the other hand, PowerShares has launched some sector indexes
that aren't available in conventional form. These might include Water,
Alternative Energy and Microcap indexes paired with associated ETFs for
example. If these types of sectors appeal to you, then these ETFs may be
your only choice.

PowerShares offerings are a bridge between active management and
conventional indexing. It's a sure thing Jack Bogle wouldn't care for them.

INTERNATIONAL ETFs

For U.S. investors initial international ETF availability was confined to
single-country ETFs. Originally offered by Morgan Stanley under the WEBS
name—for World Equity Benchmark Shares—and now part of the iShares
family, they were larely ignored as the U.S. market boomed in the late
1990s. Why go abroad when markets are roaring at home?

After the bear market ended in early 2003, what emerged was a
more global focus for investors generally. While U.S. stock sectors recovered, many overseas markets took the performance lead—some by wide
margins. Investor interest follows performance every time. U.S. investor
interest in single-country funds rose dramatically. Issues from Europe, Asia,
Asia-Pacific, and Latin America were far outpacing performance data from
conventional U.S. sectors. Japan ETF [EWJ] the most liquid and popular
single-country ETF which lingered and much underperformed through the

1990s started to rally. From the low in 2003, EWJ rallied 150 percent through the three years ending in 2006.

This rebirth of interest in overseas markets wasn't confined to just the established markets like Japan, Germany, and London. It spread to markets normally considered a backwater of investor interest. Markets from Latin America where single-country funds existed, Mexico ETF [EWW] and Brazil ETF [EWZ] also caught investor favor. From the market lows of 2003, EWW has rallied over 400 percent and EWZ nearly 800 percent! Who wouldn't want to have that performance?

New product engineers started rolling out new ETFs to accommodate increasing international ETF demand. Europe, Asia & Far East ETF [EFA] allowed investors to buy one ETF that gave them exposure to many more established global stock markets. EFA was launched in 2001 and from its low of 2003 rallied 170 percent by early 2007. In fact, EFA is now the second highest capitalized ETF listed, a reflection of the popularity of this trend.

Given the popularity of EFA and some Emerging Markets it didn't take Wall Street long to issue more regional ETFs. Emerging Markets ETF [EEM] wasn't issued until 2003, but it, too, is one of the most popular ETFs issued as measured by market capitalization, liquidity, and top of the line performance, up 280 percent through early 2007 since its launch. Other regional issues became popular as well including: Latin American ETF [ILF], Asia Pacific ex-Japan ETF [EPP], S&P Euro 350 ETF [IEV], and so on. All have been top-flight performers.

The Emerging Markets Monitor [London] has been promoting the idea of a "convergence story" whereby Emerging Markets are narrowing the performance and capitalization gap between them and more established global markets. Some evidence of this can not only be found in equity performance statistics but in fixed-income securities as well. Yield spreads, commonly regarded as the difference between various investment grade and high-yield bonds have narrowed. This means that previously lowly regarded debt from countries like Mexico are now able to issue bonds at spreads closer to U.S. Treasury Bonds and do so with ease. Just ten years ago, it would have been unimaginable for an issuer like Mexico to issue bonds at relatively narrow spreads to US Treasury's and do so in pesos versus the dollar. They did so in late 2006. Such is how things are changing.

A lot of this convergence has much to do with the emergence of China and India, or to use the now popular description, "Chindia," and to a lesser extent the BRIC countries [Brazil, Russia, India, and China]. ETFs are being issued to cover these markets collectively although we prefer to invest in them individually since there are different forces at work in each from time to time. In late 2006 India ETN [INP] was launched based on a popular Morgan Stanley index. An ETN represents an Exchange Traded Note, which is different from an ETF in that it's a debt instrument of the sponsor, Barclay's. A Russian ETF will be issued, assuming the conventional approval process is routine, in 2007 by Eaton Vance and based on a Russian index currently listed on the DeutscheBorse, the German stock exchange today lists more ETFs than any exchange in the world [although its total still trails the combined listings of the three main US listing venues].

Further there will be an increased focus on Emerging Europe, which would cover the rapidly expanding non-EU former Soviet bloc countries and markets. There is much interest here as well.

But, as always, every hot market sector gets a dose of humble pie eventually. And with Emerging Markets the declines can be swift, dramatic, and seeming to come out of the blue. In a three-week period in the summer of 2006 many markets from Latin America to Emerging Asia lost a sharp 30 percent. That's a lot of financial damage and volatility for the average investor to accept. But the important point is that it will happen again. And while those markets quickly recovered to make new highs, there will come a time when they won't recover quickly even though the fundamental growth story may persist.

INVERSE ETFs

A funny thing happened on the way down from the NASDAQ 5,500 from 2000 until early 2007; it's still only nearly half that previous high level. During the period of significant decline from 2000–2003 investors who shorted near the top made as much money on the way down, and with greater velocity, as those did on the way up. The ETF Digest for example made between 30 percent–70 percent per year just being short during that period.

One of the promoted benefits of ETFs is the ability to short them and do so without an uptick.* Unfortunately for many retail investors, being able to short available ETFs was nearly impossible for those beneath the top 10 or so in trading volume.

Why?

First, in order to short, your broker must be carrying inventory of those shares, either as a house position, or in the margin accounts of their customers, in order to lend them to you for shorting. It's expensive for

---

*The rule dating from the 1929 market crash designed to prevent momentum driven shorting. ETFs were exempt from this rule, but soon many stocks will too be given recent SEC proposals and comments.

firms to carry inventory although profitable for them to lend given potential margin income from charges. If you're working with an online discount broker and you entered an order to short a "difficult to short" [the common phrase describing this often futile effort] the order would no doubt be rejected, whether a market order or not, with a "no stock available" advice. You could reenter the order until hell froze over, but you're still going to get the same advice. Now some wire-house firms like to suggest that they'll "work the order" for you and find stock. This is nonsense to me, having gone through this experience myself. If as an FA at a major wire-house you try to accomplish this you'll only get the same answer.

Do the major firms have the capability of finding stock for you? Sure. Will they? Probably not, either when you want them to execute the transaction or if at all. Let me tell you, I've made many a call to margin clerks with a big firm and they're not going to go out of their way to find your retail client a few hundred shares. It's just not going to happen since you may as well be dealing with the post office bureaucracy.

One online firm, ETrade [and there may be others not polled by me] has stated that if you call them, they will try to find you stock to fill your order. They say it's done routinely by them but I haven't put them to the test.

There are other issues with hard to short ETFs. Stock specialists are a part of the process in accommodating retail short requests. Sometimes they're just not interested in finding stock from their order book to provide to the brokers. Further some ETFs are connected to more obscure indexes where there are no futures contracts or other vehicles for the specialist to offset their short position risk.

Finally, as we pointed out previously there are creation units that Nate Most came upon. Investors can go to the trustee of the fund and have more shares issued. The sponsors love this since more shares issued means more fee income. However, most creation units are either in 50 thousand to 100 thousand share counts. How many retail or even "mass affluent" investors have that kind of financial capacity? Not many obviously.

Therefore the promoted benefit is not being realized thoroughly by retail investors. When we presented this problem repeatedly to exchanges and sponsors they pointed to the brokers as the problems. So did the specialists. And so the buck-passing continued. In fact the exchanges just suggested that retail investors finding difficulty shorting should just turn to the options market. In my opinion, most options strategies available were never satisfactory and here I speak as an options principal. Besides options strategies were more lucrative financially to the exchange than if they had to work at helping fulfill the promoted shorting benefit.

Finally, for the burgeoning IRA and 401[k] market, not to mention other tax-exempt entities, shorting is restricted. Therefore, if you wanted to hedge your portfolio or speculate using ETFs you couldn't do it. As we outlined in chapter 1 the rollover IRA is going to be a huge market as Baby Boomers retire and receive their lump sum from their employers. They'll want tools to protect their portfolios.

The solution to this problem was the "inverse" ETF, which simply stated allow you to be short by going long. Say again? If you're not allowed to short in the aforementioned restricted accounts, then you could just buy an inverse issue, which benefits if prices related to the associated index decline. Pioneering this strategy was ProShares, an affiliated ETF sponsor to mutual fund provider ProFunds Advisors LLC. ProFunds had already had a lengthy experience at dealing with inverse issues in conventional mutual fund structures. The attraction of doing the same thing within an ETF structure was too good for them to pass up so they filed for some inverse issues with the SEC.

Approximately eight years passed while the SEC sat on their registration filing. Nothing moved in the bureaucratic process and because of the mandated quiet period, ProShares spokespersons couldn't talk about it. A pretty frustrating experience for all concerned including the ETF Digest since we were anxious to have the tools available. But finally in June 2006, the first batch of inverse ETF issues hit the Street.

- PSQ [short QQQ].
- SH [short S&P 500].
- DOG [short DJIA 30].
- MYY [short Mid-Cap 400].

Then in January 2007 two more ProShares inverse issues arrived including:

- SBB [short Small-Cap 600].
- RWM [short Russell 2000].

These six ETFs can be used by investors where they are highly correlated to portfolio exposure and hedging or speculative strategies may be employed. The good news for most investors is that now they don't have to deal with complex options strategies and margin issues that are off-putting to even sophisticated investors.

Then in spring 2007 ProShares issued several dozen more inverse and "Ultra" issues that cover more industry subsectors from the most conventional areas like MidCaps to the even Utililties.

From a business point of view, ProShares filing, tenacity, and patience really paid off for them. As the pioneer, they deservedly get all the credit for their hard work. Historically, ProFunds and Rydex Investments, both located in Maryland, also maintained an ongoing competitive relationship in unique but conventional mutual funds specializing in inverse and leveraged funds. And, as is typical of their relationship, Rydex Investments has quickly followed suit by filing for an array of similar ETF issues [66 in all] that should have some approved in 2007 with the balance in 2008. Both Rydex and ProShares are looking to file inverse and leveraged issues for fixed income and international ETFs. In fact, Rydex has already obtained SEC exemptive relief covering international ETFs. Once both companies have completed the preponderance of their offerings investors will be hard-pressed not to find product to meet their needs.

There will still be hard to short ETFs particularly for those with little liquidity or linked to odd "hard for specialists hedging" indexes. But for those sectors that are highly correlated one to another there should be an inverse issue that would work well enough to fulfill its hedging or speculative role.

ULTRA, LEVERAGED SHORT, OR LONG ETFs

If you want to add some beta [volatility] or spice to your index-based ETF portfolio, both ProShares and Rydex Investments have some ETFs for you. Both use strategies already employed within their conventional mutual fund products. These funds add double the performance of the index on either the up- or downside. Simply stated, this means you get more bang for your buck *if* you're on the right side of market trends. And if you're on the wrong side, well you lose twice the amount.

Who wants these kinds of products? Of course the issuers like them since the fees are much higher than for conventional unleveraged ETFs ranging over .75 percent per annum versus major index-based ETF fees of around .20 percent. Why are these so much higher? These ETFs involve more management work and have a narrower, more limited, investment audience.

There are many pundits who don't like or recommend them. That's probably the safe and judicious recommendation to make to the masses of investors. But there's more than just a hint of smug paternalism and a negative competitive edge to these judgments. At the ETF Digest we use Ultra series occasionally when we feel there's a real opportunity to enhance performance. But other pundits are dismissive. Charles Jaffe, a columnist with web site MarketWatch, gave out some of his annual "lumps of coal" awards in 2006 to among others ProShares for:

...a big gesture that investors should completely ignore. Late in the summer, ProFunds Group filed registration papers on 66

*new exchange-traded funds, all of them leveraged, hard-to-use and
completely unnecessary for any typical investor.*

Really? Unnecessary for *any* typical investor? This is just a completely
irresponsible and uninformed commentary. But it's a free country, right?

The anti-ETF crowd at Morningstar notes in a post by Sonya Morris,
September 25, 2006, that investors "... would do well to steer clear of
leveraged offerings altogether." Why? Because she just thinks that they're
too risky. While her comments may be helpful to conservative investors,
others more aggressive may be more inclined to make judicious use of these
products. It's still a free country that can accommodate all types of investors.
It shouldn't be a one size fits all marketplace.

COMMODITY AND CURRENCY ETFs

This is an area where the naysayers really get worked up in negativity.
And yet this area has been one of the biggest areas of sector investment
opportunity that I've seen in nearly 35 years.

Commodity trading or speculating has a poor public image conjuring
up negative images of wild pork belly trading. Currency trading has suffered
by a similar image since heretofore investing in commodities or currencies
was intimidating to the average investor and carried with it the stigma of a
poor image. Yet intuitively most investors know there's money to be made
when dealing in both areas. The problem has been how to do it easily and
minimize the perceived risks.

Previously to trade either market one needed to trade commodities
directly or in some commodity or futures pool or fund. These funds were
operated by Commodity Trading Advisors [CTAs] and Commodity Pool
Operators [CPOs]. Having been one myself, there are some serious negatives
that investors needed to overcome. First were high fees associated with the
funds that may have run more than 5 percent and included high fees charged
by CTA advisors to the fund, plus a fixed percentage of 1 percent to 3 percent
plus incentive fees from 15 to 25 percent of net profits. Further, many funds
would allow you in or out only once per month or even only quarterly.
Second, with these funds heavy leverage is often employed amounting to
perhaps 5 to 10 times the equity. Unlike with the Ultra issues from ProShares
and Rydex where only two times the index was used, with CPOs extreme
leverage can bring utter failure and fund closure.

So high costs, a lack of liquidity, and heavy use of leverage turned
average investors off.

The positive benefits however are dominated primarily by the benefit
of adding true uncorrelated portfolio diversification, which actually reduces

risk. The authoritative academic study issued in 1983 by Harvard professor John Lintner which outlined the benefits of adding managed futures assets [also known as "alternative investments," which include both commodities and currencies] to average investment portfolios. The study concluded that by adding this asset class to a conventional portfolio showed that the return/risk ratio of a portfolio of managed futures funds is higher than a well-diversified stock/bond portfolio. Come again? Well, most FAs and individual investors are taught to believe that just having a balanced stock and bond portfolio, for example, achieves diversification and reduces risk. This is not necessarily so since both markets can and do trend in the same direction. Further some pundits have advocated adding combinations of value and growth styles to achieve additional diversification. But if all these sectors are trending in the same direction you haven't accomplished any risk reduction but have just spread it around needlessly and in a costly manner.

Lintner's work proved that the asset class that added most risk reduction and better overall performance contained assets that were "uncorrelated" [moving in opposite directions generally]. The study went on to demonstrate instances when stocks and bonds suffered but managed futures performed well, given their ability to move short or long in these uncorrelated markets. In fact, it was noted that by allocating as much as 14 percent of assets to managed futures an equal percentage reduction of standard deviation [volatility] was achieved.

So enter ETFs based on both commodities and currency. This is exciting because it allows investors to conveniently add these issues to their portfolios without having to join expensive and complex CPOs or using any leverage. Now average investors can truly diversify their conventional portfolios using these products. Given the lack of leverage in the ETFs some of the benefits that Lintner noted may be lessened. But the emotional craziness often associated with futures and commodity trading has also been eliminated making it palatable for average investors. Some popular currency and commodity ETF products include:

- GLD [popular Gold ETF].
- SLV [Silver].
- DBC [PS/Deutsche Bank Commodity Index ETF].
- USO [Oil ETF].
- DBP [PS/Deutsche Bank Precious Metals ETF [An 80/20 combination of gold/silver].
- DBA [PS/Deutsche Bank Agricultural ETF].
- DBB [PS/Deutsche Bank Basic Metals ETF].

- UUP & UDN [PS/Deutsche Bank Bullish and Bearish Dollar Index ETFs].
- FXE [Rydex Euro Currency ETF].
- FXY [Rydex Yen Currency ETF].
- Other currency issues include Swiss franc, Australian pound, Mexican peseta, British pound, and the Swedish krona.

So, there's quite a few to choose from. Most investors will opt to include UUP, UDN, DBC, GLD, or DBP as their primary inclusions to portfolios since they offer broader less targeted index exposure. An example is DBC, which includes weightings in crude and heating oil, gold, copper, wheat, and corn.

Another forgotten or ignored use for these ETFS is that investors may seek to hedge their currency exposure. A simple example is the combination of Japan ETF [EWJ] that appreciated roughly 20 percent in 2005. That seemed good enough superficially, but the related Japanese equity indexes actually gained 40 percent during the same period. The difference was attributed primarily to currency differentials as the yen decline diluted the index performance for U.S. dollar investors. Being able to judiciously combine an Yen ETF [FXY] short position combined with a long EWJ position would have allowed investors to make the superior 40 percent return. Therefore hedging possibilities are now available to average investors that heretofore existed only for the benefit of institutions.

But now the same anti-ETF advisors from places like Morningstar are advising investors to avoid these issues. In the same article cited previously by Sonya Morris she states: "... it's difficult to see the investment merit of other pure-play commodity ETFs." And she goes on to say, "I think these ... have little to offer the long-term investor and are primarily aimed at speculators interested in making short-term bets on the direction of capricious commodity prices. That's a perilous game to play and one that very few investors can pull off successfully with any consistency." And she hastily adds in her dismissal, "Don't get me wrong. Commodities have characteristics that make them useful portfolio diversifiers." At the end she proceeds to recommend a leveraged Pimco Commodity Fund [PCRDX]. She obviously read something of the Lintner study but failed completely to overcome her mutual fund bias or the superior benefits of the ETF structure.

Lastly, as for currency ETFs, she states, "Very few individuals have reason to own these funds." Why? Because "making successful bets on currencies requires knowledge of global economic factors and deft forecasting." This is another silly comment, since these aren't skills unique to just currency trading—you have to know what you're doing regarding any investment activity.

ACTIVELY MANAGED ETFs?

Soon many actively managed mutual funds will be issued structured ["masquerading" might be more apt] as ETFs. Conventional mutual fund companies wish to participate in the ETF boom and see their market share being eroded by the new structure popularity.

Aside from the obvious business intentions of the issuers, the benefits to having these ETFs for investors are still murky. One could well argue that in such a new structure fees could be lower. But are mutual funds ready to cannibalize their own existing products? Is the ETF threat that great? It must be so if they intend to proceed. Another benefit is being able to conduct transaction in these funds intraday versus waiting until the end-of-day NAV calculation. So in that sense it's a more efficient and flexible process.

What are the disadvantages? There's really one, but it's a killer. The beauty of an ETF is that, to be followed and respected, it's forever tethered to an index it must track to be successful. With that link it's always easy for an investor to maintain investment transparency and know exactly what you've invested in. Having the index is the disciplining force to restrain investment management activity. Without the bond between ETF and index, you're lost.

So actively managed ETFs defy the core ETF principal and should be avoided with one possible exception. As we shall see in later chapters, there's a possibility that a convergence between actively managed mutual funds and hedge fund strategies utilizing ETFs might become a popular stand-alone product category.

WITH GROWTH COME OTHER PROBLEMS

The combination of rapid ETF issuance and the growth of electronic trading on exchanges has combined to create one problem that may well act as a brake on new ETF issuance, especially for more create products. Traditionally, stocks traded on the New York and American stock exchanges were handled by a specialist, who was, at least theoretically, responsible for maintaining an orderly market for the shares. But with the floors losing market share to electronic trading networks, the specialist firms have shrunk dramatically, laying off staff and compromising their ability to fulfill their function. For the big, liquid ETFs, that's not a problem. For the others, it can be.

One particularly egregious incident occurred in early 2007 when Claymore Securities issued their bullish and bearish Macro Oil Shares in late 2006 investors were interested since crude oil markets were hot, and being able to trade both sides of the market was a compelling feature. But problems surfaced immediately when the only specialist firm, Bear Hunter [a subsidiary of Bear Stearns], making a market in the ETFs, took a holiday leaving investors wanting to trade either security abandoned. Oil prices were dropping then and those investors wanting to buy the bearish ETF were foiled as prices for it *and* the bullish issue inexplicably rose. While the ETFs in question obviously have serious design flaws—they have consistently traded well away from the NAVs—the early-life treatment at the hands of their specialist almost guaranteed that the ETFs would fail, and it certainly undermined the chances that similar products, which might have worked better than the oil example, would never see the light of market day.

With more than 300 ETFs in registration in 2007, it would take around $1 billion to get these off the gound with some chance of success. And that's clearly not going to happen. In fact, Rydex Investments launched over a dozen Equal-Weight S&P 500 sector ETFs. After issuance some of even these well-structured ETFs found little in the way of specialist support.

ETF sponsors and issuers are turning to large Wall Street brokerage firms and even private equity investors to assume the seeding and specialist roles, something that's a simple job for iShares, a subsidiary of Barclay's Global Investors, and State Street's SPDR family. But it's much more difficult for the smaller issuers, like Claymore or First Trust.

These issues may obviously put a big breakwater in the front of the ETF tsunami. But, worry not, there are plenty of existing ETFs that will suit your investment needs already issued and trading well. Some new redundant ETF issues may not be successful given these limitations and restraints.

A DISRUPTIVE TECHNOLOGY INDEED!

Just recently I listened to an interview with a hugely popular TV stock market pundit. He was being asked about ETFs and he, as a diehard stock jockey, was quick to put them down. He argued incorrectly that if you buy "an" ETF based on a sector, you really haven't diversified your portfolio. Well, how silly! Most investors don't just buy one ETF linked to one sector, but buy a range of them to achieve appropriate diversification.

But, such is the business threat that this star felt and his competitive juices wanted to put the movement down.

The Morningstar and Lipper organizations for example, cut their teeth and made lucrative fees based on covering conventional mutual funds. The ETF industry isn't as lucrative for them. Investors following these organizations' publications pay to find out various rankings of actively managed funds and how many or few rating "stars" funds might achieve. It's only natural to want to be in a high-quality 5-star fund, right? But how do you put stars on a passive index? You can't. And there's the rub business-wise. Now Morningstar has put star rankings on a few of PowerShares Quantitative Intellidexes, which many in the investment community believe are quasi-actively managed ETFs. However, they, too, are tied to an index that the ETF tracks making ranking them difficult since to what are they compared?

The major financial advisory firms [including the brokerage, financial planning, insurance, and banking industry] are all hesitant about ETFs since they must find creative ways for firms and FAs to be paid to distribute products. The all-inclusive fee structures some firms and FAs will craft will, if accepted by investors, pay them, but not as lucratively as did the steady Evergreen Income from conventional mutual funds since charging high fees for ETF advice defeats their inherent low-cost benefits. And more forward looking FAs will have to adjust their business strategies and raise more assets to make up for inevitable losses by going off on their own as another choice.

Indexing beats active management as we've shown. For DIY investors, index-linked ETFs are the logical and most cost-efficient investment vehicles whether you're an active or passive investor.

CHAPTER 3

The Rise of Hedge Funds

*Today, if asked to define a hedge fund, I suspect most folks would
characterize it as a highly speculative vehicle for unwitting fat cats
and careless financial institutions to lose their shirts.*

—Mario Gabelli

The first hedge fund utilized a straightforward concept. It existed primarily
to manage risk by hedging "long" stock positions against relatively equal
"short" positions. Alfred Jones usually gets the credit for being the first to
implement this strategy in 1948 when he took $40,000 of his own funds
and another $60,000 from other investors and set up a partnership to test
his model.

Essentially Jones believed that by buying stronger stocks and selling
against them weaker stocks he could profit more on his long positions than
he would lose on those he was short. These transactions would ideally be
made within the same sector so that correlations would be more in sync.
His theory would reduce overall investment risk since the portfolio was
always hedged. A simple example today might find Jones "long" Toyota
and "short" Ford believing he would profit more on the former than he'd
lose on the latter.

The initial strategy worked well enough to allow Jones to alter his
investment vehicle in 1952 from a general partnership to a limited partnership. He added what was then a novel 20 percent incentive fee, which gave
the advisor a share of profits. A version of the modern hedge fund was born.

Today, Jones's initial hedged strategy is now known in the industry as
a "long/short" or "market neutral" methodology from among the dozens
of different hedge fund investment styles.

WHAT WE *REALLY* MEAN BY HEDGE FUND

The term *hedge fund* is a misnomer that has become to mean, dependent on structure and goal, what one could just call "performance partnerships." That is, investors seek out managers whom they believe can achieve high risk-adjusted investment results utilizing specific styles and strategies. Hedge fund managers are mostly notorious for the high fees they charge—typically, 2 percent of assets under management and 20 percent of new profits, although a handful charge much higher amounts—and the consequent headlines surrounding the personal income estimates of the most successful. We're not here to argue the rights and wrongs of those questions, but it does need to be kept in mind that virtually all managers report performance "after" fees, and they don't get paid until they actually make money for their clients. This contrasts with conventional mutual fund and advisory fee structures that pay flat fees whether the performance is positive or not.

To give you a good idea of the number of different hedge fund strategies, or "styles" as they are sometimes called, let's look at how two different hedge fund research firms, Lipper Hedge World [a Reuters subsidiary] and the specialist boutique Hedge Fund Research Inc. sort and evaluate different strategies. I chose these two firms because their research is widely followed, respected, and they offered two different looks at strategies.

Lipper Hedge World

Lipper Hedge World [LHW] offers a more general list of hedge fund strategies as outlined below:

> *Convertible Arbitrage.* This strategy is identified by hedge investing in the convertible securities of a company. A typical investment is to be long the convertible bond and short the common stock of the same company. Positions are designed to generate profits from the fixed income security as well as the short sale of stock, while protecting principal from market moves.
>
> *Dedicated Short Bias.* Dedicated short sellers were once a robust category of hedge funds before the long bull market rendered the strategy difficult to implement. A new category, short biased, has emerged. The strategy is to maintain net short as opposed to pure short exposure. Short bias managers take short positions in mostly equities and derivatives. The short bias of a manager's portfolio must be constantly greater than zero to be classified in this category.
>
> *Emerging Markets.* This strategy involves equity or fixed income investing in emerging markets around the world. Because many emerging markets do not allow short selling, nor offer viable futures or other

derivative products with which to hedge, emerging market investing often employs a long-only strategy.

Equity Market Neutral. This investment strategy is designed to exploit equity market inefficiencies and usually involves being simultaneously long and short matched equity portfolios of the same size within a country. Market neutral portfolios are designed to be either beta or currency neutral, or both. Well-designed portfolios typically control for industry, sector, market capitalization, and other exposures. Leverage is often applied to enhance returns.

Event-Driven. This strategy is defined as equity-oriented investing designed to capture price movement generated by an anticipated corporate event. There are four popular sub-categories in event-driven strategies:

1. *Risk Arbitrage.* Specialists invest simultaneously in long and short positions in both companies involved in a merger or acquisition. Risk arbitrageurs are typically long the stock of the company being acquired and short the stock of the acquirer. The principal risk is deal risk, if the deal fails to close.

2. *Distressed Securities.* Fund managers invest in the debt, equity, or trade claims of companies in financial distress and generally bankruptcy. The securities of companies in need of legal action or restructuring to revive financial stability typically trade at substantial discounts to par value and thereby attract investments when managers perceive a turn-around will materialize.

3. *Regulation D, or Reg. D.* This subset refers to investments in micro and small capitalization public companies that are raising money in private capital markets. Investments usually take the form of a convertible security with an exercise price that floats or is subject to a look-back provision that insulates the investor from a decline in the price of the underlying stock.

4. *High Yield.* Often called junk bonds, this subset refers to investing in low-graded fixed-income securities of companies that show significant upside potential. Managers generally buy and hold high-yield debt.

Fixed Income Arbitrage. The fixed income arbitrageur aims to profit from price anomalies between related interest rate securities. Most managers trade globally with a goal of generating steady returns with low volatility. This category includes interest rate swap arbitrage, U.S. and non-U.S. government bond arbitrage, forward yield curve arbitrage, and mortgage-backed securities arbitrage. The mortgage-backed market is primarily U.S.-based, over-the-counter, and particularly complex.

Global Macro. Global macro managers carry long and short positions in any of the world's major capital or derivative markets. These positions reflect their views on overall market direction as influenced by major economic trends and/or events. The portfolios of these funds can include stocks, bonds, currencies, and commodities in the form of cash or derivatives instruments. Most funds invest globally in both developed and emerging markets.

Long/Short Equity. This directional strategy involves equity-oriented investing on both the long and short sides of the market. The objective is not to be market neutral. Managers have the ability to shift from value to growth, from small to medium to large capitalization stocks, and from a net long position to a net short position. Managers may use futures and options to hedge. The focus may be regional, such as long/short U.S. or European equity, or sector specific, such as long and short technology or healthcare stocks. Long/short equity funds tend to build and hold portfolios that are substantially more concentrated than those of traditional stock funds.

Managed Futures. This strategy invests in listed financial and commodity futures markets and currency markets around the world. The managers are usually referred to as Commodity Trading Advisors, or CTAs. Trading disciplines are generally systematic or discretionary. Systematic traders tend to use price and market specific information (often technical) to make trading decisions, while discretionary managers use a judgmental approach.

Hedge Fund Research, Inc.

Chicago-based Hedge Fund Research [HFRI] offers a much more detailed description of strategies by breaking each area into various subsectors as outlined below:

Convertible Arbitrage. Convertible Arbitrage involves purchasing a portfolio of convertible securities, generally convertible bonds, and hedging a portion of the equity risk by selling short the underlying common stock. Certain managers may also seek to hedge interest rate exposure under some circumstances. Most managers employ some degree of leverage, ranging from zero to 6:1. The equity hedge ratio may range from 30 to 100 percent. The average grade of bond in a typical portfolio is BB−, with individual ratings ranging from AA to CCC. However, as the default risk of the company is hedged by shorting the underlying common stock, the risk is considerably better than the rating of the unhedged bond indicates.

Distressed Securities. Distressed Securities strategies invest in, and may sell short, the securities of companies where the security's price has been, or is expected to be, affected by a distressed situation. This may involve reorganizations, bankruptcies, distressed sales and other corporate restructurings. Depending on the manager's style, investments may be made in bank debt, corporate debt, trade claims, common stock, preferred stock, and warrants. Strategies may be subcategorized as "high-yield" or "orphan equities." Leverage may be used by some managers. Fund managers may run a market hedge using S&P put options or put options spreads.

HFRI Emerging Markets—Asia. Emerging Markets funds invest in securities of companies or the sovereign debt of developing or "emerging" countries. Investments are primarily long. Emerging Markets—Asia involves investing in the emerging markets of Asia.

Emerging Markets—Eastern Europe/CIS. Emerging Markets funds invest in securities of companies or the sovereign debt of developing or "emerging" countries. Investments are primarily long. Emerging Markets—Eastern Europe/CIS funds concentrate their investment activities in the nations of Eastern Europe and the CIS (the former Soviet Union).

HFRI Emerging Markets—Global. Emerging Markets funds invest in securities of companies or the sovereign debt of developing or "emerging" countries. Investments are primarily long. HFRI Emerging Markets—Global is a strategy that entails investing in emerging markets anywhere in the world, with no specific regional focus. Global funds will shift their weightings among regions according to market conditions and manager perspectives.

HFRI Emerging Markets—Latin America. Emerging Markets funds invest in securities of companies or the sovereign debt of developing or "emerging" countries. Investments are primarily long. Emerging Markets—Latin America is a strategy that entails investing throughout Central and South America.

HFRI Emerging Markets (Total). HFRI Emerging Markets [Total] is a composite index encompassing the following emerging markets substrategies: Asia, Eastern Europe/CIS, Global, and Latin America.

Equity Hedge. Equity Hedge investing consists of a core holding of long equities hedged at all times with short sales of stocks and/or stock index options. Some managers maintain a substantial portion of assets within a hedged structure and commonly employ leverage. Where short sales are used, hedged assets may be comprised of an equal dollar value of long and short stock positions. Other variations use short sales unrelated to long holdings and/or puts on the S&P 500 index and put spreads. Conservative funds mitigate market risk by maintaining market exposure from 0 to 100 percent. Aggressive funds may magnify market risk by exceeding 100 percent exposure and, in some instances, maintain a short exposure. In addition to equities, some funds may have limited assets invested in other types of securities.

Equity Market Neutral. Equity Market Neutral investing seeks to profit by exploiting pricing inefficiencies between related equity securities, neutralizing exposure to market risk by combining long and short positions. One example of this strategy is to build portfolios made up of long positions in the strongest companies in several industries and taking corresponding short positions in those showing signs of weakness.

Statistical Arbitrage Equity Market Neutral. Statistical Arbitrage utilizes quantitative analysis of technical factors to exploit pricing inefficiencies between related equity securities, neutralizing exposure to market risk by combining long and short positions. The strategy is based on quantitative models for selecting specific stocks with equal dollar amounts comprising the long and short sides of the portfolio. Portfolios are typically structured to be market, industry, sector, and dollar neutral.

Equity Non-Hedge. Equity Non-Hedge funds are predominantly long equities although they have the ability to hedge with short sales of stocks and/or stock index options. These funds are commonly known as "stock-pickers." Some funds employ leverage to enhance returns. When market conditions warrant, managers may implement a hedge in the portfolio. Funds may also opportunistically short individual stocks. The important distinction between equity non-hedge funds and equity hedge funds is equity non-hedge funds do not always have a hedge in place. In addition to equities, some funds may have limited assets invested in other types of securities.

Event-Driven. Event-Driven is also known as "corporate life cycle" investing. This involves investing in opportunities created by significant transactional events, such as spin-offs, mergers and acquisitions, bankruptcy reorganizations, recapitalizations, and share buybacks. The portfolio of some Event-Driven managers may shift in majority weighting between Risk Arbitrage and Distressed Securities, while others may take a broader scope. Instruments include long and short common and preferred stocks, as well as debt securities and options. Leverage may be used by some managers. Fund managers may hedge against market risk by purchasing S&P put options or put option spreads.

Fixed Income: Arbitrage. Fixed Income: Arbitrage is a market neutral hedging strategy that seeks to profit by exploiting pricing inefficiencies between related fixed income securities while neutralizing exposure to interest rate risk. Fixed Income: Arbitrage is a generic description of a variety of strategies involving investment in fixed income instruments, and weighted in an attempt to eliminate or reduce exposure to changes in the yield curve. Managers attempt to exploit relative mispricing between related sets of fixed income securities. The generic types of fixed income hedging trades include: yield-curve arbitrage, corporate versus Treasury yield spreads, municipal bond versus Treasury yield spreads and cash versus futures.

Fixed Income: Convertible Bonds. Fixed Income: Convertible Bonds funds are primarily long only convertible bonds. Convertible bonds have both fixed income and equity characteristics. If the underlying common stock appreciates, the convertible bond's value should rise to reflect this increased value. Downside protection is offered because if the underlying common stock declines, the convertible bond's value can decline only to the point where it behaves like a straight bond.

Fixed Income: Diversified. Fixed Income: Diversified funds may invest in a variety of fixed income strategies. While many invest in multiple strategies, others may focus on a single strategy less followed by most fixed income hedge funds. Areas of focus include municipal bonds, corporate bonds, and global fixed income securities.

Fixed Income: High-Yield. Fixed Income: High-Yield managers invest in noninvestment grade debt. Objectives may range from high current income to acquisition of undervalued instruments. Emphasis is placed on assessing credit risk of the issuer. Some of the available high-yield instruments include extendible/reset securities, increasing-rate notes, pay-in-kind securities, step-up coupon securities, split-coupon securities, and usable bonds.

Fixed Income: Mortgage-Backed. Fixed Income: Mortgage-Backed funds invest in mortgage-backed securities. Many funds focus solely on AAA-rated bonds. Instruments include: government agency, government-sponsored enterprise, private-label fixed- or adjustable-rate mortgage pass-through securities, fixed- or adjustable-rate collateralized mortgage obligations [CMOs], real estate mortgage investment conduits (REMICs), and stripped mortgage-backed securities [SMBSs]. Funds may look to capitalize on security-specific mispricings. Hedging of prepayment risk and interest rate risk is common. Leverage may be used, as well as futures, short sales, and options.

Fixed Income (Total). HFRI Fixed Income [Total] is a composite index encompassing the following Fixed Income substrategies: Arbitrage, Convertible Bonds, Diversified, High-Yield, and Mortgage-Backed.

Macro. Macro involves investing by making leveraged bets on anticipated price movements of stock markets, interest rates, foreign exchange, and physical commodities. Macro managers employ a "top-down" global approach, and may invest in any markets using any instruments to participate in expected market movements. These movements may result from forecasted shifts in world economies, political fortunes, or global supply and demand for resources, both physical and financial. Exchange-traded and over-the-counter derivatives are often used to magnify these price movements.

Market Timing. Market Timing involves allocating assets among investments by switching into investments that appear to be beginning an uptrend, and switching out of investments that appear to be starting a downtrend. This primarily consists of switching between mutual funds and money markets. Typically, technical trend-following indicators are used to determine the direction of a fund and identify buy and sell signals. In an up move "buy signal," money is transferred from a money market fund into a mutual fund in an attempt to capture a capital gain. In a down move "sell signal," the assets in the mutual fund are sold and moved back into the money market for safe keeping until the next up move. The goal is to avoid being invested in mutual funds during a market decline.

Merger Arbitrage/Risk Arbitrage. Merger Arbitrage, sometimes called Risk Arbitrage, involves investment in event-driven situations such as leveraged buy-outs, mergers, and hostile takeovers. Normally, the stock of an acquisition target appreciates while the acquiring company's stock decreases in value. These strategies generate returns by purchasing stock of the company being acquired, and in some instances, selling short the stock of the acquiring company. Managers may employ the use of equity options as a low-risk alternative to the outright purchase or sale of common stock. Most Merger Arbitrage funds hedge against market risk by purchasing S&P put options or put option spreads.

Regulation D. Regulation D managers invest in Regulation D securities, sometimes referred to as structured discount convertibles. The securities are privately offered to the investment manager by companies in need of timely financing and the terms are negotiated. The terms of any particular deal are reflective of the negotiating strength of the issuing company. Once a deal is closed, there is a waiting period for the private share offering to be registered with the SEC. The manager can only convert into private shares and cannot trade them publicly during this period; therefore their investment is illiquid until it becomes registered. Managers will hedge with common stock until the registration becomes effective and then liquidate the position gradually.

Relative Value Arbitrage. Relative Value Arbitrage attempts to take advantage of relative pricing discrepancies between instruments including equities, debt, options, and futures. Managers may use mathematical, fundamental, or technical analysis to determine misvaluations. Securities may be mispriced relative to the underlying security, related securities, groups of securities, or the overall market. Many funds use leverage and seek opportunities globally. Arbitrage strategies include dividend arbitrage, pairs trading, options arbitrage, and yield curve trading.

Sector: Energy. Sector: Energy is a strategy that focuses on investment within the energy sector. Investments can be long and short in various instruments with funds either diversified across the entire sector or specializing within a subsector, that is, oil field service.

Sector: Financial. Sector: Financial is a strategy that invests in securities of bank holding companies, banks, thrifts, insurance companies, mortgage banks, and various other financial services companies.

Sector: Healthcare/Biotechnology. Sector: Healthcare/Biotechnology funds invest in companies involved in the healthcare, pharmaceutical, biotechnology, and medical device areas.

Sector: Miscellaneous. Sector: Miscellaneous funds invest in securities of companies primarily focused on miscellaneous sectors of investments, such as precious metals [gold, silver], beverage companies, retail stores, home improvement outlets, shipping industry, weather/climate opportunities, or the entertainment/sports industry.

Sector: Real Estate. Sector: Real Estate involves investing in securities of real estate investment trusts [REITs] and other real estate companies. Some funds may also invest directly in real estate property.

Sector: Technology. Sector: Technology funds emphasize investment in securities of the technology arena. Some of the subsectors include multimedia, networking, PC producers, retailers, semiconductors, software, and telecommunications.

Sector (Total). HFRI Sector: (Total) is a composite index encompassing the following Sector substrategies: Energy, Financial, Health Care/Biotechnology, Miscellaneous, Real Estate, and Technology.

Short Selling. Short Selling involves the sale of a security not owned by the seller; a technique used to take advantage of an anticipated price decline. To effect a short sale, the seller borrows securities from a third party in order to make delivery to the purchaser. The seller returns the borrowed securities to the lender by purchasing the securities in the open market. If the seller can buy that stock back at a lower price, a profit results. If the price rises, however, a loss results. A short seller must generally pledge other securities or cash with the lender in an amount equal to the market price of the borrowed securities. This deposit may be increased or decreased in response to changes in the market price of the borrowed securities.

Fund of Funds (FOF). Fund of Funds invests with multiple managers through funds or managed accounts. The strategy designs a diversified portfolio of managers with the objective of significantly lowering the risk [volatility] of investing with an individual manager. The Fund of Funds manager has discretion in choosing which strategies to invest in for the portfolio. A manager may allocate funds to numerous managers within a single strategy, or with numerous managers in multiple strategies. The minimum investment in a Fund of Funds may be lower than an investment in an individual hedge fund or managed account. The investor has the advantage of diversification among managers and styles with significantly less capital than investing with separate managers.

HFRI FOF: Conservative. FOFs classified as Conservative exhibit one or more of the following characteristics: seeks consistent returns by primarily investing in funds that generally engage in more "conservative" strategies such as Equity Market Neutral, Fixed Income Arbitrage, and Convertible Arbitrage; exhibits a lower historical annual standard deviation than the HFRI Fund of Funds Composite Index. A fund in the HFRI FOF: Conservative Index shows generally consistent performance regardless of market conditions.

HFRI FOF: Diversified. FOFs classified as Diversified exhibit one or more of the following characteristics: invests in a variety of strategies among multiple managers; historical annual return and/or a standard deviation generally similar to the HFRI Fund of Fund Composite index; demonstrates generally close performance and returns distribution correlation to the HFRI Fund of Fund Composite Index. A fund in the HFRI FOF: Diversified Index tends to show minimal loss in down markets while achieving superior returns in up markets.

HFRI FOF: Market Defensive. FOFs classified as Market Defensive exhibit one or more of the following characteristics: invests in funds that generally engage in short-biased strategies such as short selling and managed futures; shows a negative correlation to the general market benchmarks [S&P]. A fund in the FOF Market Defensive Index exhibits higher returns during down markets than during up markets.

HFRI FOF: Strategic. FOFs classified as Strategic exhibit one or more of the following characteristics: seeks superior returns by primarily investing in funds that generally engage in more opportunistic strategies such as Emerging Markets, Sector specific, and Equity Hedge; exhibits a greater dispersion of returns and higher volatility compared to the HFRI Fund of Funds Composite Index. A fund in the HFRI FOF Strategic Index tends to outperform the HFRI Fund of Fund Composite Index in up markets and underperform the index in down markets.

HFRI also breaks out 2007 asset allocations by strategy, shown in Figure 3.1.

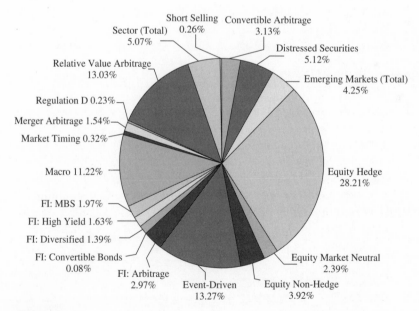

FIGURE 3.1 Estimated Strategy Composition by Assets under Management [Q1 2007]
Source: Chicago-based Hedge Fund Research, Inc.

HOT NEW SECTOR: PRIVATE EQUITY

The hottest sector of new growth is Private Equity. This strategy is the modern equivalent of the Leveraged Buy-Out sector popular in the 1980s. Today with so much liquidity available courtesy of generous central banks (see Chapter 5), funds can put together large financings to take public firms private. The strategy is to restructure the acquired firms, hold them for a period and either sell them back to the public, or spin off various restructured portions of the acquired firm.

Another aspect of Private Equity has been to become activists with corporate boards where they have taken large positions. This has been done to steer those corporations in the direction hedge fund management believes would increase shareholder value.

These are more strategies than most investors can conceivably utilize. Remember the more exotic the strategy the more likely it would be placed within institutional portfolios utilizing as many different strategies as they have assets available to invest. Their thinking goes, The more unique strategies we can add to our portfolios the more we are able to reduce overall investment risk. There really are only two strategies Long/Short [or the original hedge fund style] or Global Macro that most retail investors would find compelling for their own use. We discuss these and their construction in later chapters.

GROWTH OF HEDGE FUNDS

In 1999, hedge fund assets amounted to $363 billion, or about $60 billion less than current amounts in ETF assets. By 2002 assets had nearly doubled reaching $650 billion. It's estimated by most trade publications that hedge fund assets may by the end of 2007 approximate $1.5 trillion or achieving an asset growth rate of more than 30 percent per year; some put total assets at more than $2 trillion. But whatever the number, it's largely meaningless because most hedge fund managers, to some extent or other, leverage their investors' capital. In typical long/short equity strategies, the leverage is generally less than two times [the manager will trade, using margin or borrowed funds, $2 worth of stock for every $1 of invested capital]. Other strategies, and particularly several forms of arbitrage involving scalping nickels on hundreds of trades each day, are much more heavily leveraged. Best guess, it's possible that hedge funds worldwide control something around $6–$8 trillion, compared to the roughly $10 trillion invested in U.S. mutual funds.

The sector's asset growth will slow, if only because of the law of large numbers. In fact the TowerGroup estimates hedge fund assets will grow at an annualized rate of 15 percent between 2006 and 2008 and include roughly 10,000 funds. That's still an amazing rate.

But hedge fund growth has been both widely publicized while at the same time average investors regarded the sector as enigmatic, given the many exotic strategies and high dollar entry thresholds. Figure 3.2 shows the overall growth of hedge fund assets since 1990.

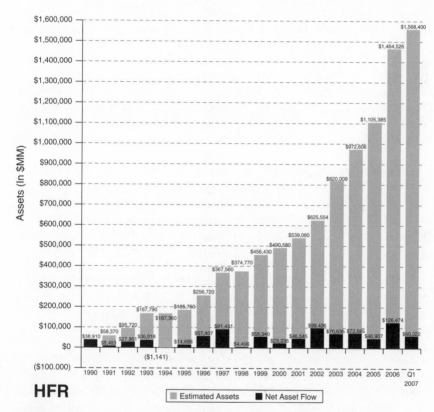

HFR

FIGURE 3.2 Estimated Growth of Assets/Net Asset Flow Hedge Fund Industry 1990 [Q1 2007]

Source: Chicago-based Hedge Fund Research, Inc.

WHO INVESTS IN THESE COMPLEX STRATEGIES?

If you want to play with the big boys, you have to be a big boy.
—Brian McQuade, Hedge Fund Center.

The usual investors include those with large pools of assets able to allocate them across a wide variety of strategies. Not many investors select just one strategy; rather they mix and match strategies hoping to achieve a more consistent rate of return with lessened risk rather than a single high return approach containing more risk.

In fact it may surprise you to learn that the three largest hedge fund investors in the U.S. are government pension plans led by Pennsylvania State Retirement System, N.Y. State Common Fund, and [CALPERS] California Public Employee Retirement System.

Hedge fund consultants exist to advise clients how to best structure an overall allocation plan utilizing the various outlined strategies that best suit their needs and objectives. Consultants are paid lucrative fees for this advice.

On the other hand large institutional clients such as government pension plans may conduct this activity in-house. They believe they have greater control and consultants are too subject to perceived conflicts of interest and perhaps force consultants into competitive bidding requirements for their services.

Other common U.S. investors might include family offices. These, as the name implies, are investment organizations just representing a specific family's overall investment activities. The family offices oversee conventional assets including personal family real estate assets and other personal property and assist the family with their estate planning, legal, and tax planning activities. With adequate assets to invest, they may seek a variety of hedge funds to augment their investment portfolios.

The wealth management divisions of large trusts and banks also assist qualified clients find and invest in a variety of hedge funds and in the process act as consultants. This activity has become a more important aspect of the banks' activities over the past decade as these organizations compete to retain clients, their assets, and fee income.

Overseas investors of all stripes, from government organizations to wealthy families seek to invest in hedge funds domiciled in many offshore countries. For many decades the ubiquitous Swiss bank was the confidential repository for many of these investors. However, over the past two decade's offshore havens from Bermuda, Cayman Islands, and Isle of Man to name a few have become popular locations for offshore hedge funds. Overseas investors like the privacy and safety these jurisdictions provided. Let's face it, many investors wanting to avoid the law or for many the IRS, achieve comfort and their more dubious goals within these structures.

WHY INVEST IN HEDGE FUNDS ANYWAY?

Figure 3.3 clearly demonstrates the rationale for hedge fund popularity: superior performance achieved with less risk. Both hedge fund indexes displayed in the figure incorporate all hedge fund performance compared to the S&P 500 Index. Notice how much smoother both the Tremont Hedge Fund Index and the Hedge Fund Research Index have been by comparison to the common stock index. Further, less volatility and risk mean better total performance overall. Quite simply, this is the reason for their popularity—less risk, better performance. What investor wouldn't want that?

Why do these funds achieve superior performance to conventional mutual funds and index investing? The answer is simple. The best money managers gravitate to this structure since the compensation is far greater than that possible from conventional activities.

As soon as a trader/money manager achieves superior success from conventional employment with a mutual fund or Wall Street trading desk, they're quickly hired away by a hedge fund or, better yet, given start-up funds by interested clients to manage money in a hedge fund structure. If they continue successfully with their unique investment strategy the financial rewards can catapult them to the top of the earnings hierarchy.

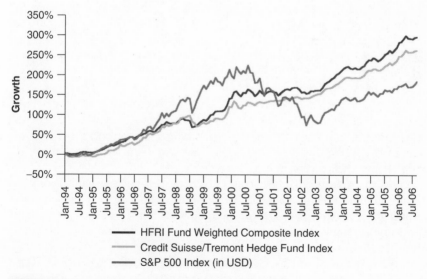

FIGURE 3.3 Smoother Growth and Outperformance
Source: Chicago-based Hedge Fund Research Inc.

BUT CAN RETAIL INVESTORS PARTICIPATE?

Putting aside the relative handful of conventional actively-managed mutual funds that implement hedge fund-like strategies, the primary hurdle for retail investors wanting to participate in "real" hedge funds is that they must be "accredited investors." The definitions are undergoing change as of early 2007. Given the notoriety of hedge funds, the government has chosen to increase the requirements for accredited investors rather than by regulating hedge funds. This, of course, is controversial and may change again in the future given the politics in Washington and/or by other events. The newest rules promulgated by the SEC in December 2006 follow.

[*Note:* These changes have not been enacted and are probably headed for the scrapheap because they would also affect venture capital and other "private investment" schemes.]

AMENDMENTS TO PRIVATE OFFERING RULES UNDER THE SECURITIES ACT OF 1933

The proposals would define a new category of accredited investor that would apply to offers and sales of securities issued by hedge funds and other private investment pools to natural persons. The proposed definition would include any natural person who (a) meets either the net worth test or income test specified in rule 501(a) or rule 215, as applicable, and (b) owns at least $2.5 million in investments, as defined in the proposed rules.

Generally, most issuers would eliminate an individual's home equity from the calculation focusing instead on "investments."

Currently to qualify an investor must be either a financial institution; an affiliate of the issuer; or an individual with a net worth of at least $1 million or an annual income of at least $200,000, and the investment must not exceed 20 percent of the investor's worth. But this will no doubt change as listed above. To be more specific the 501 rule reads currently as follows:

Rule 501—Definitions and Terms Used in Regulation D

As used in Regulation D, the following terms shall have the meaning indicated:

(Continued)

Accredited investor. Accredited investor shall mean any person who comes within any of the following categories, or who the issuer reasonably believes comes within any of the following categories, at the time of the sale of the securities to that person:

Any bank as defined in section 3(a)(2) of the Act, or any savings and loan association or other institution as defined in section 3(a)(5)(A) of the Act whether acting in its individual or fiduciary capacity; any broker or dealer registered pursuant to section 15 of the Securities Exchange Act of 1934; any insurance company as defined in section 2(a)(13) of the Act; any investment company registered under the Investment Company Act of 1940 or a business development company as defined in section 2(a)(48) of that Act; any Small Business Investment Company licensed by the U.S. Small Business Administration under section 301(c) or (d) of the Small Business Investment Act of 1958; any plan established and maintained by a state, its political subdivisions, or any agency or instrumentality of a state or its political subdivisions, for the benefit of its employees, if such plan has total assets in excess of $5,000,000; any employee benefit plan within the meaning of the Employee Retirement Income Security Act of 1974 if the investment decision is made by a plan fiduciary, as defined in section 3(21) of such act, which is either a bank, savings and loan association, insurance company, or registered investment adviser, or if the employee benefit plan has total assets in excess of $5,000,000 or, if a self-directed plan, with investment decisions made solely by persons that are accredited investors;

Any private business development company as defined in section 202(a)(22) of the Investment Advisers Act of 1940;

Any organization described in section 501(c)(3) of the Internal Revenue Code, corporation, Massachusetts or similar business trust, or partnership, not formed for the specific purpose of acquiring the securities offered, with total assets in excess of $5,000,000;

Any director, executive officer, or general partner of the issuer of the securities being offered or sold, or any director, executive officer, or general partner of a general partner of that issuer;

Any natural person whose individual net worth, or joint net worth with that person's spouse, at the time of his purchase exceeds $1,000,000;

Any natural person who had an individual income in excess of $200,000 in each of the two most recent years or joint income with that person's spouse in excess of $300,000 in each of those years and

(Continued)

has a reasonable expectation of reaching the same income level in the current year;

Any trust, with total assets in excess of $5,000,000, not formed for the specific purpose of acquiring the securities offered, whose purchase is directed by a sophisticated person as described in Rule 506(b)(2)(ii) and

Any entity in which all of the equity owners are accredited investors.

Affiliate. An affiliate of, or person affiliated with, a specified person shall mean a person that directly, or indirectly through one or more intermediaries, controls or is controlled by, or is under common control with, the person specified.

Aggregate offering price. Aggregate offering price shall mean the sum of all cash, services, property, notes, cancellation of debt, or other consideration to be received by an issuer for issuance of its securities. Where securities are being offered for both cash and non-cash consideration, the aggregate offering price shall be based on the price at which the securities are offered for cash. Any portion of the aggregate offering price attributable to cash received in a foreign currency shall be translated into United States currency at the currency exchange rate in effect at a reasonable time prior to or on the date of the sale of the securities. If securities are not offered for cash, the aggregate offering price shall be based on the value of the consideration as established by bona fide sales of that consideration made within a reasonable time, or, in the absence of sales, on the fair value as determined by an accepted standard. Such valuations of non-cash consideration must be reasonable at the time made.

Business combination. Business combination shall mean any transaction of the type specified in paragraph (a) of Rule 145 under the Act and any transaction involving the acquisition by one issuer, in exchange for all or a part of its own or its parent's stock, of stock of another issuer if, immediately after the acquisition, the acquiring issuer has control of the other issuer (whether or not it had control before the acquisition).

Calculation of number of purchasers. For purposes of calculating the number of purchasers under Rule 505(b) and Rule 506(b) only, the following shall apply:

The following purchasers shall be excluded:

Any relative, spouse or relative of the spouse of a purchaser who has the same principal residence as the purchaser;

(*Continued*)

Any trust or estate in which a purchaser and any of the persons related to him as specified in paragraph (e)(1)(i) or (e)(1)(iii) of this section collectively have more than 50 percent of the beneficial interest (excluding contingent interests);

Any corporation or other organization of which a purchaser and any of the persons related to him as specified in paragraph (e)(1)(i) or (e)(1)(ii) of this section collectively are beneficial owners of more than 50 percent of the equity securities (excluding directors' qualifying shares) or equity interests; and

Any accredited investor.

A corporation, partnership or other entity shall be counted as one purchaser. If, however, that entity is organized for the specific purpose of acquiring the securities offered and is not an accredited investor under paragraph (a)8 of this section, then each beneficial owner of equity securities or equity interests in the entity shall count as a separate purchaser for all provisions of Regulation D, except to the extent provided in paragraph (e)1 of this section.

A noncontributory employee benefit plan within the meaning of Title I of the Employee Retirement Income Security Act of 1974 shall be counted as one purchaser where the trustee makes all investment decisions for the plan.

Executive officer. Executive officer shall mean the president, any vice president in charge of a principal business unit, division or function (such as sales, administration or finance), any other officer who performs a policy making function, or any other person who performs similar policy making functions for the issuer. Executive officers of subsidiaries may be deemed executive officers of the issuer if they perform such policy making functions for the issuer.

Issuer. The definition of the term issuer in section 2(a)(4) of the Act shall apply, except that in the case of a proceeding under the Federal Bankruptcy Code (11 U.S.C. 101 et seq.), the trustee or debtor in possession shall be considered the issuer in an offering under a plan or reorganization, if the securities are to be issued under the plan.

Purchaser representative. Purchaser representative shall mean any person who satisfies all of the following conditions or who the issuer reasonably believes satisfies all of the following conditions:

Is not an affiliate, director, officer or other employee of the issuer, or beneficial owner of 10 percent or more of any class of the equity securities or 10 percent or more of the equity interest in the issuer, except where the purchaser is:

(*Continued*)

A relative of the purchaser representative by blood, marriage or adoption and not more remote than a first cousin;

A trust or estate in which the purchaser representative and any persons related to him as specified in paragraph (h)(1)(i) or (h)1(iii) of this section collectively have more than 50 percent of the beneficial interest (excluding contingent interest) or of which the purchaser representative serves as trustee, executor, or in any similar capacity; or

A corporation or other organization of which the purchaser representative and any persons related to him as specified in paragraph (h)(1)(i) or (h)(1)(ii) of this section collectively are the beneficial owners of more than 50 percent of the equity securities (excluding directors' qualifying shares) or equity interests;

Has such knowledge and experience in financial and business matters that he is capable of evaluating, alone, or together with other purchaser representatives of the purchaser, or together with the purchaser, the merits and risks of the prospective investment;

Is acknowledged by the purchaser in writing, during the course of the transaction, to be his purchaser representative in connection with evaluating the merits and risks of the prospective investment; and

Discloses to the purchaser in writing a reasonable time prior to the sale of securities to that purchaser any material relationship between himself or his affiliates and the issuer or its affiliates that then exists, that is mutually understood to be contemplated, or that has existed at any time during the previous two years, and any compensation received or to be received as a result of such relationship.

Assuming you understood all that, you can proceed. But wait, the SEC is considering raising the entry requirements for individual investors. The primary component of most proposals is to raise the minimum qualifications for individual investors as accredited investors. The primary change proposed is that investors must have assets, exclusive of residence, of $2,500,000.

Thus there are few ways for even modestly wealthy investors to participate in hedge funds. The superrich on the other hand have the millions it requires to diversify over a wide variety of hedge fund strategies. For large institutions this is relatively easy through use of consultants.

However, a FOF [Fund of Funds] strategy can enable some investors with perhaps an entry fee of one million dollars to buy-in. These hedge funds as outlined in strategies previously listed from HFRI exist to pool a variety of managers utilizing diverse strategies into one fund. They're organized by a consultant who manages and markets the fund. Investors like the approach since it gives them the opportunity to participate in a hedge fund incorporating a variety of strategies. Theoretically, the consultant/manager has skillfully chosen good managers utilizing different or even similar strategies when combined produce excellent overall returns to the partner investors.

The downside to FOFs is that fees are higher since the consultant must charge a fee for their services, which when added to the individual manager's fee would reduce returns to investors. Further, some consultants force prospective manage rs to share fees with them to mitigate overall costs. The negative is that the better managers won't participate since they won't need to share fees with anyone. This naturally reduces the pool of talent available to both consultant and investor.

A Northern Trust 2007 survey reported that households with $10 million or more in investable assets report that 31 percent of their portfolios are allocated to alternative investments such as private equity, hedge funds, and commodities. [In fact, all three cited sectors should be part of hedge funds.] Households below that threshold maintain alternative investment allocations of seven percent. Further fully half of investors cited improved portfolio diversification for using alternative investments and hedge funds.

Also an interesting result of the survey is that GenX millionaires were more apt to own ETFs versus Mature Generation [age 61+]. And, GenX millionaires are more likely to own Emerging Market funds, managed futures, and high-yield bond funds. Most of these are also staples within many hedge funds.

HEDGE FUND DISASTERS

Many investors are aware of the collapse of Long-Term Capital [LTC] in 1998. Its demise rocked stock markets and caused billions in losses for investors. The LTC strategy was extremely aggressive and doesn't fit neatly with most of the strategies outlined. Possibly "Fixed-Income: Mortgage Backed" would fit since they were trading heavily in those markets. However, their strategy involved using enormous leverage that served them well when they were on the right side of markets, but when wrong caused a collapse.

John Meriwether was a former Salomon Bros. whiz who founded LTC. He parlayed $4.8 billion in capital to control $140 billion in stocks and bonds, plus derivatives with a value of $1 trillion [240-for-1 leverage]. His associates were Nobel economics prize winners Myron Scholes and Robert Merton.

Meriwether's undoing was a major bet on the spread between two different bond maturities. Without going into the trade details, suffice it to say the spreads went against him in a big way. In some of these trades, LTC had put up zero, that's right, "zero," margin. Given the enormity of the positions the government stepped in and cobbled together a group of Wall Street firms to take over LTC and work off their positions. And, wouldn't you know it, those firms made a lot of money off those positions.

In August 2006 another hedge fund Amaranth began the month with nearly $9 billion in assets. Its primary trading focus became energy markets and the volatile natural gas sector in particular. By the time August ended, the fund had lost 35 percent and was forced to close. What happened was similar to LTC in the sense that a huge directional bet was made on one market sector, natural gas, moving their way. The opposite happened and billions were lost. The fund was shut down.

Worse still are some crooks portraying themselves as bona fide hedge fund operators who steal money from unsuspecting investors. They get caught eventually and if the assets can be recovered they're returned to investors. But, more often than not, those assets will have disappeared for good. A case in point is that of Kirk Wright who bilked investors, including some NFL players, out of millions through his International Management Associates. Typically, after investors deposited funds with him he would send phony statements stating that the fund had more than $150 million in assets when there was only $150 thousand. At its height, Wright collected $110 million from clients. Wright disappeared and was on the lam until arrested in Miami Beach in May 2006. The total recoverable assets were only $200 thousand.

The Wright case is a typical scheme to steal from unsuspecting or even gullible investors. It usually ends with the guilty parties getting caught, which always make me wonder why they bother since they know jail time awaits.

TO REGULATE OR NOT

The fear of hedge funds is overblown, based on a misunderstanding of their role in the international financial system. In reality, hedge funds do not increase risk; they manage it—and policymakers, rather than clamping down, should make sure hedge funds have the tools to perform this function well.
—Sebastian Mallaby, *Foreign Affairs*, January/February 2007

Whenever trading scandals occur or an industry becomes hugely successful the urge to regulate it becomes more popular. It seems a natural knee-jerk reaction for most politicians and government agencies. Beyond the enormous growth of the industry, the number of hedge fund manager fraud is growing and there's a desire by some sponsors to make the funds available to smaller investors and pension funds. But the hedge fund industry is also powerful politically with many of the most successful fund managers' important patrons to politicians from both political parties. Their influence is enormous.

Furthermore the hedge fund industry is a world to itself since many of the most powerful players move their operations to popular offshore jurisdictions like Bermuda, Cayman Islands, Isle of Man, and so forth. From those bases their clients are more secure from snooping from the ubiquitous IRS. And, should the government want to regulate the hedge fund managers, these jurisdictions also exempt them from registration.

The SEC tried to regulate domestic hedge funds by requiring advisors with 15 or more investors and who don't close the funds to new investors before the deadline to register as investment advisors under the 1940 Investment Advisors Act by February 1, 2006. This would have subjected the funds to all manner of compliance and reporting requirements. Further the SEC would be entitled to conduct routine audits and inspections to ascertain that these funds were following federal securities laws.

Registration in this manner would be very costly to the funds in legal fees associated with initial registrations. Even heavier costs would result from the red tape associated with continuing reporting and a host of compliance issues. Some third-party firms are sprouting for funds to outsource many of these tasks. This is costly to the funds and most likely would be passed on to investors.

In June 2006 the U.S. Court of Appeals vacated the SEC's rule requiring hedge fund registration after determining that the SEC rule, based upon its interpretation of "client," was arbitrary. And while the SEC may appeal the ruling, thus far it seems to be backing away from the registration issue altogether. Many firms that had begun the registration process cancelled continuing work on their applications. Many firms that had registered are now withdrawing their registrations.

It now seems that the SEC is dropping the registration requirements entirely. But that doesn't mean there isn't pressure. State regulators and some politicians aren't giving up on the registration goal. State regulators are the toughest bunch to deal with given that 50 different states can create 50 different rules to supersede the SEC. For many investment managers dealing with these bureaucrats is a nightmare. Further some state regulators are extremely aggressive while others more accommodating. So, how to deal with them is a challenge.

The current status of the registration process is in limbo. Senator Chuck Grassley [R, Iowa] has introduced legislation again to repair the defects in previous legislation that the courts rejected. Perhaps this legislation will pass but then be tested in the courts again. But no matter, it seems that hedge fund managers won't be registering any time soon. In fact many managers who did register are now deregistering. Why go through regulatory hell if you don't have to?

HEDGE FUNDS ARE HERE TO STAY

Even with threats of regulation, occasional hedge fund blow-ups a la Amaranth and Long-Term Capital and threats of regulation hedge funds will continue to grow in popularity with the wealthiest investors.

The only question is how will the average investor be able to participate? Answering that question and providing solutions is at the heart of this book.

CHAPTER 4

A Convergence Story

Mutual Funds, ETFs, and Hedge Funds

With mutual funds threatened by the growing popularity of ETFs, it shouldn't be a surprise that there would be an effort to compete. Further the popularity of hedge funds makes them candidates for mainstream investors in either an ETF or mutual fund format. And DIY investors now have the ETF issues and tools necessary from which they can construct their own hedge funds. Given these circumstances it shouldn't surprise one that these products would converge in one form or another.

In order to help FAs earn a living from the popular ETF boom, firms have either constructed "wrap-type" products or structures where retail investors can buy and sell ETFs for a flat fee. That might mean a 1 percent annual fee for example. But doesn't this defeat the low cost feature and attraction of ETFs? Yes. However, if your FA adds value in constructing all ETF portfolios and as an investor you value this, then why not? Many investors like having a personal relationship with an advisor whom they perceive as competent and trustworthy. As we've discussed previously while many investors want greater control over their financial affairs they also want some help. Most clients in this category are willing to pay for this service a qualified FA can provide.

The mutual fund industry has also joined in by offering all ETF funds. For example, the Huntington Rotating Markets Fund [HRIAX] utilizes ETFs exclusively to construct portfolios that rotate assets from sector to sector according to the models of the fund manager. Fees for the fund run 1.50 percent in sales load with a recurring management fee of 1.42 percent which presumably FAs can utilize. In the same category is the Wayne Hummer Pathmaster Domestic Equity Fund [PDEAX]. It has a 5 percent front-end load [sales charge] while charging 1.5 percent annual management fees. Some FAs will likely gravitate to these high-cost funds. Are these funds a good idea? Yes, but only if the performance meets and satisfies investor expectations.

Some mutual funds using ETFs are issued with a "target" date that could meet investor education or retirement requirements. For example, the Seligman TargETFund 2025 [STKAX] is more heavily oriented to equity ETFs initially and rotates to a heavier weighting in bond ETFs the closer to maturity [2025] it gets. This fund carries a load of 4.75 percent and an annual management fee of 1.26 percent. The Federated Target ETF 2025 carries an expense ratio of .77 percent but has a front-end load of 5.50 percent. So, if you want help and are willing to pay these funds may work for you. Remember, given the heavy upfront fees, these funds are not something you can easily walk away from should your own situation change, or if you become dissatisfied with the fund's performance. It's also worth keeping in mind that the whole "target date" concept is relatively recent, and it remains to be seen whether the idea has legs, or will later be supplanted by the next investment fad du jour.

MUTUAL FUNDS ADOPTING SOME HEDGE FUND STRATEGIES

According to Morningstar there are now more than 100 mutual funds currently offer some variation on the traditional hedge fund long/short or market neutral strategy, but it's hard to tell how many are using ETFs, rather than stocks, bonds and derivatives, a category that includes both conventional equity and index options, and more complex "swaps" keyed to the performance of, for example, an investable hedge fund index. Many funds in this category like the higher beta [volatility] of individual stocks versus an ETF. For example, the best performing stock within a sector will generally outperform the worst performing stock within a sector by a significant margin. So a *correct* long/short bet within a sector will, assuming the same level of risk, outperform, the ETF's directional bet on the overall sector.

Experienced mutual fund managers in this area will likely continue to use what's worked best for them in the past. However, given all the new ETF issues available, managers skilled at making overall sector selections may opt to utilize ETFs as the tools of choice. By way of example, suppose a manager felt by whatever means used to make these evaluations, that the financial sector would underperform the energy sector. Presumably, the manager would be long energy and short an equivalent amount of financial. The ETFs of choice might include Energy ETF [XLE] and Financial ETF [XLF]. If the manager was correct then more money would be made on the long position versus the short position even if they both declined in value. When you articulate a market neutral approach, you're arguing that the direction of the overall market is irrelevant to your positions. The market could go to hell in a basket and as long the relationship between the two sectors goes in your favor, you should be making money ... or, at worst, losing considerably less than the overall market.

FUTURES INVESTMENT STRATEGIES IN HEDGE FUNDS

Futures are one of the most misunderstood, and consequently overlooked, investment fields in today's financial markets. For most individual investors, commodities trading is associated with high risk and the wild trading of pork bellies and soy beans, for example. Who can blame them? The area is rife with tales of fortunes being made and lost in just a few days. Most people view the area as pure gambling and would be just as well off in a casino where at least they'd have the cards in their own hands and get a complimentary cocktail or two for their trouble.

The fact is that a diversified managed futures portfolio—a subset of the "hedge fund" universe—has proven a valuable addition to conventional portfolios. As we described in Chapter 1, many studies have proven that adding a small percentage of managed futures to a conventional portfolio reduces overall portfolio risk. The reason is that these assets are uncorrelated to typical stock and bond trends. Therefore if customary stock and bond markets are trending in one direction, managed futures will often trend in an opposite manner, or at least do something different.

Until recently, investing in managed futures usually meant participating in so-called commodity pools, which are limited partnerships created by major Wall Street firms. Their structure has been effective since the investment area is regulated by the Commodity Futures Trading Corporation [CFTC], which would not permit these funds to be structured as mutual funds, which are regulated by the SEC. The partnerships usually have higher entry thresholds than conventional mutual funds; $25,000 tends to be the "bottom line," although many will allow smaller sums for IRA accounts. Investors normally come and go each month, although a few still offer only quarterly redemptions.

The general partner of the fund is the sponsoring firm, or a specially created entity intended to limit the sponsor's liability. The general partner charges a hefty fee, which may exceed 3 to 5 percent per annum to manage and distribute the fund. He also hires the manager, or managers, who carry the somewhat archaic title of Commodity Trading Advisors [CTAs] who in turn charge their own fees, usually 2 percent per annum, for management, plus an incentive or performance fee, which may exceed 20 percent of new capital appreciation. But despite the fees good CTAs and partnerships often overcome high fee structures with performance exceeding double-digit annualized returns.

Another aspect of Commodity Pools is the common use of leverage that generally may run 4 to 1 more or less. The greater the level of leverage the better the returns when the CTA is right, but when they are wrong losses can quickly mount. Risks rise proportionately to the use of leverage and therein is the principal drawback for most retail investors.

All these considerations make commodity pools a tough sell, with all but the most experienced investors struggling with the complex trading concepts, high fees, and leverage. By way of another anecdote, I remember taking a CTA around to visit clients 25 years ago. One client asked the advisor if he would invest in such a product or fund. The advisor bluntly responded: "I wouldn't touch this with a 10-foot pole." This was both funny and not a sales oriented statement by the CTA but the client perceived it as both. Nevertheless, the client decided to go ahead with the investment because he felt the CTA was honest and eventually became one of the CTA's best clients.

RYDEX INVESTMENTS LEADS A BIG CHANGE

In March 2007 Rydex Investments launched the Rydex Managed Futures Fund [RYMFX]. The Rydex fund creates a new opportunity for investors to be involved with a nonleveraged, more liquid, and lower-cost investment structure to parallel the more expensive limited partnerships outlined above.

RYMFX per its brochure "seeks to provide investment results that closely track the daily performance of the Standard & Poor's Diversified Trends Indicator [S&P DTI]." It goes on to say, S&P DTI is a way to identify and potentially capitalize on momentum in the financial and commodity futures markets. The investment model calculates the averages of prices in the futures markets and gives signals to indicate whether a position should be held long or short. The index is comprised of 14 sectors from around the world, with 50 percent allocated to financial futures and 50 percent to commodity futures. Each of the 14 sectors has the potential to be long or short based on price momentum. The exception within the model is energy because of political issues, economic changes, and other risk factors fairly unique to that sector. The S&P DTI will never short the energy sector, but it may take a neutral [or "flat"] position. The 14 sectors are rebalanced monthly, which result in the portfolio being reset to its 50/50 commodity–financial weighting.

The index follows a quantitative and rules based method to establish long or short positions in each constituent sector. The back-tested index dates back to 1985. The index method, per an interview I did with Edward

Egilinsky, Managing Director for Alternative Strategies at Rydex consisted of utilizing a seven-month technical look-back period with a heavier emphasis on the most recent 90-day period. Naturally, without divulging the strategy's details beyond that, this is about as much as they would reveal.

RYMFX features an annual fee of 1.65 percent, high certainly by ETF standards, but not uncommon for mutual funds, and decidedly lower than fees charged by conventional limited partnerships. Further the fund is offered in an H class structure in addition to A and C classes. The H class is designed as a no-load fund, which is targeted at both DIY investors and FAs with the latter adding an overall advisory fee.

What to make of this fund's investment approach compared to typical commodity funds? Almost all current registered CTAs and their funds are technically oriented, meaning they follow chart analysis rather than any fundamental considerations. Why? Because most CTAs utilize leverage and most markets being traded are too fast moving to deal with fundamental considerations. Additional considerations include agricultural commodities where weather, disease, planting issues, international tensions, tariffs, and so forth alter conditions dramatically. A freeze in Florida affects citrus, hurricanes sugar, drought grains and livestock, war many markets and other acts of God beyond analytical capabilities. Futures contracts, which are the tools investors use, are structured to expire monthly or quarterly for example. Fundamental analysis may not be useful given these types of structures and circumstances.

The only sector where fundamental analysis is most helpful is perhaps in financials where overall economic conditions may be useful. However this is mitigated by leverage since timing becomes more important when risk management is paramount.

It's unclear at this time whether the Rydex strategy will be successful. Not being able to short energy is surprising. That may be the result of both the monthly expiration of energy contracts combined with the monthly rebalancing that the fund employs. However, it's much more likely that in back-testing the S&P DTI it was proven that shorting utilizing their methodology just wasn't effective.

"Nonleveraged" means investors don't have to worry so much about risk-taking. However, at the same time, good performance when markets are trending in the right direction is compromised. It's an obvious trade-off.

Most investors don't like being stuck in underperforming funds that feature limited or highly restricted liquidity opportunities. In other words, most conventional limited partnerships will allow you in or out only once per month while some may limit the additions and redemptions to quarterly or longer. Most of this is due to accounting issues unique to partnerships since many are audited based on opening and closing net asset values each month. Generally retail investors have never liked this type of inflexible lock-up. Clearly the Rydex fund will be beneficial allowing investors in or out daily.

The Rydex fund is just the first entry in the managed futures market. Will others follow? They will if Rydex is able to raise significant assets competitive instincts being what they are.

The big question is will successful CTAs wish to join by registering such an offering? That's even more difficult to say since Rydex fees are low by CTA standards and obviously they wouldn't want to cannibalize their existing products. Nevertheless they may find unique ways to structure products based on the lack of leverage, which would make the products unique from existing funds.

The problem with the Rydex fund is their lack of experience with this type of product and also the methodology they're using. It's quite unique being based on a new back-tested index developed by S&P. How effective this strategy will be only time will tell.

POWERSHARES ACTIVELY TRADED ETF

No ETF provider has been more active in issuing novel and cutting edge ETFs than PowerShares, which was acquired by large mutual fund provider and distributor AMVESCAP in 2006. They have led the way in designing quasi-actively managed indexes [Intellidexes] in conjunction with the American Stock Exchange upon which they've issued dozens of ETFs.

Most ETF market pundits have accepted their Dynamic/Intellidex indexes. Others have wanted to let these uniquely structured ETFs demonstrate their worth over time and even a variety of market cycles.

But now PowerShares has taken the first step in introducing an ETF that could easily be considered an "actively managed" fund with some hedge fund characteristics. Per their web site (www.powershares.com):

> *The PowerShares DWA Technical Leaders Portfolio (Fund) is based on the Dorsey Wright Technical Leaders™ Index (Index), which includes approximately 100 U.S.-listed companies that demonstrate powerful relative strength characteristics. The Index is constructed pursuant to Dorsey Wright proprietary methodology, which takes into account, among other factors, the performance of each of the 3,000 largest U.S.-listed companies as compared to a benchmark index, and the relative performance of industry sectors and subsectors. The Index is reconstituted and rebalanced quarterly using the same methodology described above.*

The prospectus allows for a more detailed description of DWA's methodology as follows.

PRINCIPAL INVESTMENT STRATEGIES

The Adviser will seek to match the performance of the Technical Leaders™ Index. The Technical Leaders is comprised of stocks of approximately 100 U.S. companies that are selected pursuant to a proprietary selection methodology of Dorsey Wright & Associates ("Dorsey Wright" or the "Index Provider"), designed to identify companies that demonstrate powerful relative strength characteristics. Relative strength characteristics are based upon each security's market performance. The companies are selected from a broad mi-cap and large-cap universe. As of December 31, 2006, the Technical Leaders Index included 100 companies with a market capitalization range of between $2.1 billion and $72 billion. The Fund will normally invest at least 90 percent of its total assets in common stocks that comprise the Technical Leaders Index. The Fund's investment objective and 90 percent investment policy are nonfundamental and require 60 days' prior written notice to shareholders before they can be changed.

The Technical Leaders Index is adjusted quarterly and the Fund, using an "indexing" investment approach, attempts to replicate, before expenses, the performance of the Technical Leaders Index; a figure of 1.00 would represent perfect correlation. The Fund generally will invest in the stocks comprising the Technical Leaders Index in proportion to their weightings in the Technical Leaders Index. However, under various circumstances, it may not be possible or practicable to purchase all of those stocks in those weightings. In those circumstances, the Fund may purchase a sample of stocks in the Technical Leaders Index. There may also be instances in which the Adviser may choose to overweight another stock in the Technical Leaders Index, purchase securities not in the Technical Leaders Index which the Adviser believes are appropriate to substitute for certain securities in the Technical Leaders Index or utilize various combinations of other available investment techniques in seeking to track the Technical Leaders Index. The Fund may sell stocks that are represented in the Technical Leaders

(Continued)

Index in an anticipation of their removal from the Technical Leaders Index or purchase stocks not represented in the Technical Leaders Index anticipation of their addition to the Technical Leaders Index.

DORSEY WRIGHT TECHNICAL LEADERS INDEX METHODOLOGY

The Dorsey Wright Technical Leaders Index methodology is designed to identify those stocks that have powerful relative strength characteristics. The methodology evaluates companies quarterly, then ranks them on a proprietary algorithm. Stocks that are selected receive a modified equal weighting.

INDEX CONSTRUCTION

The Technical Leaders Index includes companies selected pursuant to a proprietary methodology of Dorsey Wright designed to identify companies that demonstrate powerful relative strength characteristics and are listed on the NYSE, American Stock Exchange ["AMEX"] or quoted on the NASDAQ. The 3,000 largest U.S. Stocks [by market capitalization] traded on the NYSE or AMEX or quoted on the NASDAQ are ranked using a proprietary relative strength methodology. The methodology takes into account, among other things, the performance of each of the 3,000 companies in the eligible universe as compared to a benchmark index and the relative performance of the industry sectors and subsectors. Approximately 100 of these stocks are selected for inclusion in the Technical Leaders Index. Stocks that are selected receive a modified equal weighting.

From Figure 4.1, you can see the impressive overall returns. However, you should also note the roughly 45 percent decline in performance during the bear market of 2000 to 2002. In that circumstance, allocating assets to an overall declining Relative Strength Indicator [RSI] model would be a losing game since all RSIs were in a declining state.

— Dorsey Wright Technical Leaders™ Index: $44,724
— S&P 500: $18,733

FIGURE 4.1   Index Performance [Growth of $10,000]
Source: PowerShares Capital Management LLC.

POWERSHARES PRIVATE EQUITY ETF

No hedge fund sector in 2006–2007 has been hotter than private equity. It's hard to find good data on capital flows to the sector since it is private but it shouldn't surprise anyone that capital committed to the sector is in the hundreds of billions. So it stands to reason that active issuer PowerShares would find a way to structure an ETF product utilizing the private equity focus capitalizing on the trend. The question becomes how to issue such a fund that accurately mirrors and performs as well as the prominent players in this area.

All during the equity market rise from the summer lows of 2006 to the peaks in early 2007 one activity dominated all others—mergers and acquisitions currently being described as private equity. In the go-go 1980s this activity was described as LBOs or leveraged buy-outs. What is occurring in this era is really the same thing. Shrewd investors like Kohlberg, Kravis & Roberts, now the public company KKR Financial, were active in taking over companies by using debt. They would reorganize the company and restructure management. In so doing they felt they were better able to optimize performance and more importantly shareholder value. To cover debt expenses they might spin-off or sell various parts of a company retaining what they believed were the most valuable. After operating the retained portion for a few years perhaps, they would resell the company to the public in the form of an initial public offering [IPO].

Nothing really has changed today except the name of the activity. The private equity story would not be complete without some discussion of the high levels of liquidity during the past few years. A primary source of cheap money was sourced first to the United States where a "carry trade" existed. A "carry trade" exists when short-term borrowing costs are low and longer-term costs are higher—a rising yield curve. Investors could borrow cheap and invest in longer-term securities at higher rates locking in the difference. Some borrowers could just as easily speculate. This condition in the United States ended when the yield curve flattened [short and long-term interest rates were equal] and eventually inverted [short-term rates were higher than long-term rates]. When that happened the U.S. carry trade ended. However the carry trade just moved from the United States to Japan where for the past decade Japanese short-term interest rates have been at almost 0—that's right, 0 percent. This meant that if you had the clout astute firms like KKR could borrow extensive funds cheaply to finance their acquisitions. In the 1980s, most of this activity was financed by "junk bonds" at very high rates.

In the 1980s, owing to the higher interest costs of carrying junk bonds firms like KKR would be most anxious to quickly reorganize companies and sell them off in pieces to pay off the debt. This was known as the "super nova theory" of investing; meaning the sum of the parts was greater than the whole.

In current private equity transactions, companies like KKR aren't as pressed to sell the companies as borrowing costs are low. Further the rapidly expanding amounts of assets in hedge funds allowed for well-heeled partners who were willing to be long-term equity as opposed to debt investors. This was even more cost-effective and ultimately lucrative to firms like KKR.

The following is PowerShares' description of their private equity ETF [see Table 4.1]:

The PowerShares Listed Private Equity Portfolio (Fund) seeks to replicate the Red Rocks Capital Listed Private Equity Index[SM], which includes more than 30 U.S. publicly listed companies with direct investments in more than 1,000 private businesses. This gives investors diversified exposure to a wide range of growth and value-oriented listed private equity companies in a single product. The LPE Index[SM] is rebalanced and reconstituted quarterly and fund holdings are disclosed every day, giving investors a much higher level of transparency than is often available in traditional private equity funds.

TABLE 4.1 Fund Holdings as of 3/15/2007

Industry Sector	Symbol	Company	% of Fund
Consumer Discretionary 3.24%	TRY.B	Triarc Cos. Inc. (Cl B)	3.19%
	JMBA	Jamba Inc.	0.05%
Energy 0.71%	NGPC	NGP Capital Resources Co.	0.71%
Financials 71.67%	LUK	Leucadia National Corp.	9.12%
	ACAS	American Capital Strategies Ltd.	8.11%
	SIVB	SVB Financial Group	7.86%
	KFN	KKR Financial Corp.	6.20%
	ALD	Allied Capital Corp.	6.05%
	CSE	CapitalSource Inc.	6.03%
	AMG	Affiliated Managers Group Inc.	4.30%
	AINV	Apollo Investment Corp.	4.13%
	CIT	CIT Group Inc.	3.97%
	ARCC	Ares Capital Corp.	2.57%
	MCGC	MCG Capital Corp.	2.32%
	CODI	Compass Diversified Trust	2.10%
	CSWC	Capital Southwest Corp.	1.80%
	TICC	Technology Investment Capital Corp.	1.12%
	BPFH	Boston Private Financial Holdings Inc.	1.08%
	GAIN	Gladstone Investment Corp.	1.05%
	GLAD	Gladstone Capital Corp.	0.93%
	MVC	MVC Capital Inc.	0.90%
	HTGC	Hercules Technology Growth Capital Inc.	0.76%
	TINY	Harris & Harris Group Inc.	0.76%
	PSEC	Prospect Energy Corp.	0.51%
Health Care 4.10%	MLNM	Millennium Pharmaceuticals Inc.	4.10%
Industrials 5.35%	MIC	Macquarie Infrastructure Co. Trust	4.39%
	UTK	UTEK Corp.	0.96%
Information Technology 10.55%	CMGI	CMGI Inc.	4.44%
	ICGE	Internet Capital Group Inc.	2.62%
	SFE	Safeguard Scientifics Inc.	2.56%
	JUPM	Jupitermedia Corp.	0.93%
N.A. 1.45%	HQH	H&Q Healthcare Fund	0.80%
	HQL	H&Q Life Sciences Investors	0.54%
	Cash	Money Market	0.11%
Utilities 2.94%	PNW	Pinnacle West Capital Corp.	2.94%

Fund Holdings are subject to change.
Source: PowerShare Capital Management LLC.

While many would find the area compelling based on news reports of KKR and others making a killing from their activities, it should be remembered that the area contains high risks. The "yen carry trade" could end abruptly. The assets held by each of these companies may at some point be exceeded by their debt holdings. A more positive view however comes from the diversified holdings within the index even though 70 percent is within the financial sector.

COMMODITY ETFs DIRECT

Other than choosing actively managed mutual funds most DIY investors would want to establish their own positions utilizing the new ETF tools that are available. The next few sections outline these areas.

The first ETF to invest in a commodity directly was Streettracks Gold ETF [GLD]. This launch in late 2004 was followed quickly by competing iShares Gold ETF [IAU], which has been less well received than [GLD]. The latter is the result of the typical "me too" ETF investor behavior where investors go with the first offering ignoring the subsequent offerings that are less liquid and not unique enough to capture their interest.

[GLD] has been a stunning success. Many attribute the rise in gold prices from 2004 to 2007 to the demand for the metal resulting from these funds. Previous to the [GLD] launch gold investing for investors was confined to futures and options trading [the leverage and continuous contract rollover was off-putting to most individual investors], precious metals stocks [which also could be dissatisfying due to the unreliability of various company prospects], and numismatic coin collections [marked by heavy sales expenses and little liquidity]. A liquid ETF tracking the price movement of gold overcame previous gold investing deficiencies. It shouldn't be too surprising that subsequently the more speculative and volatile silver issue, [SLV] iShares Silver ETF was launched in April 2006.

In lieu of using a managed futures product such as the Rydex Managed Futures fund, there now exists commodity ETFs where investors can structure their own allocations and do so using whatever strategy suits them best. Leading the way in this regard has been Deutsche Bank [DB], which has created a wide variety of commodity indexes upon which ETFs have been based.

Again, as described previously, the reason to add this type of product to conventional portfolios is to reduce risk and increase overall performance by adding uncorrelated assets to a conventional portfolio of stocks and bonds.

To assist with marketing of their products, PowerShares and DB have joined forces, with the former using their marketing clout and asset management remaining within the domain of DB. This has been a convenient relationship for both since DB had the expertise in the area but not the marketing network and PowerShares needed the products.

DB's products fall into several areas. First, there is the broad-based commodity index [DBLCIX], which contains six specific commodity sectors: crude oil [35%], heating oil [20%], gold [10%], aluminum [12.50%], wheat [11.50%], and corn [11.50%]. The index is what ETF, DBC is linked to. Investors seeking to add commodities can utilize this ETF in whatever weighting they choose. Alternatively there is the more widely known index-linked ETFs based on the popular Goldman Sach's Commodity Index [GSCI] launched by Barclays GSG [iShares GSCI]. However, GSCI as of this date is weighted 71 percent to energy, which may be too heavily weighted toward that sector for some. The DJ AIG Commodity Index has an ETF trading in London currently which no doubt will be brought to the United States eventually. Its weightings are even more unique with only 33 percent to energy, 18 percent to grains, 18 percent to industrial metals, and only 8 percent to precious metals.

Our own opinion is that DBC is based on DB's historical back-tested research superior to other broad commodity indexes despite using fewer market sectors. Other ETFs contain many more subsets but the overall weightings of DBC seem to accomplish better returns using fewer sectors. The index history in Table 4.2, compares DB Commodity Index to GSCI and the DJ–AIG Commodity Index.

DB also features more targeted commodity issues including:

- DB Base Metals ETF [DBB], which is evenly divided among aluminum, zinc, and copper.
- DB Agricultural ETF [DBA], which is divided evenly among corn, wheat, soybeans, and sugar.
- DB Energy ETF [DBE], which is divided unevenly by Light Sweet crude oil, Brent crude oil, heating oil, RBOB gasoline, and a small 10 percent weighting to volatile natural gas.

TABLE 4.2 Fund Performance and Index History (%)*

Index	1 Year	3 Year	5 Year	10 Year	Inception
DB Commodity Index	17.00	28.76	27.74	13.65	10.85
GSCI	−15.09	7.73	14.79	4.69	−17.13
DJ-AIG	2.07	10.58	16.10	6.98	3.21

*As of December 31, 2006.
Source: PowerShares Capital Management LLC & DB Commodity Services.

- DB Gold ETF [DGL], which tracks gold and has as its primary advantage a much lower price than GLD, for example.
- DB Silver ETF [DBS] tracks silver prices but does so in a much lower price manner. Some retail investors find SLV's $130 price difficult for them to acquire round lots whereby DBS is currently at $25 making it more appealing. However, the price doesn't alter the percentage moves.
- DB Precious Metals ETF [DBP] tracks a relationship of 80 percent gold to 20 percent silver.
- DB Oil ETF [DBO] tracks light sweet crude oil and does so at a lower share price, which may also have more retail appeal.

In the popular energy markets, crude oil also has several ETFs beyond the DBO issue from which to choose. U.S. Oil Fund LP [USO] was launched first. Oddly to some observers it tracked the movement of West Texas Intermediate Crude oil market in lieu of the more conventional Light Sweet Crude oil market that we're most familiar with. That was an initial turn-off since WTIC pricing is much under the radar. But interestingly instead of tracking the price of oil in dollars, USO tracks the percentage movement of the spot price. It seems an effective method and based on trading volumes, nearly 5 million shares per day, USO is the most popular oil ETF available.

There have been some unintended consequences from some oil ETFs. Claymore Securities launched a bullish [UCR] and bearish oil ETF [DCR] allowing investors to either make a directional bet that oil prices would rise or fall. Unfortunately for Claymore something nasty happened after the launch on January 16, 2007. That day crude oil prices dropped 3 percent but DCR was up 2 percent while UCR was also down 2 percent. Huh? Well, that was a bite in the shorts literally, eh? Claymore was quite embarrassed by it and correctly blamed specialists for poor market making. Nevertheless their series of oil ETFs got a black eye and now investors must stand aside and see how these issues perform over the next year or so before one can confidently use them again. Unfortunately with confidence low so, too, is volume and that will hurt in the long run as investors shun both series.

CURRENCY ETFs DIRECT

Previous to currency linked ETFs becoming available, investing in those markets for retail investors was as difficult as with commodities. The only route for individual investors was through previously outlined expensive and leveraged commodity and futures pools. Currency trading was the domain for large banks and other institutions accustomed to dealing with large sums daily in the inter-bank market.

Taking the lead in currency ETFs was Rydex Investments. They launched a series of ETFs including:

- Rydex Euro Currency ETF [FXE].
- Rydex British Pound ETF [FXB].
- Rydex Swiss Franc ETF [FXF].
- Rydex Swedish Krona ETF [FXS].
- Rydex Canadian Dollar ETF [FXC].
- Rydex Mexican Peso ETF [FXM].
- Rydex Australian Dollar ETF [FXA].
- Rydex Yen ETF [FXY].

Why are these important? In the first place they're necessary for hedging purposes. For example, in 2005 the Nikkei 225 Index in Japan gained nearly 40 percent, but Japan ETF [EWJ] gained 20 percent. While a respectable return for the ETF, naturally an investor would like the return of the index more. The difference was the value of the yen, which had deteriorated by an equal amount. So if FXY had been available the investor could have shorted it in an appropriate amount to hedge yen currency risks.

Finally, our DB friends have issued a very important bullish UUP and bearish UDN Dollar Index series. This really allows investors to hedge or speculate against a rising or falling U.S, dollar. It's an extremely important issue for investors since there is continued and widespread conjecture that the U.S. dollar may fall sharply at some point. If investors wish to protect themselves or profit from such an event, how would they do it without the benefit of UDN?

INVERSE ETFs DIRECT

A funny thing happened when trying to take advantage of shorting opportunities in various ETFs—most retail investors found they couldn't. Almost every ETF issued carries the same benefit as stated on promotional material alleging you may engage in "short selling without an uptick."

So then, what's the problem?

We didn't give it much thought until late 2003 when we tried to short TLT [Lehman Bros. 20-year Treasury ETF] and couldn't. Subscribers to our newsletter who also tried were told the same thing by their brokers—"no stock available." How could that be, I wondered? TLT was trading then over a million shares per day so it seemed there was plenty of liquidity. Some authorities on the subject like ETF creator Nate Most was equally disappointed given that specialists couldn't be the problem since there existed adequate options and futures contracts where they could hedge their risk in executing two-way trading. Then we were told that the specialist firm Speer Leeds wasn't really making a market for the public as much as they were for their new owner Goldman Sachs. I remember being told by one industry professional that "all the stock you need for shorting is sitting on the trading desks at Goldman Sachs." In other words, GS had their own uses for both the specialist and TLT.

Well, that's not a good thing, I thought. But is that the only problem? No. It turns out that more than other sources of difficulty brokerage firms were really the problem.

In order for brokers to have any stock or ETF available for shorting they have to be carrying it in inventory, or if not available, be willing to find the security for you. It seems simple enough but it isn't. Brokerage Stock Loan Departments aren't necessarily a profit center. It costs money for them to carry stock in inventory. Most firms maintain a "hard to short list" that detail which securities are readily available from inventory. Should you ask them for a security from that list to short, the immediate reply would be "no stock available" and the client order would be rejected. If you're an online trader entering such an order and received that reply, you may as well forget about it. You can enter the order until the cows come home and you'll just keep getting the same response.

Some online firms including ETrade for example claim that when you receive such a response you are able to call their desk and they will "try to find you the stock." Now if you think that a large brokerage firm can do any better, you're sorely mistaken. I can remember when being a broker at a large firm calling the margin clerks myself hoping to find stock for clients. You may as well be calling the post office since you're not going to get very far "working the order" in that manner. The same thing occurred when I had my own firm and cleared transactions with Bear Stearns—no chance.

Let's be clear, when it comes to shorting the largest ETFs issued like the Cubes and Spyders isn't a problem. But beneath the top half dozen or so in trading volume, you'll start running into problems. The lower into the bowels of the ETF roster you move the more difficult to short it is for retail investors. This is especially true for many exotic PowerShares, Claymore, and First Trust issues. But large issuers like Barclays and State Street aren't any better with some of their own issues. In fact when I complained to Barclays about our inability to short TLT they just said, "It's a broker issue, now go away."

Institutional investors don't have this difficulty since they are able to go directly to the trustee and have new shares issued in denominations of 50 to 100 thousand shares. All the issuers and sponsors love accommodating them since with new shares being issued they earn more fees. Retail investors are left to deal with the issues already in float. So cynically sponsors brush off investor complaints.

Anyway given the way markets have performed since the 2002 low who wants to be short anyway, right? If the markets ever experience a bear market again, retail investors will be mighty steamed if many try to short "difficult to short" ETFs all of a sudden.

The solution came in the form of ProFunds' breakthrough "inverse" ETF products, the first of which were launched in the summer of 2006. While only a first step featuring six basic issues, they opened the door for an easier and more reliable way for retail investors to overcome existing shorting difficulties. These novel ETF issues took ProFunds the better part of a decade to secure SEC approval given their novel nature and the glacial pace at which the SEC moves. In early 2007 another batch of inverse issues came to market and competitor Rydex filed for dozens of similar issues immediately thereafter.

Again, not every ETF that's difficult to short will have a companion inverse issue—at least not for a long time. However, many market sectors with inverse issues can be highly correlated to other sectors not having a companion inverse issue. If so, then a highly correlated inverse ETF can be used against the issue you might own.

Why engage in such tactics? Many individuals would like to hedge their portfolios against an overall market downturn. Such an event could drag or sink all sectors. Utilizing inverse ETFs becomes a risk reduction tactic that is a lot easier to incorporate than using options or other more complex and more expensive methods.

The other unique benefit is for tax-exempt accounts like IRAs, 401[k]s, foundations and other entities restricted from shorting. As we demonstrated in Chapter 2, the inverse issue allows previously restricted accounts to go short by going long. Huh? When you buy an inverse ETF you make money when the associated sector declines. This solves the shorting prohibition for this class of investors. At the same time, it opens a huge market for issuers such as ProFunds and Rydex.

NEW MARGIN RULES

On April 2, 2007, new margin rules promulgated by the SEC will go into effect. The new rules permit brokers to calculate the overall risk of a portfolio rather than that for each security within the portfolio.

Currently margin requirements are 50 percent for each security with a maintenance margin of 25 percent. Under the new rule investors will have to put up just 15 percent. That's a pretty stunning change!

Why is this happening? First, there are overseas competitive pressures where investors in some cases don't need to deposit any margin amounts. U.S. brokers and exchanges need to compete more ably. Second, it was felt that an overall portfolio risk assessment would better represent actual risk rather than considering each component at previous margin rates.

For example, some hedging strategies involving options or futures have their own set of margin requirements. Yet engaging in such strategies reduces overall portfolio risk. Therefore, rather than viewing each security it was felt that a measuring overall risk would be more realistic.

The SEC conducted a two-year pilot program beginning in July 2005. San Francisco-based Fimat USA LLC was one of the first brokers to participate in the program. According to an interview appearing in *Investment News* from January 8, 2007 with Doug Engmann, Fimat CEO:

> It gives a lot more flexibility to the customers in terms of being able to hedge positions and use options creatively to trade. The main impact of that is we'll have a generally safer system, because people can now hedge and get the benefit on their hedging from reduced margin.

But the changes also require brokers to assume more risk as well. No doubt that calculating or evaluating these risks will be more difficult and perhaps even subjective. However, brokers must utilize SEC pricing models when making these calculations.

Since a lot of this activity had moved offshore where margin restrictions were less severe the exchanges felt that regulating this area was better than seeing the business go away.

The Chicago Board Options Exchange [CBOE] web site articulates the rules changes and benefits as follows:

> The new portfolio margining rules have the effect of aligning the amount of margin money required to be held in a customer's account to the risk of the portfolio as a whole, calculated through simulating market moves up and down, and accounting for offsets between and among all products held in the account that are highly correlated (for example, options on the S&P 500 Index (SPX), can be offset against options on the S&P 500 Depositary Receipts (SPY), or options on DIAMONDS (DIA) can be offset against SPX options). The longstanding practice for strategy-based margins is to require margin based on set formulas for various strategies (i.e., some spread strategies require a certain minimum

margin), regardless of what other offsetting positions were held in the account and regardless of potential market moves. For some positions the margin requirements may not change significantly, but for other positions, such as owning a protective put against a long stock position, the difference may be sizable. This is appropriate in that the margin calculation accounts for the fact that the risk of one position (long stock) is offset by the other (long put).

And The Options Clearing Corporation outlines the features and benefits as follows:

This expansion of customer portfolio margining helps U.S. equities markets take a major leap forward allowing securities firms to participate on a level playing field with the futures and international equities markets as it relates to customer margining. Current margin rules governing U.S. equity markets follow a strategy-based approach requiring broker-dealers to identify approved hedged positions (or strategies) and imposing a set margin requirement for each position. Portfolio margining allows broker-dealers to group products based on a related underlying asset into portfolios with the margin requirement based on the risk of the portfolio as opposed to a set amount.

This risk-based approach is based on OCC's TIMS margin methodology, which determines the maximum loss associated with a portfolio given a percentage move in an underlying asset. A portfolio containing an offsetting position in the derivative and underlying asset reflect less market risk and requires less equity to collateralize the account. This provides additional leverage to customers' capital available for reinvestment. The approach has been the standard for U.S. futures and international securities markets for years.

It may well be for retail accounts that new margin rules will vary from firm to firm. Some firms will want to take a wait and see attitude while others will jump right in fearing competitive pressures. The initial beneficiaries of this change will be hedge funds. In fact, during the initial pilot program minimum account equity mandates was $5 million, but that has now been dropped. As brokers get more familiar with the processes and gain experience no doubt these services will be passed on down to retail investors in one form or another. Each firm is free to set more stringent requirements but. of course, not less.

THE ZERO COMMISSION

As we noted in Chapter 1, the zero commission is starting to catch on with more brokers than just upstart firm Zecco.com. Bank of America and Wells Fargo have matched the zero commission boom in their own ways. Nevertheless, combining this with major wire-house firms eliminating commissions in exchange for a flat annual fee has allowed investors to use these tools that add to cost-effective trading possibilities when trying to employ more active hedge fund strategies.

CONVERGENCE WELL UNDERWAY

There have been dramatic changes in the investment marketplace. The explosive growth of ETFs has included many diverse issues. These new issues have done much to open markets previously either difficult for retail investors to enter or impossible. These would include unleveraged commodity and currency sectors, inverse series, actively managed, private equity, and globally focused issues.

Mutual funds have found a way to utilize ETFs utilizing hedge fund like structures and strategies including many long/short funds mushrooming into existence. Mutual funds have also found a way to offer Alternative Investments through the Rydex Managed Futures Fund which allows investors another important and typical hedge fund component never previously available to retail investors. And zero commission structures allow for cost-effective trading previously only a province of major institutional traders and large hedge funds.

In a breakthrough development that confirms the "convergence theme" Man Financial has filed to issue the Man Dual Absolute Return Fund. It will be structured as a "closed-end" mutual fund and will become the first publicly-listed hedge fund in the U.S. within a few months. The fund intends to manage the majority of its assets in a long/short style with a much smaller balance devoted to macro strategies. The sketchiness of this information is due to the mandatory SEC "quiet period" that the offering is currently in.

During a quiet period we must speculate to fill in the blanks from the SEC filing. But, no doubt, barring any regulatory glitches or delays this fund will be available before 2007 ends. An interesting question will be how Man Financial, which is delegating the management of the fund to Tykhe Capital LLC of New York, will allocate between the various strategies outlined in the prospectus. They will no doubt charge the fund a performance fee similar to the 2 percent fixed and 20 percent incentive fee common to most hedge funds. Curiously, the SEC frowns on mutual funds charging any performance/incentive fees. One could infer readily that Man Financial intends to pay these fees, if merited, directly to Tykhe while reported net performance after fees to shareholders. Will this pass SEC muster? We'll see, but the important issue taken from the theme of this book and chapter is that for the first time hedge funds are going mainstream. If they are successful in doing so, the convergence story becomes even more real.

In June 2007, according to the *Investment News* article "Hedge Funds Face Potential Challenge," it was announced: "A handful of firms have begun constructing so-called replication indexes that use multiple baskets of liquid securities to generate returns that mimic those of major hedge fund indexes." The basic strategy is to invest primarily in a blend of ETFs and futures contracts to achieve performance and results comparable to typical hedge fund strategies. Further, and of perhaps more significance, the fixed fee will be only 1 percent and performance fees will not exceed 10 percent. That's a major reduction from the customary 2 percent fixed and 20 percent performance fees structure.

According to Jerome Abernathy, Managing Partner, Stonebrook Structured Products LLC, they have begun the process of launching an ETF that replicates the hedge fund index performance. Abernathy stated, "We think the best use for this product is to deliver hedge-fund like returns for retail investors. The promised land for this is an ETF." Merrill Lynch, Goldman Sachs, and JP Morgan Chase are also assembling indexes that could be eventually suited for ETF product construction and issuance.

Just remember one thing: These types of products may be "dumbing-down" hedge fund investing. After all, the best managers will still command the highest fees while providing superior returns. Putting indexes together that mimic hedge fund performance is a project that may only dilute performance for each strategy undertaken. You can never buy the best performance on the cheap. However, taken together, products and strategies are now becoming more readily available for retail and institutional investors. Only regulatory restraint and new product engineers' imagination will hold back the tide of new issues and products. And time will tell if any of these products will be any good.

CHAPTER 5

The Bullish Bias Gets a Makeover

The essence of the bullish bias* is based on one premise: Over long time periods stock prices go up. You've heard this a gazillion times no doubt. It might be more correct to say: Over long time periods stock market *indexes* go up. As we've learned indexes get readjusted with losers being tossed and winners taking their place. After all you could hold some losers yourself that will *never* go up or even succeed as going enterprises, which is why indexes are less risky.

Stock indexes rise over long periods due primarily to one reason: the earnings growth of their constituent companies. Since indexes get rebalanced frequently [quarterly, semiannually, and annually] with winners being added and losers being ejected it stands to reason that most companies within the relevant index experience rising earnings. As earnings rise so, too, do [PE] price to earnings ratios.

The P/E ratio is arrived at by dividing the stock or share price by the earnings per share. It's also used to determine how many years it will take for earnings to cover the current stock price. For an index or an individual stock there are two ways to view PEs. One is the "lagging" PE, which is based on known current earnings. The other is the more misleading "forward looking" PE, which consists of Wall Street analysts' guesses. As most know, these estimates are just educated guesses and are often off-base, especially at the peak of an earning cycle when the analysts expect the rate of profit increase to continue ad infinitum. So when you hear different PE numbers for the same index being bantered about, try to know whether these are based on current or lagging data or someone's view, whether a consensus number or not, of the future.

---

*Note: You might wonder why, given this book's theme, we would even discuss this subject. However, it's fundamentally important that investors understand the contemporary structure of today's investing environment *before* developing and adopting any investment strategy.

Typically investors are willing to pay higher and higher prices for shares where earnings are consistently increasing. It's a straightforward concept.

OTHER CONTRIBUTING FORCES

Much of this area is changing, less clear, or not obvious. The financial media in particular add to bullishness. Let's face it, the ad revenues most in the financial media receive come from financial services firms with products to sell. Always featuring upbeat commentators, guests and news are, more often than not, dominant. It just makes sense. Editorially these companies are not interested in driving away or turning off their revenue makers.

Even the old venerable and hugely popular public television series *Wall Street Week with Louis Rukeyser* usually featured guests that had a bullish outlook and/or had a story and products to sell. While a public television production the show nevertheless had Wall Street firm sponsors.

The same situation exists today with popular CNBC television programming. Most of their featured shows have very few, if any, bearish, or even mildly cynical, guests or commentary. Again their sponsors are financial services firms with products to sell. They're conflicted.

And sometimes they're contracted. The notoriously bullish Jim Cramer, host of the popular, currently successful CNBC *Mad Money* show, is prohibited from shorting stocks. He made this startling revelation when answering a question on his Street.com web site May 15, 2006 when he said: "First of all, I am not allowed to short stocks per my deal with CNBC ... " Probably not many people are aware of this or what it means. Why would CNBC insert such a clause in Cramer's contract? The answer might be multi-faceted, but to me the obvious answer is that CNBC doesn't want Mr. Mad Money to be projecting negative market images that would turn off advertisers with bullish products to sell.

Then there are of course the "sell side" stock analysts, who frankly are paid to be bullish. They hang around the companies they cover too much, hearing only one side of a story, develop friendships, and are often seduced by their comments. After all the companies don't want their stock price to decline since so many senior level managers are compensated with stock options that pay generously as their stock rises in value.

Analysts are also conflicted by their employers' desire to gain lucrative investment banking business relationship with the companies the analyst covers. The conflicts of interest are obvious, and continue despite the huge settlements paid out in the wake of the "research" scandal uncovered during the 2000–2003 bear market. Even though firms have erected Great Walls of China to separate analysts from their investment banking counterparts, the wink and nod factors still exist. The pressure from the investment banking side for revenues is intense as most executives from that sector are paid substantial bonuses from underwriting or other profits. And as a major profit center senior management overseeing both business areas want them to grow and increase profits for the firm.

Prior to the bear market of 2000–2002, it was rare to impossible to note an analyst giving an outright sell for any company's stock they covered. The most severe negative rankings or recommendations they would provide varying by firm were classifications such as "hold," "neutral," or "underperform." Why so timid? Because they didn't want to offend the management of companies they covered. Neither were they willing to take the heat from their peers in investment banking or senior management.

"Sell" rankings would only be given to companies that were likely to go out of business. That would be a safe classification since there was little in the way of banking opportunities. But even that's starting to change given reorganization or distressed securities opportunities the investment banking sectors might enjoy.

COMMISSIONS OUT, FEES IN

When Wall Street firms relied on commissions as a major component of earnings especially at the retail level, no one seemed to care if investors were buying or selling. The important thing was commission revenues.

As outlined in Chapter 1, the structure of Wall Street firms has changed dramatically at the retail level. Out are the days of encouraging active trading for commissions and in are building a recurring fee business. With the new structure modeled on financial plans clients are now advised to stay with the plan and keep funding it. And why not? This is the only way to keep the "evergreen income" coming in and growing.

It's a pretty rigged structure and theme that encourages investors to "invest for the long term" and ignore market ups and downs. This behavior now completely dominates investing at the retail level. It's also reflected in the message Wall Street firms convey to their Fas, which goes: "Keep the casino exits difficult to find as usual." That message may be too harsh, but it does reflect the hard facts.

As we also learned in Chapter 1, the online trading industry is trying to offer services similar to the full service firms also for a fee. Charles Schwab for example has been promoting their advisory relationships with participating registered investment advisors [RIAs] quite successfully. Just as at the wire-house level, Schwab receives a hefty share of the fees the RIA charges and they don't have to share those fees with any FAs. Ameritrade also offers some advisory services and others will be joining in as well. So here's another case of business model convergence between wire houses and online discount firms.

But given this fee-based structure the same incentives apply. Keep investors in the game and faithful to whatever plan they have bought into. To do this, firms must not be singing any bearish tunes. All public communications must contain bullish happy talk on all matters. If you're thinking anyone from these firms is going to come out and start telling investors to sell that would be disruptive to fee income models and would occur rarely.

Also, firms are gearing up for the great avalanche of IRA rollovers from Baby Boomers who are going to be retiring over the next decade. Many have pension and 401[k] plans currently that will be distributed when employees retire. It's estimated trillions of dollars will be available for investment. But this doesn't contribute that much since much of this money will only enrich FAs and firms without theoretically affecting markets. This is because it's the same money currently invested and is just being recirculated, although retiring investors may—in fact, should—be choosing. One aspect of it though is that retiring investors may choose a more conservative investment scheme emphasizing bonds over stocks, for example.

The standard business practices at banking trust departments serve as the basis for the captive asset models on Wall Street today. It's impossible for me to recall how many trust beneficiaries have complained about the lousy performance of their assets held at trust departments. These are truly captive assets since the trust outlines and describes the trustees' authority over the account. While they might politely listen to beneficiaries' complaints they are in complete control over the investment decisions. They can be removed only for breaching normal fiduciary guidelines. That makes their decision making ultra-conservative since they don't want to lose the fee business. After all it was only in the past 30 years or so that stocks were considered suitable investments by the so-called "prudent man rule." The rule has evolved from allowing only Treasury and investment grade bond ownership, to dividend paying stock ownership and with the advent of the Employee Retirement Income Security Act [ERISA] the demands for more flexibility grew.

The current prudent man rule definition runs something like this: A standard of conduct that requires a fiduciary to discharge his or her duties with care, discretion, intelligence, skill, prudence, and diligence under the circumstances then prevailing that a prudent man acting in a like capacity and familiar with such matters would use in the conduct of an enterprise of a like character with similar goals.

So now it's a matter of interpretation. To meet client demand and remain relevant some large trust companies and more sophisticated banks are even helping their clients find suitable hedge funds and alternative investments, which seems a bold departure from the old prudent man rule. These steps can be justified based on studies like the Lintner study that justifies academically the risk lowering benefits of employing these strategies.

But no matter how you view the overall industry there is a battle for fees. And it's become an industry dependent on optimism to keep investors in the game at all costs.

RECURRING FEES

With the explosion of ERISA-based accounts one thing is certain, employers and individual investors need to keep adding funds to their plans each year. These plans include IRAs, 401[k]s, profit-sharing, or other forms of retirement or savings accounts.

Most of these contributed funds are geared to an established investment plan. These plans generally don't have a large allocation to cash. Why is that? Generally because investors have been sold on the belief that markets will always rise and sitting on the sidelines is a waste of opportunity. More distasteful to firms, dependent on how the account fees are structured, is that cash fees are lower. For example, if your FA is receiving a percentage of fees generated by the account, the lowest fee producer will be cash. If the account is structured as a "wrap account" where the fees are based on a fixed percentage of all assets, then having high cash balances shouldn't be an issue. But often it can be since the financial culture is geared toward being fully invested at all times as opposed to trying to time markets. Remember, FAs are focused more on raising assets than being market experts. Having to make those types of decisions is a distraction that slows them down from their primary business model mission—gathering assets.

When investment performance is good, adding more funds to the plan is not an emotional problem for most investors. When times are more difficult FAs have to work harder to remind investors of their mantra, "invest for the long term and quit worrying." From a client's perspective this is just human nature while the FAs urgings are based on deeply engrained training.

THE GREENSPAN AND BERNANKE PUT

There's a variety of definitions of the Greenspan and Bernanke Put. First there's a relatively simple one from Investopedia:

A description of the perceived attempt of then-chairman of the Federal Reserve Board, Alan Greenspan, of propping up the securities markets by lowering interest rates and thereby helping money flow into the markets.

Investors assumed that they would be able to liquidate their stocks at a set price at or before a future date as if there was a built-in put option. They believed that Greenspan would manipulate monetary policy and continue to maintain market stability. While the former Fed chair's actions did have an effect on the markets, it was not necessarily his objective.

The term was coined in 1998 after the Fed lowered interest rates following the collapse of the investment firm Long-Term Capital Management. The effect of this rate reduction was that investors borrowed funds more cheaply to invest in the securities market, thereby averting a potential downswing in the markets.

The new Fed Chairman Ben Bernanke came to his job much like a new coach following a legend. After all Greenspan had occupied the office for almost two decades and was arguably the most influential Fed chairman in history. Presidents of both political parties were fearful of not reappointing him lest they frighten investors.

However Bernanke came to his position with even better academic credentials than his predecessor and was widely regarded as a genius. His early statement to ease market fears of a change in leadership was a commitment to "continuity." In other words, maintaining the policies of his predecessor. As such he also adopts what is now the Bernanke Put, which argues that the Fed is there to bail out investors should things go awry. Enhancing this put are previous statements that are attributed to him which include his willingness to "drop money from helicopters" to cure market difficulties. This is where his nickname, "Helicopter Ben" originated.

It should be apparent that both chairmen were and are willing to use their powers to stimulate markets in a bullish direction, which only reinforces and enhances the "bullish bias."

MONEY SUPPLY SHENANIGANS

What is M-3?

One of Bernanke's first major moves was to eliminate from view popular M-3 statistics from public scrutiny. This was done in March 2006. First, what is M-3?

The Federal Reserve had traditionally published prior to March 2006 three measures of money supply growth. M-1, which calculates currency and checking accounts; M-2, which includes M-1 plus savings deposits, CDs, and money market funds; and M-3, which is M-2 plus large-denomination time deposits, balances in institutional money funds, repurchase liabilities issued by all depository institutions, and Eurodollars held by U.S. residents at foreign branches of U.S. banks worldwide.

Why is this important? Many investors saw the removal in nefarious terms: that the government was trying to hide from scrutiny excessive monetary inflation.

Nobel prize winning economist Milton Friedman, perhaps one of three [John Maynard Keynes and John Kenneth Galbraith being others] most consequential economists of the twentieth century argued that the money supply should continually expand at a consistent rate of 3 percent annually. Clearly as M-3 data reflected excessive growth, authorities decided to drop it after it reached a level of annual growth exceeding 8 percent.

John Williams of Shadow Government Statistics and others have been able to recreate the measurement by cobbling together available data to reflect what M-3 would appear as if it still existed.

As you can see in Figure 5.1, both M-3 and M-2 now exceed Friedman's suggested monetary growth targets with M-3 as of March 2007 running at nearly 11 perent and M-2 pushing 6 percent. Why does this matter? Because high money supply growth is inflationary and too much money being printed by authorities can and has produced asset bubbles. Finally, like anything else governed by the laws of supply and demand, too many dollars make them less dear.

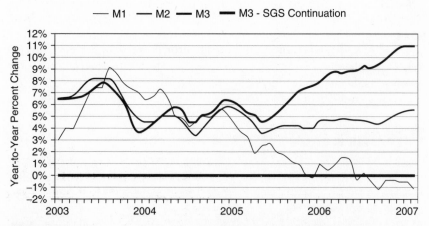

FIGURE 5.1 Annual Money Supply Growth—with M-3 Continuation
Sources: Shadow Government Statistics, Federal Reserve Board.

The bottom line is that pushing out so many dollars stimulates markets, since it creates additional liquidity that needs to be invested thus adding to the bullish bias.

EXCESS LIQUIDITY AND STOCK BUYBACKS

With the government printing presses running hot, much of this excess liquidity finds its way to corporations. With this corporations can do several things: invest in research and new product development, pay shareholders increased dividends, or buy back outstanding shares in the open market.

In the past few years corporations have chosen the stock buyback as their primary manner to deal with all this cash. In fact in 2006 owing to stock buyback activity and private equity transactions the overall supply of stocks was reduced by $600 billion. Fewer shares with liquidity high means higher stock prices. This activity has proven a convenient consequence or addition to the bullish bias.

But is this a bad thing? Yes and no. Obviously for corporations it helps to lift their stock price, all other things being equal. This is a good thing for investors and management, who are paid stock option bonuses based on how their stock performs. But it's only a short-term positive since fewer shares only temporarily lower P/Es. For example, if a company's earnings are flat on fewer shares the company's P/E will drop, but overall progress for the company doesn't exist. It's deceiving to shareholders in that manner. But it's a direct result of too much liquidity in the system caused by a generous Fed.

I'm not on any corporate boards to understand the accounting model for each firm as to why one would choose stock buybacks versus raising dividends with excess cash. Founders and/or insiders with low-cost basis stock would benefit more it would seem from stock dividends given current tax law. For example, someone like Bill Gates would benefit from a large tax advantaged dividend and still keep all his stock. He could also claim a tax deduction for the money received if he gifted it to his foundation. Now how cool is that?

I'M FOREVER BLOWING BUBBLES

One consequence of the attitude and behavior of former Chairman Greenspan has been the creation of asset bubbles and an unwillingness to deal with them in a timely fashion. First, there was the stock market bubble. Greenspan tried to jawbone markets lower in 1996 with his famous "irrational exuberance" testimony. The bearish effect was temporary [lasting just a day or two] and thereafter Greenspan let markets rise in bubble-like fashion.

The notion that the Fed could save markets from any disaster was first noticed in 1998 with the financial collapse of Long-Term Capital Management [LTCM]. With trillions at risk the Fed stepped-in, cut interest rates, and helped organize a bailout of the firm's liabilities. This was a classic example of the Greenspan Put at work.

However, when the stock market bear market of 2000–2003 began the Fed started to cut interest rates belatedly not doing so until the rout was well underway. The Fed cut rates aggressively so that the discount rate was cut from 6 percent to a measly 1 percent. The consequence? A housing bubble that is being popped as this is written.

Bernanke inherited the housing bubble from Greenspan and how will he handle it? It seems a no-win situation since some have suggested he'll either let home prices fall risking a drop in consumer confidence and spending [nearly two-thirds of present economic activity] if he does, which could foster a recession. Or he cuts interest rates dramatically so that mortgage rates drop substantially making homes affordable based on lower interest rates exclusively. In doing the latter he risks igniting more inflation.

And in early 2007 subprime mortgage problems [low-quality mortgages issued requiring either no money down, limited or no income verification, and poor credit history] are hitting the market negatively. To solve the problem he may choose to rev-up the helicopters to drop money on the system as his solution.

Again, this is another example of the bullish bias at work.

BYE-BYE GLASS – STEAGALL

Senator Couzens: Did Goldman, Sachs and Company organize the Goldman Sachs Trading Corportation?

Mr. Sachs: Yes, sir.

Senator Couzens: And it sold its stock to the public?

Mr. Sachs: A portion of it. The firms invested originally in ten per cent of the entire issue for the sum of ten million dollars.

Senator Couzens: And the other ninety per cent was sold to the public?

Mr. Sachs: Yes, sir.

Senator Couzens: And what is the price of the stock now?

Mr. Sachs: Approximately one and three quarters.

—from the Senate Hearings of Stock Exchange Practices, 1932

After the market crash of 1929, many rule changes and agencies were created to cure problems that many felt caused the great crash. The Glass-Steagall

Act of 1933 authorized bank deposit insurance [FDIC] and prohibited banks from owning brokerage firms, trading or owning shares and underwriting new stock issues. It was created as many banks failed due to their ownership of shares bankrupting many depositors in banks that at the time had no insurance.

The Securities and Exchange Commission [SEC] was created by law in 1934. It promulgated many rules regarding trading, brokerage registration and compliance, margin standards, and so forth.

When in the 1970s brokerage firms began offering money market accounts to their clients complete with check writing and debit/credit cards banks objected. This was an invasion of their space by brokers and represented unfair competition as bank lobbyists complained.

In 1986 the Fed, given their regulatory jurisdiction over banking, decided to reinterpret Glass-Steagall prohibitions and allow banks to have up to 5 percent of their gross revenues from that investment banking business.

Then in 1987 over the objections of then-Fed Chairman Paul Volcker the Fed voted to allow banks to handle the underwriting business including commercial paper, municipal revenue bonds in addition to previously approved municipal general obligation bonds and mortgage-backed securities. The then-vice chairman of Citicorp, Thomas Thobald argued that three outside checks on corporate misbehavior had emerged since 1933: "a very effective SEC; knowledgeable investors and sophisticated rating agencies."

When Greenspan became chairman in 1987 he had previously been a board member of JP Morgan. In 1989 the Fed board approved an application by JP Morgan, Chase Manhattan, Bankers Trust, and Cititcorp to expand the Glass-Steagall loophole to include dealing in debt and equity securities.

In December 1996 Greenspan supported a Fed decision to permit bank holding companies to own investment bank affiliates.

And then in 1997, with Greenspan looking the other way by offering no comment, Bankers Trust bought the brokerage and investment bank Alex. Brown & Company, in the first of many similar transactions.

Finally in October 1999 the Financial Services Modernization Act was passed engineered by Treasury Secretary Robert E. Rubin, President Bill Clinton, and Citigroup's Sandy Weill and John Reed, which effectively repealed Glass-Steagall. A few days later Rubin accepted a job at Citicorp as Weill's chief lieutenant. Well, membership has its privileges doesn't it?

The modern Wall Street firm was born.

"DA BOYZ" AND PRIMARY DEALERS MERGE

Just who are these guys?

"Da Boyz" earned this moniker and reputation given their insider knowledge, trading skills, and sheer dominance over all trading issues on Wall Street and now globally as well. The archetypical group is led by well-known firms such as Goldman Sachs, Lehman Bros., Bear Stearns, and others. Their trading desk operations are profit centers. Over the past few years, trading desk or "proprietary investment" profits have soared. These profits in 2006 for example now exceed revenues/earnings from all other sources, including investment banking and captive asset fee income.

Almost every firm, doing business as Da Boyz, have trading desk profits that are similar [although smaller] than super trading results from industry leader Goldman Sachs. Goldman's earnings reported March 2007 from the previous quarter totaled $3.15 billion of which 74 percent was derived from trading. That's not chump change, is it? Other firms reporting similar results are Lehman Bros. and Bear Stearns since they're more focused on their core business than, say, Citigroup, which has more diverse operations including widespread banking and retail brokerage operations. These activities dilute positive trading results.

The bottom line is that large brokerage firms have become trading machines. Since we never get detailed earnings breakdowns sufficient enough to know what trading styles were utilized [why would they want to share that information?] to achieve these spectacular results, one style you can rest assured is utilized to some extent is "program trading." A simple definition of the strategy [courtesy of Answers.com] is "the large-scale, computer-assisted trading of stocks or other securities according to systems in which decisions to buy and sell are triggered automatically by fluctuations in price."

According to data published by the New York Stock Exchange [NYSE] the average percent of all trading volume devoted to program trading has been more than 30 percent of all volume. See Figure 5.2. From the typical detailed trading breakdown in Figure 5.3, it's clear which firms dominate this activity either for their account or on behalf of their clients.

So we can readily infer one technique that Da Boyz are using to make a lot of dough. But are these earnings from trading unusual? If investment banking activity is lower than normal it stands to reason that trading as a percentage of overall revenues would be higher. Then again these firms have another more powerful contributor and partner to their bottom line [ahem, you and me] since they're now, thanks to Greenspan and Clinton, primary dealers.

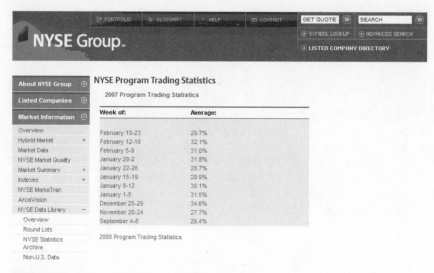

FIGURE 5.2   Early 2007 Program Trading Statistics
Source: NYSE.

What is a primary dealer? According to the Federal Reserve Bank of
New York:

> *The primary dealer system has been developed for the purpose*
> *of selecting trading counterparties for the Federal Reserve in its*
> *execution of market operations to carry out U.S. monetary policy.*
> *The designation of primary dealers has also involved the selection*
> *of firms for statistical reporting purposes in compiling data on*
> *activity in the U.S. Government securities market. These changes in*
> *the administration of these relationships have been developed after*
> *consultation with the Federal Reserve Board, the Federal Open*
> *Market Committee, the Treasury and the Securities and Exchange*
> *Commission.*

Let me try to give it to you in plain English. When the Fed and/or
Treasury wish to add/decrease reserves to the banking system they turn
to a handful of large prequalified institutions consisting of banks and
broker/dealers. As to the latter they are now one and the same. These
activities are called "open market operations" and can manipulate the
money supply indirectly while more commonly known interest rate changes
are both public and direct.

PROGRAM TRADING PURCHASES AND SALES

Trading on NYSE (Average Daily - Millions)	Current Week	Previous 52 Week Average*
Buy Programs	475.3	544.1
Sell Programs	496.4	548.2
Total Programs	971.7	1,092.3
Total NYSE Volume+	2,830.5	3,334.2
Program Trading as % of Total NYSE Buy + Sell Volume	34.3%	32.8%

Trading By Executing Market (Percent)	Current Week	Previous 52 Week Average·
NYSE	42.9%	46.7%
Other Domestic	56.6%	48.6%
Non-U.S. Markets#	0.5%	4.7%
Total: Average Daily - Millions of Shares	2,267.5	2,344.7

#Does not include program trading activity by non-U.S. sub sidiaries of NYSE member firms.

NYSE Program Trading - 15 Most Active Members Firms
(Millions of Shares)

	Index Arbitrage	Other Strategies Subject to Rule 80A(c)**	All Other Strategies	Total	Principal	Customer Facilitation	Agency
Lehman Brothers, Inc.	12.2	-	779.8	792.0	113.1	68.8	610.0
Goldman, Sachs & Co.	1.0	-	469.1	470.1	261.6	15.5	193.1
Morgan Stanley & Co. Inc.	3.9	-	431.6	435.5	132.7	-	302.8
Merrill Lynch, Pierce, Fenner, & Smith, Inc.	-	-	378.1	378.1	190.7	40.6	146.8
UBS Securities, LLC.	-	-	280.7	280.7	256.8	-	23.9
Credit Suisse Securities (USA) LLC.	15.6	-	257.4	273.0	131.5	5.9	135.6
Deutsche Bank Securities	18.3	-	182.7	201.0	32.8	9.0	159.2
Bear Stearns	6.9	-	181.7	188.6	12.6	-	176.0
RBC Capital Markets Corp.	38.5	-	127.7	166.2	-	-	166.2
BNP Paribas Brokerage Services Corp	-	-	142.0	142.0	-	-	142.0
Banc of America Securities LLC	2.8	-	134.2	137.0	51.6	14.6	70.7
Interactive Brokers LLC	-	-	86.0	86.0	-	-	86.0
SG Americas Securities, LLC	15.9	-	27.2	43.1	40.0	-	3.2
JP Morgan Securities, Inc.	-	-	39.3	39.3	22.4	1.6	15.3
Citigroup Global Markets	-	-	38.1	38.1	5.8	9.6	22.7
Total for 15 Member Firms	115.1	0.0	3,555.6	3,670.7	1,251.6	165.6	2,253.5
Total for All Firms Reporting	146.5	-	3,740.6	3,887.1	1,282.3	165.6	2,439.2
% of Total	3.8%	0.0%	96.2%	100.0%	33.0%	4.3%	62.7%
% - Average (Previous 52 Weeks)*	4.8%	0.0%	95.2%	100.0%	32.9%	6.6%	60.5%

+ Total NYSE volume is the sum of shares bought, sold and sold short on the NYSE, including its crossing sessions.
*Average is previous 52 week rolling average. For non-expiration weeks this includes 40 non-expiration weeks; for monthly expirations this includes 8 monthly-expiration weeks;
for quarterly expirations this includes only 4 quarterly expiration weeks. Totals may not sum exactly due to rounding.
**See Appendix

Note 1: NYSE program trading totals include purchases and sales during regular trading hours as well as during Crossing Sessions II and IV.
Note 2: Program Trading Totals in this report include from member submissions through September 13. Subsequent changes to these data may occur.

NYSE Research
September 2007

FIGURE 5.3 The Major Firms [also Primary Dealers] Engaged in Program Trading
Source: NYSE.

Here are some of the qualifications to be a primary dealer [if you wish to make application] that are more curious than mere capacity per the same previously cited authority:

As in the past, all primary dealers will be expected to (1) make reasonably good markets in their trading relationships with the Fed's trading desk; (2) participate meaningfully in Treasury auctions, and (3) provide the trading desk with market information and analysis that may be useful to the Federal Reserve in the formulation and implementation of monetary policy.

And it continues:

In evaluating a firm's market-making performance with the trading desk, the FRBNY will look to the amount of business of various types actually transacted and the quality of the firm's market-making and market commentary. Dealers that do little business with the Fed over a period of time, that repeatedly provide propositions that are not reasonably competitive, and that fail to provide useful market information and commentary, add little to the Fed's ability to operate effectively and will be dropped as counterparties for at least six months.

In evaluating participation in Treasury auctions, the Fed will expect a dealer to bid in reasonable relationship to that dealer's scale of operations relative to the market, and in reasonable price relationship to the range of bidding by other auction participants. Any decision to suspend a primary dealer designation because of inadequate auction bidding will be taken in close consultation with the Treasury.

As you can see by reading between the lines, the operative term is "play ball or you're finished." The Fed wants participating primary dealers to bid on short-term loans such as repurchase agreements and other commitments in a fair and consistent manner from their view.

Just who are the current primary dealers today? Following is the current list, courtesy again of the Federal Reserve Bank of New York:

BNP Paribas Securities Corp.
Banc of America Securities LLC
Barclays Capital Inc.
Bear, Stearns & Co., Inc.
Cantor Fitzgerald & Co.

Citigroup Global Markets Inc.
Countrywide Securities Corporation
Credit Suisse Securities (USA) LLC
Daiwa Securities America Inc.
Deutsche Bank Securities Inc.
Dresdner Kleinwort Wasserstein Securities LLC.
Goldman, Sachs & Co.
Greenwich Capital Markets, Inc.
HSBC Securities (USA) Inc.
J. P. Morgan Securities Inc.
Lehman Brothers Inc.
Merrill Lynch Government Securities Inc.
Mizuho Securities USA Inc.
Morgan Stanley & Co. Incorporated
Nomura Securities International, Inc.
UBS Securities LLC.

With the exception of a few, most firms are household names.

DOES THE FED OR TREASURY MANIPULATE MARKETS?

There are many conspiracy theories that argue in the affirmative. Naturally, the government doesn't want markets to suffer or the economy to weaken. Their primary job is the *orderly* management of the nation's money supply. Or, as mentioned previously, Milton Friedman's admonishment that the money supply expand consistently at 3 percent per year.

However, beginning with the stock market crash in 1987, the President's Working Group on Financial Markets was organized. The group has been euphemistically called the PPT, or Plunge Protection Team, by many conspiracy theorists. They believe the Fed entered the futures markets directly in 1987 by buying heavy amounts of S&P 500 futures contracts to cause a short squeeze driving prices higher that stemmed the market crash. Is there any proof of this? No, just the observation that some record-breaking buy transactions took place out of the blue over the next two trading days. But the Fed did respond directly to the crash by flooding the banking system with reserves and stating publicly that it was ready to extend loans to their primary dealer network if necessary.

The President's Working Group on Financial Markets [PPT] has four members: the Secretary of the Treasury, chairmen of the Federal Reserve Board, the US Securities and Exchange Commission, and the Commodity Futures Trading Commission. It obviously takes advice from sources including the President's National Economic Council, the chairman of the Council of Economic Advisors, the comptroller of the currency, and the president of the New York Fed Bank. Traditionally, it has met only in times of emergency, essentially functioning as a war room for handling financial accidents, in keeping with its main goal of keeping the markets operating in the event of a crash and preventing a banking panic.

Current Treasury Secretary Paulson has asked the Working Group to meet more frequently [monthly] than previous quarterly only meetings. This further gets the conspiracy buffs energized thinking that there will be a more active attempt to manipulate markets higher. Since there are no reports or minutes of these meetings publicly available no one can prove anything nefarious about these meetings.

But when the Fed engages in "open market operations" that either add or drain reserves [liquidity] to the primary dealer networks, theorists have more than just an inkling as to what will happen as a result. Remember, the primary dealers are now also brokers in a big way. Do they route reserves to their trading desks to speculate with? Well, why not?

The Fed conducts these operations through a variety of methods with the "repo" or repurchase agreement being the primary tool. A repo is a temporary loan that the Fed offers for bid to the primary dealers. The loans have a set term and a negotiated rate of interest. The terms can range from one day to several weeks and interest rates are often around or beneath the discount or Fed Funds rate. A typical offering looks like the ones in Figure 5.4a and 5.4b.

So in one day there were two operations conducted totaling $18 billion with one expiring in one day while the other lasted for two weeks. You can see for yourself that there was healthy competition for the funds and most were done at a variety of rates.

Another new twist added in 2002 is that the Treasury has begun conducting temporary loans using surplus tax receipts to loan out until they're needed for budget commitments. An example appears in Figure 5.5.

The two most important things to remember about this activity are how these funds are used and, while done less frequently, if these loans are forgiven. In the first case, there are many legitimate reasons why the primary dealers need the liquidity to meet normal banking demands whether to meet temporary reserve requirements or lending needs there is nothing unusual about this. If the funds get routed to trading desks and Da Boyz get to trade your money ["your tax dollars at work"] for a few days, well; more power to them.

There's another more important result that can take place from these activities—sometimes these loans are forgiven. When that happens money is created out of thin air, which expands the money supply and enriches the primary dealers. Not a bad deal, I'd say.

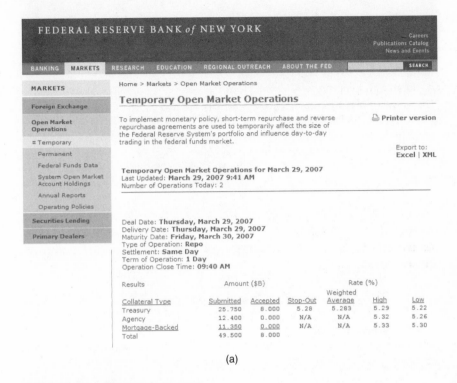

(a)

Deal Date: **Thursday, March 29, 2007**
Delivery Date: **Thursday, March 29, 2007**
Maturity Date: **Thursday, April 12, 2007**
Type of Operation: **Repo**
Settlement: **Same Day**
Term of Operation: **14 Days**
Operation Close Time: **08:30 AM**

Results	Amount ($B)			Rate (%)		
				Weighted		
Collateral Type	Submitted	Accepted	Stop-Out	Average	High	Low
Treasury	12.500	2.917	5.17	5.178	5.20	5.05
Agency	9.050	3.607	5.25	5.259	5.27	5.20
Mortgage-Backed	15.050	3.476	5.27	5.277	5.28	5.24
Total	36.600	10.000				

(b)

FIGURE 5.4 (a) Short-term Repo and (b) Two-week Repo
Source: Federal Reserve Bank of New York.

DEPARTMENT OF THE TREASURY
FINANCIAL MANAGEMENT SERVICE
WASHINGTON, D.C. 20226

**TREASURY TAX AND LOAN INVESTMENT PROGRAM
TERM INVESTMENT OPTION AUCTION RESULTS**

CONTACT: Investment Management Division
Thompson Sawyer: 202-874-7150

Auction Date:	March 26, 2007
Auction Number:	310
Placement Date:	March 27, 2007
Maturity Date:	March 30, 2007
Term:	3 Days
Treasury's Offered Amount:	$3,500,000,000
Total Accepted Amount:	$3,509,000,000
Total Bid Amount:	$5,823,000,000
Bid-to-Cover Ratio:	1.66
Highest Bid Rate:	5.480%
Lowest Accepted Bid Rate:	5.230%
Percentage Allotted at Lowest Accepted Bid Rate:	2.86%

FIGURE 5.5   Typical Short-Term Loan Results from Treasury Auction
Source: Department of the Treasury.

I forgot to mention another interesting fact in this discussion: Two out of the last three Treasury Secretaries were from Goldman Sachs, Robert Rubin [Clinton Administration] and current Treasury Secretary Henry Paulson. Is there anything wrong with that? No, but it just clearly demonstrates connections and attitudes that further support the bullish bias.

TIME TO CONNECT THE DOTS

Let's review the factors old and new that support the bullish bias.

- Higher earnings should over time drive stock prices higher, which is especially true within indexes.
- The financial media are highly dependent on advertising revenue from financial services firms with product to sell. Positive stories and attitudes are a priority as an editorial consequence.

- Sell side stock analysts are generally conflicted since their employer wants eventually to do other business with the firms the analysts cover. Analysts also tend to remain too close to companies to maintain a more objective arm's length opinion.
- The switch from a commission to fee-based business models for most firms argues that maintaining and enhancing recurring fee business has become the paramount mission of the modern Wall Street firm especially at the retail level.
- The so-called Greenspan and Bernanke Put means the government is ready, willing, and able to interfere to prevent markets from a sharp decline or crash.
- The growing money supply data has created too much liquidity, which naturally drives demand to "buy, buy, buy."
- The demise of Glass–Steagall has created a new kind of primary dealer able to speculate and trade in markets whether thru program trading or other means. The explosive nature of rising earnings from this source provides clear evidence.

So the bullish bias is more robust than ever and investors should be aware of its power to move markets higher. But that doesn't mean the business cycle has been defeated or that speculative excess won't be punished. Just remember the poor Japanese experience from 1990 thru today or the U.S. bear market of 2000–2003.

THE NEW ROBBER BARONS

One hundred years ago President Teddy Roosevelt was known as the "trust buster" as massive wealth had been concentrated in the hands of a couple of dozen fabulously successful families. Rockefeller, Carnegie, Mellon, and Vanderbilt dominated business activity and society pages. Their concentration of business control over industry, banking, and transportation was legendary. We've all read articles about and seen examples of their extravagance and wealth in the mansions they built and lifestyle lived.

Today a new set of robber barons have risen to dominance and fame. You'll find most of them at the senior level of many Wall Street firms, Fortune 500 companies, and as hedge fund operators whether in popular Connecticut or overseas in Bermuda, London, Zurich, Geneva, Singapore, or Hong Kong to name but a few locales.

These major players are insiders to the flow of the best information. With the exception of some Middle East countries, they control the world's business. They're either involved in private equity takeovers of major firms, thanks to the current liquidity bubble, or running investment banks as primary dealers and controlling communications.

Frequently we read about what appears to most as annual compensation that rivals only lottery winners. With Da Boyz at Goldman Sachs alone, total bonuses paid in 2006 were $26 billion. Is it any wonder that property prices on Park Avenue and other nearby environs continue to soar while the rest of the country is mired in a housing slump? It was noted recently that a London hedge fund manager was building a $500 million yacht; another was going to market a $150 million house in Montana; there is a private jet order backlog; and many are on a binge to acquire sports teams to satisfy their egos and raise their visibility.

Warren Buffett recently accused hedge fund managers of being the Pied Pipers of Performance and that their fees are exceeded only by their arrogance. Well, Buffet's a low-key operator living somewhat modestly in Omaha. He doesn't get the nouveau riche pretentiousness demonstrated by most of these operators. It's interesting theater, but it turns many people off.

Why am I writing about this at all? Because these interests are so entrenched politically on both sides of the aisle that their stature will continue to grow and dominate markets and investing.

TWO JOKERS IN THE DECK

While the basic business cycle will ultimately trump efforts to manipulate it, the structure of the bullish bias has two jokers that can succeed at foiling the best efforts of the powerful consortium that make up the players in the bullish bias: hedge funds and bloggers.

With nearly $2 trillion in assets and inherent aggressiveness these funds can derail the structural bullish bias. Now not all hedge funds are structured to play both sides of the market. As we've seen many are involved in such unique strategies as convertible arbitrage, distressed securities, and private equity among others. Many funds aren't structured to short markets aggressively if they smell or generate shorting signals. It's difficult to know by strategy how assets are allocated among the 9,000 different hedge funds in existence. But trust me; there are plenty of assets in a variety of hedge funds to be opportunistic to short markets.

One interesting change at Goldman Sachs [GS] occurred in the early 1990s when Robert Rubin was running the firm. For the first time a firm allowed their trading desks to trade against their clients' positions. This is unique since GS was and is a clearing firm for many hedge funds. That is, the hedge fund makes its trades thru GS and other firms to settle at GS as the custodian of hedge fund assets. Trading deliberately or otherwise against your clients' positions sounds devious and unethical. But it's now a common practice. To get around this, hedge funds now have multiple custodians and brokers trying to disguise their activities.

Making this even more interesting for example is that GS operates and manages one of the world's largest hedge funds, GS Alpha Fund, with more than $12 billion in assets. Are they geniuses? No, since in 2006 Alpha lost nearly 12 percent while as we've seen GS itself made vast sums. A conflict? Probably not since the missions are different as trading desks typically engage in ultra-short term programs trading while Alpha's mission is quite different and longer-term. Nevertheless the opportunities for conflicts of interest are clear enough to make a hedge fund manager uncomfortable and cautious in trading practices.

As in politics and other fields, bloggers are making inroads and competing with the mainstream financial media. Bloggers have no set bias, but it seems many of them have contrarian views to the conventional spiel that Wall Street tends to utter.

How influential are they? In the same way as bloggers affect positively or negatively the MSM for example, they are a rising force. With so many online investors searching for help their influence will rise, confounding the conventional Wall Street spin while at the same time shining a light on issues that the mainstream financial media chooses to ignore.

The power of these two wild cards is difficult to determine, but they can have an impact that balances and disrupts biased views.

WHAT BEARS ARE UP AGAINST

So now you should be more aware of the enormity of the bullish bias. The forces arrayed against bears consist of a large and diverse army with one thing in mind: Drive equity markets higher.

That doesn't mean that the powerful combination of these institutions can prevent or undo normal business cycles and subsequent bear markets, but it does mean that going against the bullish bias has never been more difficult.

You'll need more help understanding and dealing with these new financial alliances and realities like never before. Hopefully succeeding chapters provide more help.

Strategies

CHAPTER 6

Market Neutral

Our mandate is to find the 200 best companies in the world and invest in them, and find the 200 worst companies in the world and go short them. If the 200 best don't do better than the 200 worst, you probably should get in another business.
— Julian Robertson, Tiger Fund

Market Neutral is a strategy that usually involves simultaneously taking a long position combined with a short position in relatively equal amounts. It could include strategies involving convertible arbitrage, fixed income arbitrage, merger arbitrage and equity market arbitrage. Why would you do that? In order to reduce or neutralize overall market risk. Sounds simple enough—but is it?

Of course not.

The most popular strategy for most investors is equity arbitrage, which is the original and basic hedge fund approach that we outlined in Chapter 3. It generally involves pairs trading, where an investor makes decisions to be long a strong company stock from within a given sector while shorting a weaker one from the same sector. Therefore the investor's goal is to profit on the increasing spread for his positions irrespective of overall market movement. Both stocks within the trade could rise or fall but so long as the spread is moving in favor of the combined position, the investor profits. Theoretically the investor doesn't care what the overall stock market is doing.

Choosing positions can be done from a fundamental or technical perspective. Using a fundamental approach generally means making valuation

FIGURE 6.1 Intel Stock: Weak or Oversold?
Source: Chart courtesy of StockCharts.com.

decisions. An astute practitioner would most likely identify a company with positive earnings growth and future prospects and purchase it against a short position in a company with the opposite characteristics within the same sector.

Let's say for example, a portfolio manager utilizing this strategy concluded that within the semiconductor sector [INTC] Intel's future prospects were superior to competitor [AMD] Advanced Micro Devices. The logical portfolio position would be long INTC and short AMD. Another view

FIGURE 6.2   AMD Stock: Oversold But the Trend Is Down
Source: Chart courtesy of StockCharts.com.

might be that the [P/E] Price/Earnings Ratio of the former combined with its book value make one of the stocks described more attractive than the other. This is a pure valuation judgment and may not contain other aspects beyond this calculation. Ironically, it may be that employing this approach might put each investor on the other side of the previous trade: long AMD and short INTC.

Technical analysis might also be employed in a variety of ways, with equally different and conflicting results. These conflicts would be the result of utilizing different technical approaches to the same issues. For example, in Figures 6.1 and 6.2, one could reach two different conclusions: oversold meaning a buying opportunity or a sign of continuing weakness and staying short the right approach.

Market Neutral strategies are a favorite among investors concerned more with the management of risk versus high performance. What follows are typical strategies employed to accomplish this.

THE NORTHWEST QUADRANT

The ultimate goal for any portfolio manager is to achieve the highest rates of return combined with the lowest risks. In the industry this would mean putting your strategy and long-term results in the "northwest quadrant," as demonstrated in Figure 6.3 where the lower axis represents risk and the upper reward.

Theoretically, removing overall market risk should put skilled practitioners of market neutral disciplines into the box on the upper left. The lower axis represents risk and the other return. Clearly the highest return with the lowest risk is something most investors would find compelling.

Having your portfolio with these potential performance characteristics is what makes this strategy appealing for most institutional hedge fund investors, and would be compelling for retail investors.

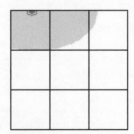

FIGURE 6.3 Investors
Seek the Highest
Return with Lowest
Risk
Source: Chart courtesy
of StockCharts.com.

EVEN HERE, RISKS REMAIN

Risks in market neutral approaches are numerous, since there are so many diverse and complex strategies within the field. Since one man's feast is another's famine, performance and risk can vary dramatically from one manager to another. This section runs through some of the typical pitfalls.

Trading costs can be more expensive, since most approaches tend to be more active. However, given current low commission structures now available most of these considerations have become concerns of the past.

Tax issues can become more dominant given the activity. This may be especially true given the likelihood of more short-term gains taxed as ordinary income versus more favorable long-term capital gain treatment. Further other tax considerations may result from the lack of tax-favored dividends from most approaches and models. But if the account is structured as a retirement account, foundation, pension plan, or other tax-favored entity, taxes are not a consideration.

Last, there can be "style drift" issues whereby managers may exhibit emotional bias toward specific issues versus maintaining a systematic and disciplined approach. If this occurs volatility may increase and the style would lose its effectiveness. Julian Robertson's Tiger Fund sported 32 percent compound rates throughout the 1980s and most of the 1990s. At the end he erred by betting against the "irrational technology craze" and lost 19 percent, closing his fund at $6 billion which at one point was $26 billion.

ETFs AND MARKET NEUTRAL STRATEGIES

ETFs can be employed within the market neutral strategy since so many diverse sector issues exist to utilize. Some investors believe that being in the right sector is primary to achieving good performance. As we've discussed previously, given their diverse components indexes are inherently less risky than individual stocks.

Many U.S. equity markets have ETF issues based on broad sectors, like the S&P 500 ETF [SPY], commonly referred to as the SPYDR. And within SPY are subsector ETFs that break the index down with different issues. For example, the following is a list of SPYDR sector ETFs now both available and popular.

- Select Sector SPDR Consumer Discretionary ETF [XLY].
- Select Sector SPDR Consumer Staples ETF [XLP].

- Select Sector SPDR Energy ETF [XLE].
- Select Sector SPDR Financial ETF [XLF].
- Select Sector SPDR Health Care ETF [XLV].
- Select Sector SPDR Industrial ETF [XLI].
- Select Sector SPDR Materials ETF [XLB].
- Select Sector SPDR Technology ETF [XLK].
- Select Sector SPDR Utility ETF [XLU].

FIGURE 6.4   Consumer Sector of S&P 500 [WMT] and [HD]
Source: Chart courtesy of StockCharts.com.

It's important to remember that these ETFs are "weighted," meaning the largest companies carry the heaviest weighting within each sector. For example, Microsoft would carry the heaviest weighting in XLK while smaller companies within the sector a lesser amount. Recently Rydex Investments launched an equally weighted version of the same SPYDR sectors that appeal to a different group of investors seeking a different and perhaps better view of an overall sector. But in any event, Figures 6.4 through 6.12

FIGURE 6.5 Consumer Staples Sector of S&P 500 [PG] and [MO]
Source: Chart courtesy of StockCharts.com.

FIGURE 6.6 Energy Sector S&P 500 [XOM and CVX]
Source: Chart courtesy of StockCharts.com.

look at varying long-term monthly charts so you are able to spot trend and performance differentials among these subsectors.

You might view some sectors as having similar patterns one to another but the percentage differences might be significant enough to make a difference. Therefore while the broad S&P 500 Index might be rallying or declining some sectors are doing better than others. This presents opportunities to market neutral approaches where it might be possible to be long [XLU] Utilities ETF versus a short position in [XLK] Technology ETF

FIGURE 6.7 Financial Sector S&P 500 [C and AIG]
Source: Chart courtesy of StockCharts.com.

despite the fact that both may have been trending higher over the past few years. The difference of course is that you would have made more money on the long position versus what you may have lost on the short position making the arbitrage profitable.

Even more opportunities exist within subsectors. For example in highly popular and volatile technology sectors there are subsets that offer unique opportunities as well. The popular Cubes or QQQQ [NASDAQ 100 Index ETF] has also been broken into separate subsets with ETFs created and

FIGURE 6.8   Healthcare Sector S&P 500 [MRK and PFE]
Source: Chart courtesy of StockCharts.com.

issued linked to unique indexes not necessarily representing the QQQQ precisely but generally.

Examples featured in Figures 6.13–6.17 include [IGW] GS Semiconductor ETF, [IGV] GS Software ETF. [IGN GS] Network ETF, [IBB] NASDAQ Biotech ETF and [HHH] ML Internet Holders. Many arbitrage opportunities are available within the technology sector.

HHH [Figure 6.17] has a long history. However, now we recommend using new issue [FDN] First Trust DJ Internet Index ETF. FDN better

FIGURE 6.9 Industrial Sector S&P 500 [CAT and BA]
Source: Chart courtesy of StockCharts.com.

represents the important Internet sector as outlined next but just has a short trading history making the chart comparisons more difficult.

"Holders" have both potential benefits and shortcomings. Unlike ETFs, Holders are a trust created by Merrill Lynch. As a trust, they are unable to add new issues to their holdings and therefore are not dynamic.

When you think of investing in Internet-based stocks for example, it wouldn't be unusual to think of Google first as the preeminent company. But, since Google became a public company after HHH was issued, it isn't

FIGURE 6.10 Materials Sector S&P 500 [DD and DOW]
Source: Chart courtesy of StockCharts.com.

and can't be included as a Holder. Naturally, for most investors it seems odd to invest in the Internet space and not have Google as a component.

Why would anyone want HHH then? Because a trust has its advantages when industry consolidations occur. For example, HHH is heavily weighted by EBAY, YHOO, and AMZN to name a few. Given all the industry consolidation via private equity as in 2006–2007, if one of these companies is bought out or taken private a windfall could accrue to holders. That's the upside, which is of course speculative.

FIGURE 6.11   Technology Sector S&P 500 [IBM and MSFT]
Source: Chart courtesy of StockCharts.com.

In the long run, it's probably better to deal in a contemporarily consti-
tuted and balanced index-based ETF than a Holder.

ALPHA STRATEGIES

Delving into this area could be a waste of time for most investors, as it
can be arcane. But since it's a term bandied about frequently and *may*
incorporate some market neutral or long/short techniques we'll mention it.

FIGURE 6.12 Utilities Sector S&P 500 [TXN and ED]
Source: Chart courtesy of StockCharts.com.

According to Investopedia:

Alpha is what would be deemed "excess return." In a regression equation, one part describes how much the market's movement adds to your portfolio's return; the remainder of the return is deemed alpha. This is a measurable way to gauge a manager's ability to outperform the market.

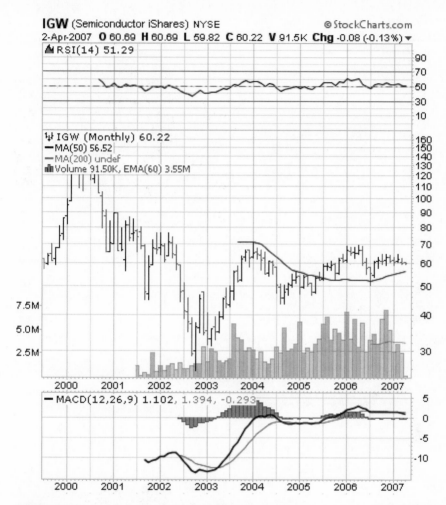

FIGURE 6.13 Semiconductor iShares [INTC and AMD]
Source: Chart courtesy of StockCharts.com.

It's still a mouthful isn't it? Basically, alpha is just a measure of a fund's risk relative to a particular market index. An alpha of 1.0 means the fund outperformed the market by 1 percent. A positive reading is the extra return to investors for the additional risk taken rather than a passive return from the relevant market index.

Beta is the opposite. Overall market risk and volatility has a measurement of 1.0. The higher the number rises above 1.0, the greater the volatility

FIGURE 6.14 Software iShares [MSFT and ORCL]
Source: Chart courtesy of StockCharts.com.

and risk. For example, a typical Emerging Market index would carry a high beta, while a more staid Utility index a low measurement.

Now if a strategy is incorporated to outperform the S&P 500 Index, then the difference created by beating the index becomes the alpha produced. Each benchmark selected that the strategy is intended to beat becomes the bogey that produces alpha, if any.

FIGURE 6.15 Networking iShares [CSCO and JNPR]
Source: Chart courtesy of StockCharts.com.

If you're an average investor you probably don't hear much about this feature or investment goal. But for institutional investors, it's become a big deal.

How is it related to market neutral or long/short strategies? It is and it isn't. There are many strategies used to achieve alpha from manager to manager. Some of these will incorporate market neutral or long/short techniques and others won't.

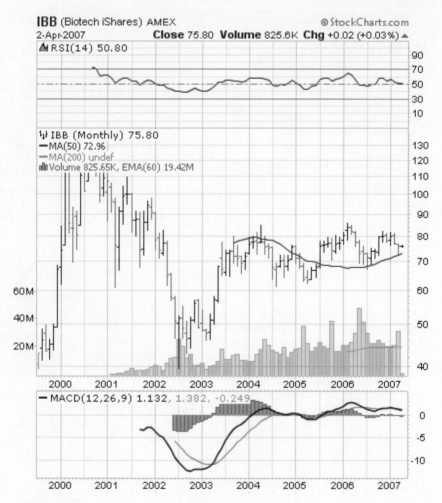

FIGURE 6.16 Biotech iShares [AMGN and IMCL]
Source: Chart courtesy of StockCharts.com.

The bottom line for most investors is that alpha is more of a measurement than a technique. So if you start to hear about it, you might just ignore it and concentrate on ultimate performance.

The largest hedge fund utilizing alpha measurement features and techniques is Goldman Sachs' Global Alpha. It has nearly $10 billion in assets. However, it lost 11.6 percent in 2006 after returning 40 percent the previous year. This means while you gained a substantial sum in percentage terms

FIGURE 6.17 Internet Holders [YHOO and EBAY]
Source: Chart courtesy of StockCharts.com.

the previous year, in dollar terms, you gave half of it back the next year. That's how deceiving percentage returns can be.

MARKET NEUTRAL MUTUAL FUNDS

There are now hundreds of mutual funds issued utilizing market neutral strategy and FAs can offer them for investors to use. While their

TABLE 6.1 Random Sampling of Available Market Neutral Mutual Funds

Fund	Ticker	1-Year Return (%)	Annualized 3-Year Return (%)	Expense Ratio (%)
Diamond Hill Focus Long-Short A	(DIAMX)	17.8	24.7	1.78
Schwab Hedged Equity Investor	(SWHIX)	11.6	n/a	2/0
TFS Market Neutral	(TFSMX)	10.8	n/a	2.49
Hussman Strategic Growth	(HSGFX)	5.5	11.8	1.24
Calamos Market Neutral Income A	(CVSIX)	2.2	4.5	1.32
James Market Neutral	(JAMNX)	1.6	5.6	1.95

strategies aren't designed to incorporate ETFs as their dominant tools, many funds within this category use them occasionally. In what way are ETFs used?

Many mutual funds whether focused on market neutral strategies or not utilize ETFs for getting invested quickly in a sector. Suppose for example XYZ Fund thought the overall Tech sector was going lower. They might short the Cubes as an efficient way to put a position on immediately. Then they might target individual stocks to short within the sector that they felt were going to much underperform the overall sector. They then short those stocks closing the Cube and trade proportionately as they do so.

At this time there are no pure ETF market neutral mutual funds that I'm aware of. A Fox News essay has isolated a few, shown in Table 6.1. It's important to note that variations of performance from this sample are primarily due to different objectives: growth versus income, for example.

A more detailed summary of market neutral mutual funds can be found at the Morningstar web site (www.morningstar.com), where more than 100 such funds are listed.

CONCLUSION

Why would investors find a market neutral strategy attractive? In bull markets, market neutral funds don't keep up with overall indexes. Like any other approach, it's not for everyone; their primary attraction is that over time a well-executed strategy should provide consistent growth and a smoother less volatile ride.

Let's move on to another style that may be even more dynamic and risky depending on the folks at the controls—Global Macro.

CHAPTER 7

Global Macro

It is becoming increasingly obvious around the world that economic or investment analysis can no longer be conducted on a purely domestic basis. The speed with which capital is capable of moving means that any economy can be disrupted by international capital flows due to external considerations.
  —Martin Armstrong, Princeton Economics International

The most notorious hedge fund managers are practitioners of the Global Macro approach. In fact the large Goldman Sachs Global Alpha hedge fund, cited in the previous chapter, utilizes their own version within this category.

Most investors know or have heard something good or bad about famous traders such as George Soros, Stanley Druckenmiller, and Michael Steinhardt. Further we all know about famous hedge fund blow-ups from Long-Term Capital Management to current Amaranth hedge funds.

Global Macro is about making often highly leveraged bets across various investment classes from international stock and bond markets to currencies and commodities. Many decisions traders make using this strategy fundamental and subjective. They study macroeconomic issues and events from various countries that may provide enough information for them to form judgments, reach investment conclusions, and place bets. They may also try to determine how an event in one corner of the world could affect markets elsewhere.

Successful examples include how Druckenmiller predicted correctly and quite lucratively how the fall of the Wall in Germany would boost the value of the deutsche mark. Felix Zulauf correctly anticipated the decline of the U.S. stock market in 1987 by noting that a fall in the U.S. dollar would hasten a decline, as tight money then combined with high stock valuations were incompatible. George Soros bet nearly $10 billion of borrowed funds that the British pound would be devalued and he was correct. Later Soros took on what he believed was the overvalued Malaysian currency that rattled that government creating a PR battle between him and the Malaysian prime minister. Further many saw that a crisis in the small country of Thailand in 1997 created a contagion that spread throughout Asian markets.

So these are all very bright and skilled players who when right can make fortunes but when wrong can as quickly lose the same amount.

When they're wrong they make headlines and scare conventional investors who fear that a financial accident of great magnitude could disrupt markets which can negatively affect markets and their portfolios. These situations have occurred.

LTCM BLOWS UP

Long-Term Capital Management [LTCM] was founded by John Meriwether a former vice-chairman and head of bond trading at Salomon Bros. To his board he added 1997 Nobel prize winning economists Myron Scholes and Robert Merton. The initial annual returns of LTCM exceeded 40 percent but in 1998 it lost $4.6 billion in just a few months creating a market crisis.

The strategy employed by LTCM was an arbitrage model based on complex mathematical models designed to exploit differentials from various bond markets that primarily used U.S., Japanese, and European government bonds. In what they termed "convergence trades," LTCM believed that ultimately price and yield differentials in percentage terms from one bond series to the next would converge and become identical. Naturally, this convergence would be erratic in nature and to be successful their mathematical models were employed to determine how best to capture it.

Employing arbitrage strategies developed by their mathematical models they would buy one bond and short another hoping to profit upon convergence. They did well at this for a time and more investors sought them out based on previously published excellent returns. However, as their asset base increased dramatically, they were pressed to undertake new trading strategies that were not in keeping with their original bond oriented trading regime.

One thing has always been true in this business: Once you reach trading capacity in your existing model, don't accept new funds that stretch your abilities. This maxim was lost on the principals of LTCM as ego and/or greed allowed them to accept new funds and then later develop a trading strategy—a classic cart before the horse situation. Frankly, those funds and managers who decline new investments achieve a level of prestige in the industry. If you can't get in, it must really be good for those who are already in. Typically, if and when the fund reopens to new investments, investors are lined up to put money in.

So LTCM had to come up with a new strategy as an add-on to their existing convergence model for bonds. What to do? They turned to trading stocks via the S&P 500 using options to take advantage of volatility, meaning for them they were "short long-term volatility" hoping to capture its unwinding.

Since the differentials in positions were very small, LTCM needed to add great amounts of leverage to produce adequate returns. High amounts of leverage increase risk, naturally. Therefore at the start of 1998 LTCM had assets of nearly $4.8 billion but was leveraged to approximately $125 billion. Even scarier was that the firm had derivative positions to the staggering sum of $1.25 trillion [that's right, trillion]. These derivatives were largely comprised of interest rate swaps and equity options.

In May 1998 net returns for their fund started to fall and by June the declines totaled nearly 17 percent hitting their fund to a drawdown of nearly $500 million.

By August everything started to come apart. When the Russian government defaulted on their debt investors rushed out of Japanese and European bonds to the perceived safety of U.S. bonds. The unusual event undid the convergence strategy as massive divergence occurred causing huge losses to LTCM's fund amounting to nearly $1.85 billion.

As the fund's equity started to implode, leverage actually "increased." By the end of September the fund's equity dropped from $2.3 billion to $600 Million. As news of this spilled out to the media, financial markets started to sell off. In a state of concern that LTCM's situation would cause a financial panic, the Federal Reserve stepped in and organized a bailout of $3.625 billion with funds from the major creditors, who were large Wall Street investment banks. These firms were also primary dealers to the Fed, who wielded tremendous influence with their members. In other words, "you will do this or else!" In the end, the creditors who injected these funds made extraordinary amounts of money managing and unwinding LTCM's positions. Why? Because eventually the fund's convergence strategy worked as their long-term bets paid off as the crisis faded and normalcy returned to markets. The fund's investors? They received just pennies on the dollar.

What got LTCM into such trouble was excess leverage, new strategies but not their original bond market convergence strategy. Had they not been so leveraged they could have, like their creditors subsequently, ridden out the unusual crisis.

GUNSLINGERS

How do you lose a small fortune in the markets? Start with a big one.

—Old Wall Street maxim

The image the average investor must come away with is twofold: It would be cool and have some cache to be with the winners but at the same time the risks are abhorrent. Most investors don't have what it takes financially to run with this crowd. Even if some investors have the $1 million entry fee they aren't willing to lose it all, either. That's why only the largest investors can play. These are the superrich, who can easily lose that much money and still continue to play the game. It reminds me sometimes of a movie scene from the baccarat tables in Monte Carlo. The hero loses $1 million, brushes it off as no big deal, walks off with the pretty girl, and still can play again the next night.

No, mainstream investors want to invest more globally but without the high stakes risk strategies employed by these boom/bust players. It's more fun to watch Texas Hold 'Em on TV than endure the pressure involved in playing yourself.

THINK GLOBAL, INVEST GLOBAL

The move toward global investing is rapidly becoming more common even as some investors are doing so reluctantly and with caution. It may be difficult to know if the computer based financial plans used by many FAs for clients will include heavy allocations overseas. After all most of these models are based on old sector performance data that may not be either forward looking or contemporary.

One theme borrowed and modified from the *New York Times,* Thomas Friedman: "The investment world is flat."

As of March 2007 the combined European market capitalizations eclipsed that of the United States for the first time in modern history. Further, owing to reforms of Sarbanes-Oxley stemming from accounting malfeasance after the U.S. stock market fell in 2000 [Enron, WorldCom, and so forth], London has now surpassed New York as the premier financial center. London doesn't have these protections or requirements and so companies wishing to go public may do so there. And they have.

In the United States, ETF issues geared to overseas investing has grown faster than any other sector. Popular [EFA] MSCI Europe, Asia, and the Far East is now the second or third largest ETF in terms of assets in the United States. Other overseas ETFs are also extraordinarily popular including: [ILF] Latin America ETF, [EEM] MSCI Emerging Markets ETF, and single country funds like [EWA] Australia, [EWJ] Japan, and [EWW] Mexico to name just a few. Mostly listed on the American Stock Exchange [AMEX], many of these ETFs, particularly in the single-country fund area have existed for quite some time but languished with little trading volume during the 1990s as investors focused on the U.S. stock market boom. Just on the AMEX alone there are more than 50 such overseas oriented issues. The New York Stock Exchange [NYSE], not to be left out of the game, is becoming more competitive with dozens of new issues listed there as well.

Furthermore, many overseas ETFs are becoming more specialized in subsectors with diverse issues focused on value, small-cap, and dividend models, for example. Therefore investing overseas is becoming like that in the United States with nearly as many different approaches there as in the United States.

Why is this focus overseas occurring? One thing that hasn't been discussed frequently as a stimulus revolves around the end of the Cold War. Until the Soviet Union collapsed in 1990 Europe was divided between Eastern and Western Bloc countries not just politically but economically. After the fall, it didn't take as long as some felt for the European Union to be formed and the subsequent single currency, the euro, replaced many different currencies from German deutsche marks to Spanish pesetas. This more homogenous economic structure unencumbered by Cold War politics and attendant economic barriers freed individuals and business to seek economic growth.

Also previous to the collapse of the Soviet Union, much of the world apart from Europe was also either with the West or the Soviets. Even the so-called "non-aligned" nations were primarily with the Soviets. Here, too, after the Soviet collapse, many nations whether in Asia or Latin America were also freed from the political constraints of Cold War politics. They could move forward with economic growth and most did.

In the fall of 2006, our newsletter The ETF Digest [www.etfdigest.com] began a series of quarterly podcast interviews with well-regarded London research firm the Emerging Markets Monitor [EMM]. [These interviews are available for listening without cost or registration from our public homepage.] They presented a core argument of a "convergence story" taking place among all global markets especially including Emerging Markets. The basis or theme is that many markets previous to around 2000 were valued at pre-Cold War levels and were deemed too economically backward, corrupt, and too volatile for consistent investment results.

Even when evaluating credit risk it was common before and during the global bear market of 2000–2002 that spreads [the difference in yield between Emerging Market debt and, say, U.S. Treasury debt] to be more than 200 to 300 basis points. That is, if U.S. Treasury bonds were yielding 7 percent, Emerging Market debt would need to yield 9 to 10 percent for buyers. Today this is changing. Interest rate spreads are narrowing to half the previous levels. Why? Some of this [others might argue "all"] is due to the high levels of global liquidity needing and perhaps rationalizing a home. But equity markets too were leading the way higher. In fact, the succeeding equity bull market returns in established markets [whether in the United States or established overseas markets] were dwarfed by returns garnered by Emerging Markets.

In the United States, 9/11 had many overseas investors perceiving the event as primarily a U.S. problem. The war between radical Islam and the West would have to be fought by the United States. It was regarded callously as not a problem for the rest of the world including Asia [led by China and India] to Latin America. So while the United States fought an economically costly war the rest of the world got on with their business.

The evidence is clear and is clearly demonstrated by performance history as demonstrated in Figures 7.1 through 7.7. First, let's look at returns from mainstream United States and some established overseas markets.

While the established markets turned in excellent performances during this four-year post-bear market period, you'll note the clear superior performance of Germany versus its established market peers.

During the same period, other overseas market ETFs—especially in the Emerging Market sector—did much better than their established market counterparts, especially in the United States. Furthermore these have been the leaders in both performance and popularity over the same investment period. See Figures 7.8 through 7.10.

There were individual single-country ETFs that performed as well or better than even the broad regional issues, shown in Figures 7.11 through 7.14. And no, I'm not just cherry-picking the best ones. Is it any wonder that overseas investing is popular, given the evidence of superior performance?

Austria has benefited from the end of the Cold War and the European Union [EU]. It is regarded now as the financial center for emerging and former Iron Curtain countries. Spain and other smaller economies within the EU have prospered with the new financial integration. Spain even had to abandon its popular siesta practice of closing shop and taking several hours off while the rest of Europe was working. Imagine hard working Germans calling Madrid for business in the afternoon and finding them "out to lunch." The work obsessed Germans weren't going to tolerate that.

The "Chindia" [China and India] story continues to captivate investors and much of the growth in other markets stems from the economic vibrancy and demand sourced to these two countries.

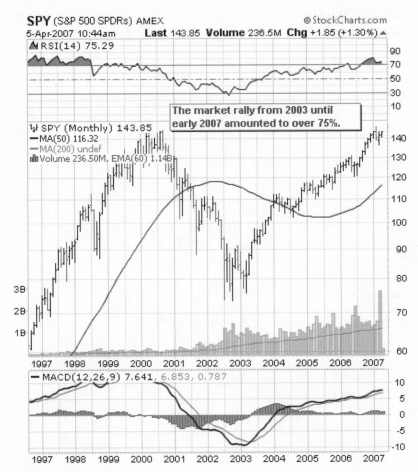

FIGURE 7.1   Monthly Chart S&P 500 ETF
Source: Chart Courtesy of StockCharts.com.

Latin America prospers as it is able to meet the demand for raw materials globally from China and India. Australia's market is booming since it, too, is a supplier of key minerals to feed the appetite also from the same source.

TRADE GLOBAL

Overseas investing has become so popular with U.S. investors that online discount broker E*Trade has launched a program that allows clients to conduct transactions in global markets. In an interview with E*Trade

FIGURE 7.2   Monthly Chart Mid-Cap ETF
Source: Chart Courtesy of StockCharts.com.

Vice-President Christopher Larkin the firm acquired multinational broker
TIR Holdings Ltd. In so doing, they also obtained registrations to conduct
business in 42 different stock markets around the globe. Beginning in April
2007 they proposed offering these services to their clients in a few of the
most popular and largest markets including Canada, London, Germany,
Japan, and Hong Kong.

E*Trade will set up accounts for you and allow you to fund it yourself
with whatever currency is applicable, if you have your own source to

FIGURE 7.3 Monthly Chart Russell 2000 Small Cap ETF
Source: Chart Courtesy of StockCharts.com.

acquire it. Or, conversely, they will obtain the currency of choice for you based on a sliding scale. Larkin stated as an example, that if you deposit approximately $50,000, they will obtain the currency at a cost of around 75 basis points. Then in addition they might charge $15–20 for stock transaction commissions.

Previously, for individuals to do business overseas with their U.S. broker they had to deal with two issues: high commissions and currency expenses and complications. Many overseas markets were, and some still are, highly

FIGURE 7.4   Monthly Chart NASDAQ 100 ETF
Source: Chart Courtesy of StockCharts.com.

protective of their brokerage industry. This protection was especially geared
to keep large international investment banks out of lucrative deals but also to
keep out primarily U.S. discount brokers. Many overseas brokers were still
behind the times when it came to brokerage commissions. Charging pre1975
U.S. commissions kept broker revenues high based on commission-only
business models. They didn't want U.S. discount firms disrupting their
lucrative life.

FIGURE 7.5 Monthly Chart London Stock Index—FTSE
Source: Chart Courtesy of StockCharts.com.

I remember dealing with Hong Kong brokers 20 years ago when I owned my own brokerage firm. Our customer accounts were cleared and held by Bear Stearns. They had no brokerage license to deal in Hong Kong securities directly. If my customers wanted to buy stocks trading only in Hong Kong [without any American Depository Receipts, or ADRs] Bear Stearns would route the trades to a third-party Hong Kong broker with whom they had a relationship of sorts. The upshot was that clients would need to pay Bear Stearns commissions plus those of the Hong Kong broker. And Hong Kong

$DAX (German DAX Composite) INDX   © StockCharts.com
4-Apr-2007 **O** 6911.13 **H** 7076.21 **L** 6891.80 **C** 7073.91 **Chg** +156.88 (+2.27%)▲

RSI(14) 81.46

$DAX (Monthly) 7073.91
—MA(50) 4728.18
—MA(200) 3808.28
Volume undef

Germany did the best @ 180%.

MACD(12,26,9) 601.620, 529.629, 71.991

FIGURE 7.6   Monthly Chart German Stock Index—DAX
Source: Chart Courtesy of StockCharts.com.

brokers then were charging nearly 2 percent for each transaction. Even if
we reduced our commissions beneath 1 percent, clients were paying nearly
3 percent per round turn. Also there were ridiculous mark-ups for currency
conversions. These might amount to another 3 percent, which was pretty
silly since the Hong Kong dollar was pegged to the U.S. dollar making high
mark-ups owing to volatility risks unnecessary. Our solution was to find
our own Hong Kong broker, which we did and negotiated better fees with
them. But still costs were high. So you can readily see that this was an often
prohibitively costly affair.

FIGURE 7.7 Monthly Chart Japan Stock Index—Nikkei 225
Source: Chart Courtesy of StockCharts.com.

But remember, "The investment world is flat." Overseas brokers couldn't hold on to antiquated and protective business models. Various online firms negotiated with some overseas markets and obtained entry. However, costs for investors were still high relative to heavily discounted U.S. rates. These were transitional baby steps.

Eventually E*Trade will allow their clients to trade in all 42 markets directly, which means that a U.S. client can buy a German or Malaysian ETF trading within those countries directly. Now that's a big change!

FIGURE 7.8 Monthly Chart EAFE—Europe, Asia, and Far East
Source: Chart Courtesy of StockCharts.com.

SO YOU WANNA BE A GUNSLINGER, TOO?

The average investor has no interest in putting on large leveraged positions. For most this type of trading was too stressful and overwhelming. The only avenue for retail investors to raise the risk level of their investment activity was investing in futures and options trading directly or through an investment in a managed futures fund. But even these ventures were too risky for most.

FIGURE 7.9 Monthly Chart MCSI Emerging Markets ETF
Source: Chart Courtesy of StockCharts.com.

Enter the SEC, which changed the rules in April 2007 to accommodate risk takers. As we mentioned in Chapter 4, the embedded market bullish bias got a further lift when the SEC altered margin rate calculations and rules making it easier for individuals to increase risk through added leverage. The key change was to allow brokers and investors to engage in "portfolio margin" calculations versus previous "position margin" rules.

The basic impact of the rule change was to lower margin deposits from 50 percent for each position to 15 percent based on what regulators

ILF (Latin America 40 Index iShares) NYSE   © StockCharts.com
5-Apr-2007 11:03am   **Last** 185.17 **Volume** 581.9K **Chg** +6.81 (+3.82%) ▲

RSI(14) 78.68

ILF (Monthly) 185.17
—MA(50) 95.42
—MA(200) undef
Volume 581.90K, EMA(60) 2.93M

A return of 500%.

MACD(12,26,9) 23.647, 21.659, 1.988

FIGURE 7.10 Monthly Chart Latin American 40 Index ETF
Source: Chart Courtesy of StockCharts.com.

and brokers deemed overall portfolio risk. Further the SEC had restricted this activity to accounts with assets exceeding $5 million. This eliminated most retail clients from participating. But the SEC decided to drop this restriction allowing its application to any investor. Some people think this is like eliminating the age limit for casino gambling. Is this too paternalistic a view? Time will tell.

The biggest initial impact is to investors incorporating options transactions to their investing strategies. Let's say you wish to buy 1,000 shares of

FIGURE 7.11 Monthly Chart Spain ETF
Source: Chart Courtesy of StockCharts.com.

XYZ stock for $100 and at the same time buy puts against the position. Old margin would require a $50,000 deposit on XYZ and the full amount on the option, which, if the option was $1,000 you would need to deposit the full amount or $51,000. The new rules could reduce the deposit to only a little more than $4,000. This is a dramatic change.

From an article posted April 5, 2007 at TheStreet.com by Steven Smith:

> *Some of the key features of the new amended plan proposed by the Chicago Board of Options Exchange and the NYSE that were*

FIGURE 7.12 Monthly Chart Austria ETF
Source: Chart Courtesy of StockCharts.com.

approved by the Securities Exchange Commission *last December, but went into effect on April 2 include:*

- *Removing the $5 million account minimum, but most brokers still can impose their own minimum account balances and trading experience thresholds.*
- *Portfolio margining will be expanded to include all equities and their related options, not just index products. It also*

FIGURE 7.13 Monthly Chart Mexico ETF
Source: Chart Courtesy of StockCharts.com.

*will allow some cross margining of "highly correlated prod-
ucts." For example, options on the* S&P 500 Index *can be
offset with options on the* SPDR Trust *(SPY). It will also
include some similar futures contracts, and there will no
longer be a need to have a separate cross-margining account.
(http://www.thestreet.com/pom/pomrmy/10348598.html)*

Smith went on to say that not all firms would implement these rules,
since to do so requires a complete overhaul of their internal margin rules and
monitoring. As he says, "It will be a headache" to implement and manage.

FIGURE 7.14 Monthly Chart Australia ETF
Source: Chart Courtesy of StockCharts.com.

However, competitive pressure will force many firms to participate since it's anticipated that trading volumes will increase and firms won't want to lose customers by not offering their own models.

CONCLUSION

For most retail investors, the first two strategies discussed in this part— Market Neutral and Global Macro—may not be very compelling or suitable.

The next chapter should provide a more palatable compromise between the two.

In any event, ETFs are the primary tool to build and implement both hedge fund strategies since so many diverse issues now exist combined with high levels of liquidity.

Most FAs won't find many attractive mutual funds employing the Global Macro theme for one main reason: fees. The best managers will opt for a private hedge fund structure. Within a hedge fund good managers can charge lucrative incentive fees not "yet" available to mutual fund managers. I emphasize *yet* since with margin rule changes and competition from both ETFs and hedge fund structures you can be assured there will be some mutual fund lobbying for changes to allow them to compete. So the convergence story of hedge funds, mutual funds, and ETFs will continue.

CHAPTER 8

Doing It Their Way

The market's job is to derail the systems traders. Some of them are going to make money, but that can't go on forever.
—Richard Dennis, *Stocks & Commodities*, October 2004

In Chapter 3, we outlined dozens of typical hedge fund strategies including their various subsets. Frankly the most notorious and successful players in the hedge fund game are often difficult to pigeonhole. They operate using their own unique strategies and methods crossing back and forth to other set models. You might be able to lump them into Global Macro, but that's just a convenience since each has their own approach utilizing perhaps bits and pieces of all previously outlined strategies.

The important result is that some achieve excellent performance. The most successful are often led by enigmatic individuals, some of whom wish to remain out of the limelight. Others have more flair and make a news splash given their vast fortunes and notorious spending.

Many successful hedge fund operators can be categorized in the following manner:

- *Trader*. Seeks to exploit short-term volatility in the price of a security and may incorporate complex program trading strategies whether from Wall Street trading desks or through organized funds. Since this strategy is more technically based most traders don't have a fundamental opinion about market conditions or the stocks they might utilize. The only thing that matters to a trader is the perceived momentum and direction of trends and their ability to capitalize on them.
- *Stock Picker*. Tends to take just the opposite approach from a trader since they tend to focus on fundamental analysis of various companies,

overall indexes, and macroeconomic considerations from different countries including currency levels. Stock pickers usually are in positions for the long-term seeking to have prices meet their fundamentally based objectives. Some stock pickers become "activists" and personally intervene with targeted companies trying to effect change. Recent examples include Carl Icahn with Motorola and Kirk Kerkorian with General Motors. Not all succeed in these latter activities. But in their analysis they believe targeted companies are poorly managed and their strategies are designed to unlock more shareholder value through a variety of techniques including spin-offs and management changes. With spin-offs, they're often described as the "super nova" of investing where the sum of a company's parts are worth more than the whole.

- *Distressed Investor*. These investors swarm over companies in serious trouble or perhaps already in bankruptcy. A case in point would be United Air Lines [UAL], which fell into bankruptcy and a variety of investors, including pilots and machinists, vied to put together plans to take the company out of bankruptcy that the chief bankruptcy court judge or trustee might approve. We featured the demise of [LTCM] Long-Term Capital Management hedge fund in Chapter 3. The creditors, although almost forced by the government, took over the assets of the fund for pennies on the dollar. They knew what they were doing assuming these obligations since most of them were both creditors and market professionals. Ultimately these buyers made billions of dollars by assuming the positions at a low basis owing to the crisis atmosphere that drove these prices lower. Once the crisis abated, prices for the affected securities rose dramatically generating profits for the rescuing firms. This was as successful a "distressed" securities intervention as ever recorded.

- *Quantitative Investor*. Sometimes referred to as "robo-traders" and "quants" they may behave like traders. The major difference is that for the quants the human element is completely subservient to complex mathematical formulae and software programs. The trader on the other hand combine their experience with technical factors and perhaps even news events.

Many hedge fund operators practice just one methodology while others embrace many different strategies making them difficult to pigeonhole. The bottom line for all is the desire to excel using their own style and abilities. The best, despite large egos, keep an open mind to new techniques and strategies.

SELECTED TRADER PROFILES

- Steve Cohen, SAC Capital Advisors, manages approximately $12 billion. He lives secretly and is reputed to be a great trader. One notorious example of Cohen's style is the public battle conducted between SAC and public company Biovail. SAC was disseminating negative research information on the company and selling it short. Biovail sued, alleging that SAC was publishing erroneous information about the company's condition. The outcome of a protracted lawsuit isn't as important as the tactics and style utilized by SAC. Within what strategy outlined is this? Opportunistic? There isn't one per se.
- Kenneth Griffin, Citadel Investment Group, is another opportunistic trader with $13 billion in assets. The Chicago-based fund has become so successful that it was able to sell its own bond offering in 2006 which made Griffin and his firm less secretive. According to an April 15, 2007, *New York Magazine* article, Citadel made big profits when Amaranth Hedge Fund collapsed. Amaranth was long volatile natural gas futures contracts and when those prices collapsed Citadel must have taken the other side of the trade. Sure, it's a ruthless business. The sharks will feed off the wounded and dead.
- Michael Novogratz, Fortress Investment Group, is another trader with $4.6 billion in assets. Their current claim to fame is they were the first hedge fund manager to become a public company after launching an initial public offering [IPO] in February 2007. The shares were expected to price between $16 and $18.50 but came to market at the high-end $18.50. When they opened for trading to the public, they did so at $35 or a 67 percent gain. It's assumed that others like Citadel will follow.

    The downside for Fortress is that now they must answer to shareholders in addition to their fund investors. That means privacy and secrecy have been swapped for some quick cash for the founders. Would you then infer that their best days are behind them?

SELECTED STOCK PICKERS PROFILES

Who doesn't want to be a great stock picker? That's as cool as being a great trader, one would think.

- Eddie Lampert, ESL Investments has $18 billion in assets. He's a Buffett-type investor who takes over companies like Sears and

AutoNation. And he doesn't just buy the companies, he manages them as well.

- Daniel Loeb, Third Point, based in Manhattan with $4 billion in assets, is part of the "activist" movement. They take positions in companies they feel are poorly managed and go after management in a vocal and aggressive manner.
- James Chanos, Kynikos Associates with $3 billion in assets, is described as a deep thinker who made himself famous shorting Enron early. Say no more.

SELECTED DISTRESSED SECURITIES PROFILES

- David Tepper, Appaloosa Management with $5 billion in assets, was previously a junk bond trader with Goldman Sachs like so many others who got their start there. In 2007 he got involved with the Delphi Automotive restructuring, which is the kind of deal that would attract a distressed securities practitioner.
- Stephen Feinberg, Cerberus Capital Management with $19 billion in assets, worked at Drexel Burnham Lambert when Michael Milken was doing his junk bond financings. Like other distressed securities funds they're becoming more buyout oriented and private equity deals.
- David Shaw, D.E. Shaw & Company with $26 billion in assets, have been more active in the quantitative investment style; however, like most good entrepreneurs they have jumped into the private equity sector, which often can bridge into distressed securities.

SELECTED QUANTITATIVE PROFILES

- James Simons, Renaissance Technologies with $24 billion in assets, is the leading fund employing complex algorithms investing by computer. Known as "black box" investing Renaissance has a very high level of performance results and maintains the highest fee structure at 5 percent fixed and 44 percent of capital appreciation. That's a pretty impressive stiff fee but Simons has produced spectacular after-fee performance.
- Ray Dalio, Bridgewater Associates with $30 billion under management, is also often viewed as one of the leading proponents of black box investing.
- Mark Carhart, Goldman Sachs Asset Management, operates $10 billion hedge fund Goldman Sachs Global Alpha and others totaling $32 billion. Of course given Goldman's excellent trading reputation you'd

expect their flagship fund Global Alpha to excel. In 2005, it returned 40 percent but in 2006 managed to lose nearly 12 percent and the losses continued through the first quarter of 2007 where an additional 5 percent was lost. That's 17 percent, which in dollar terms means fund investors gave back more than half of everything they made in 2005. If the past is any guide, Carhart & Company will be leaving Goldman to set up their own hedge fund.

OTHER FAMOUS HEDGE FUND PRACTITIONERS

We couldn't deal with this topic without adding famous and now difficult to pigeonhole money managers like Paul Tudor Jones, Bruce Kovner, Louis Bacon, and Richard Dennis to our list of notable and successful market operators. Each of these men started their careers trading commodities almost exclusively. That would normally categorize them in a style best known as Alternative Investing and [CTAs] Commodity Trading Advisors.

Most of these men initially utilized variations of trend-following techniques, a sophisticated-sounding catchall phrase that simply meant "going with the flow." Many of the best practitioners would readily admit knowing little about fundamental economic forecasting. Some would say their approach is more humble yielding to market trends over their personal opinions. And letting technical systems work beyond their personal beliefs is their first key to successful trading results. To deal successfully in highly leveraged markets, risk management is of primary importance. A surfing analogy would be getting on a developing big wave early, riding it well, and not wiping-out.

As some CTAs' success grew more client money found a way to them. But trading capacity in certain markets was limited. Grain markets like wheat, corn and soybeans could handle only so many contracts at any given time, so successful CTAs had to start dealing in other markets. Conveniently the rise of financial market sectors especially in the 1990s and accompanying futures contracts [stock indexes, currencies, and fixed income markets] allowed most CTAs to expand their opportunities to those markets. Further trading was expanded from the United States to include overseas markets, dramatically increasing trading capacity. Most traders then employed staff to deal in 24-hour trading operations. Making these changes greatly expanded trading capacity to apply their successful techniques to overseas sectors.

- Smart traders like Paul Tudor Jones have transitioned even further from pure quantitative trend-following techniques in commodities and futures markets to fundamental global equity investing, venture capital, and event-driven strategies. His Greenwich, Connecticut, firm, The Tudor Group and its affiliates, now manage more than $15 billion in assets.

- Bruce Kovner is founder and chairman of Caxton Associates, which currently manages nearly $10 billion in assets and is also closed to new investors. His current style is global macro but like so many before him he got his start trading commodities. It's said he borrowed $3,000 to trade soybeans and watched the value rise to $50,000 before it dropped to $22,000 before he sold. This was his first lesson in risk management. Kovner is a highly private man who doesn't give interviews.

- Louis Bacon founded Moore Capital Management in 1986, which manages roughly $8 billion in assets. He is a discretionary trader in what would be a global macro strategy. He trades markets in the United States, Europe, and Asia and includes Paul Tudor Jones as a close friend. Like Jones he's a philanthropist giving generous gifts to support environmental causes.

- Richard Dennis is no longer a major player but his volatile commodity trading was legendary. He perhaps is most famous for his Turtle Trader experiment. He and a fellow trader William Eckhardt wondered if Dennis's belief that trading could be learned or if success was the result of innate ability. To put his theory to the test, Dennis put an ad in the paper for applicants to test his belief. He said, "I'll train traders like Singapore raised turtles."

More than 1,000 applied and from this field 13 ultimately were selected. They included a willing but eclectic bunch who were evaluated for all manner of skills including cardplaying abilities. Dennis incubated them, gave them some funds to trade, and approved systems to utilize. After a period they were set free to pursue their fame and fortune. Some succeeded while others failed. One thing that was true of Dennis and his Turtle group: Their systems were marked by extreme volatility.

INSIDER TRADING BUILDING PERFORMANCE?

A lot of the hedge funds are just trading on inside information. They're not trading. They're shooting fish in a barrel.
—Richard Dennis, *Stocks & Commodities*, October 2004

On March 1, 2007, the SEC charged 14 defendants in "a brazen insider trading scheme that netted more than $15 million in illegal insider trading profits on thousands of trades, using information stolen from UBS Securities

LLC and Morgan Stanley & Co., Inc." The complaint continues: "... the defendants also include three hedge funds, which were the biggest beneficiaries of the fraud."

Surprised? You shouldn't be. These are just the folks who got caught. And this is the type of scandal that starts as a drip, drip, drip of negative news and mushrooms to something larger like the mutual fund market timing scandal beginning in 2002. Prosecutors get the first accused to rat out others in these schemes. Their plea bargain deals either reduced their penalties or for the lucky ones, vacated them completely.

This could be just the tip of the iceberg. If you find a little of this kind of activity, you'll know there's probably a lot more of it going on. According to SEC Chairman Christopher Cox, "Our action today is *one of several* [emphasis added] that will make very clear the SEC is targeting hedge fund insider trading as a top priority."

The current complaint revolves around unlawful trading ahead of upgrades and downgrades by analysts at both UBS and Morgan Stanley. Brokers would tip off their hedge fund clients before these potentially market-moving events, positioning trades most likely at other firms ahead of the news. According to the complaint, "The ringleaders of the UBS part of the scheme went to great lengths to hide their illegal conduct, first through a clandestine meeting at Manhattan's famed Oyster Bar and eventually the use of disposable cell phones, secret codes, and cash kickbacks before the scheme unraveled."

The analysts and brokers involved in the scheme received a share of the profits from the participants. Some of the brokers even traded on the information for their own accounts at small participating brokerage firms.

Steve Luparello, an executive vice-president for market regulation at NASD stated in *BusinessWeek* ("More Heat on Hedge Funds," February 6, 2006), "Hedge funds misusing nonpublic information is a growing issue."

According to the same article:

Regulators are cracking down on funds that participate in private placements and then take advantage of the information they glean. The biggest case thus far has been that of Hillary L. Shane, the manager of hedge fund FNY Millennium Partners LP. The NASD and SEC charged her in May with fraud and insider trading for allegedly agreeing to buy unregistered shares as part of a private placement in Maryland security systems outfit CompuDyne Corp. (CDCY) and then short-selling the registered stock, betting that it would fall in value.

Investment bank Friedman, Billings, Ramsey Group Inc. (FBR) invited Shane to participate in the placement on the condition that *she treat the information as confidential. Shane has paid a $1.45 million fine to settle charges brought by the SEC and the NASD.*

This article also points to another story from London where:

... the Financial Services Authority is investigating abuse of confidential borrower information. The case everyone is talking about: a probe into whether a trader at GLG Partners LP, a London hedge fund, improperly used information provided by Goldman, Sachs & Co. (GS) in advance of a security offering by Sumitomo Mitsui Financial Group Inc. in 2003. The FSA is concerned about any instances where parties who are made insiders then use that information to trade in related securities," says spokesman David Cliffe. The crackdown is just beginning.

Another tactic to gain insider information was sourced by the *Wall Street Journal* and reported by SOX First [a management and compliance service]. An article by Brody Mullins and Kara Scannell ("Hedge Funds Seek Tips in D.C.") published in the *Journal* on December 8, 2006, noted that "hedge funds are hiring lobbyists for their so-called 'political intelligence units' to pick up market-moving information. The lobbyists, many of them lawyers with public policy expertise, are charging anywhere between $5,000 and $20,000 a month for passing on the information. For the hedge funds, it's just a small investment that can deliver big profits."

The article concludes: "To my way of thinking, the only way you can address this problem is to have more disclosure about the links between Washington and lobbyists. The lobbyists would have to disclose more information about their clients, and vice-versa. Otherwise, Washington will continue to fuel flagrant insider trading."

Many experienced investors know intuitively when something's about to occur with a company's stock. High volume options trading can often precede a market-moving event in shares of a company. According to a March 2, 2007, Bloomberg article ("SEC Freezes Profits from Suspected TXU Insider Bets"), "...trading in options to buy shares of TXU Corp. surged more than sevenfold on Feb. 23 before CNBC said the company would be acquired in the largest-ever leveraged buyout. This week, the volume of options trading to buy shares of Hyperion Solutions Corp. rose almost sixfold before Oracle Corp. yesterday said it will buy the company for $3.3 billion."

In an April 5, 2007 column in MarketWatch, David Weidner wrote:

Feb. 15 started out as just another day in the life for Birmingham, Ala.-based Compass Bancshares Inc. But after the market opened, the stock was one of the hottest on Wall Street.

The share price of the regional bank at one point topped $66, more than $5 above its already record high. By the end of the day shares were up 7.4% to an adjusted close of $65.96 and had a volume of 3.9 million shares—eight times its recent daily volume.

Wire reports in the U.S. said money managers and traders were "hearing" that the company was about to be sold. Sure enough, the next day Compass announced it accepted a $9.6 billion buyout from Spain's Banco Bilbao Vizcaya Argentaria.

The trading at Compass in mid February underscores an obvious truth on Wall Street. In the world of mergers and acquisitions there are two kinds of people: Those who know and us.

Famously in March 2007, Mad Money's Jim Cramer revealed the many market manipulative practices he routinely engaged in when running his hedge fund. (It's all there for you to watch on YouTube.) A remarkably successful money manager when he ran the $450 million Cramer Berkowitz hedge fund, Cramer in the webcast shared tips on how to drive a stock price down so that a short-position—a bet that a stock price would drop—remains profitable.

"I think it's important for people to recognize that the way that the market really works is to have that nexus of: Hit the brokerage houses with a series of orders that can push [the stock] down, then leak it to the press, and then get it on CNBC—that's also very important. And then you have kind of a vicious cycle down. It's a pretty good game."

Mr. Cramer said he had used some of the tactics himself, including lying to bozo reporters to get them to report misinformation on particular stocks. He singled out CNBC's Bob Pisani. He separated legal activities from illegal ones (such as fomenting), and never quite says he ever took part in the latter.

However, seconds later, he acknowledged, "I'm not going to say that on TV," referring to his show on CNBC.

Cramer later said that "no one else in the world would ever admit that, but I don't care." *He added that the strategy—while illegal—was safe enough because "the Securities and Exchange Commission never understands this."*

According to the SEC, illegal market manipulation is defined as follows:

... intentional conduct designed to deceive investors by controlling or artificially affecting the market for a security. Manipulation can involve a number of techniques ... [such as] spreading false or misleading information about a company ... or rigging quotes, prices or trades to create a false or deceptive picture of the demand for a security. Those found guilty of manipulation are subject to criminal and civil penalties.

As Cramer says:

Now, you can't "foment." That's a violation. You can't create yourself an impression that a stock's down. But you do it anyway, because the SEC doesn't understand it [emphasis added]. That's the only sense that I would say this is illegal. But a hedge fund that's not up a lot [this late in the year] really has to do a lot now to save itself.

Hmm. "So you do it anyway because the SEC doesn't understand it." This just means in his arrogant opinion, they're stupid.

So he mocks and scorns the SEC. His friend, Harvard classmate and former investment client Eliot Spitzer, the former New York attorney general, now governor, responsible for cracking down on illegal trading activity with mutual funds and hedge funds, must be embarrassed by Cramer's brazen bragging. Or is he?

So who's kidding whom?

SO IF IT'S A GAME FOR THE BIG BOYS, HOW CAN WE PLAY?

The aforementioned must be disturbing, intimidating, and off-putting information for investors thinking they can compete with both dirty and big players. The bottom line is you can't. Inside information isn't known by the same people all the time. Various players know something at one time but are in the dark at others. The individual investor doesn't have the money to buy good information, either.

Late actor James Coburn was once asked to describe his fellow movie star and buddy Steve McQueen. "Steve was the essence of cool," said Coburn.

Many investors wish they could be savvy and hip traders using the styles described in this chapter. Even conservative investors inwardly wish to be the same as they no doubt probably regard superficially conservative investor Warren Buffett in that light as well. He makes strategic bets that make the style cool if not the man.

Being cool just won't be available to individual investors. You'll have to keep your day job, I'm sorry to say. But fear not, for you there are hedge fund structures and techniques that most investors and financial advisors can utilize and embrace. After all, that's the purpose of this book.

CHAPTER 9

Trading—Do I Have To?

*I always say you could publish my trading rules in the newspaper
and no one would follow them. The key is consistency and
discipline. Almost anybody can make up a list of rules that are
80% as good as what we taught our people. What they couldn't
do is give them the confidence to stick to those rules even when
things are going bad.*

—Richard Dennis, Turtle Trader

If you want to manage your own hedge fund, you'll have to trade. Period.
All hedge funds have elements and varied levels of trading activity.

Choosing a trading style to call your own can be an intimidating
process if you're unfamiliar with it. Most inexperienced investors have an
image of frenetic floor traders conducting their business at various stock
and commodity exchanges. Or, perhaps you know of the boom and bust
outcomes for the day traders of the late 1990s and early 2000. All this can
be a turn-off.

One thing remains true about trading: It's not for everyone. But there
isn't a hedge fund style that doesn't require some trading whether it's fast or
slow paced. In this chapter we look under the hood at more trading styles
with more information as to how they work. And we discuss how each
might appeal to different investors given their own unique circumstances
and tastes. We even examine what's purported as the non-trading and
currently popular Lazy Investor approach. Is it really that effective?

ONE TRUE THING

An easy statement is that almost all investors would have wanted to be out
of the stock market in 2000 rather than endure the long protracted decline

that lasted until the spring of 2003. If you were and still are an investor in the NASDAQ Index, even with the more recovery in prices, the Index is still as of April 2007 at half its previous high.

If you *had* gotten out of the market, you could have done something else like rest in cash, shorted some ETFs, or dabbled in real estate until markets started their recovery in 2003. Even if you had to pay taxes on all those gains earned until 2000, you still would have had a significantly larger asset base to reinvest when things finally turned around in 2003.

To best see how being more vigilant and proactive would have made a major difference, study Figures 9.1 through 9.6. They show long-term

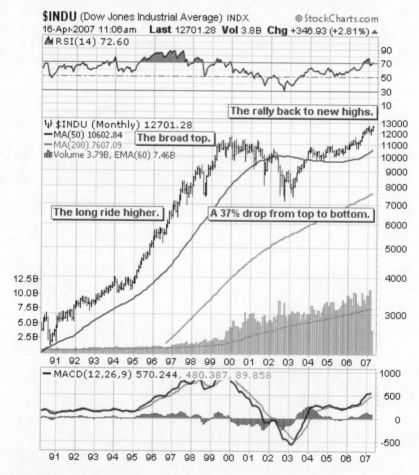

FIGURE 9.1 Monthly Chart Dow Jones Industrial Average (DJIA)
Source: Chart courtesy of StockCharts.com.

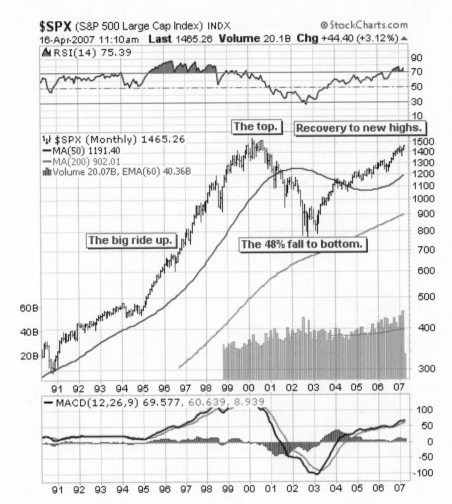

FIGURE 9.2 Monthly Chart S&P 500 Index
Source: Chart courtesy of StockCharts.com.

monthly charts of six leading indexes: the Dow Jones Industrial Average, the S&P 500 Index, the NASDAQ Composite Index, 30-year U.S. Treasury Bonds, a popular real estate ETF, and a representative real estate housing bubble chart. From these disparate market charts you could easily reach the following conclusions as to smart or profitable portfolio moves:

- Selling out of stocks in 2000.
- Shorting stocks from 2000–2003.
- Buying back stocks in 2003.

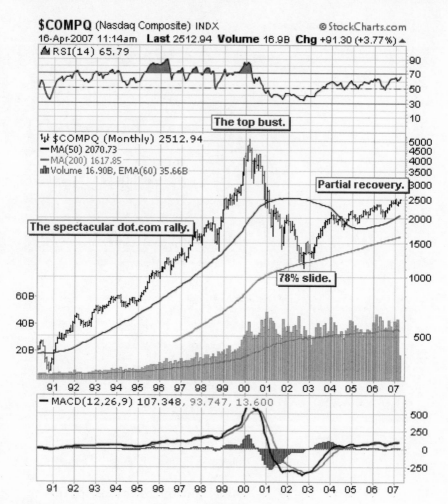

FIGURE 9.3 Monthly Chart NASDAQ Composite Index
Source: Chart courtesy of StockCharts.com.

- Balancing bonds with large-cap stocks primarily.
- Sitting in cash from 2000–2003.
- Buying real estate in 2000.
- Selling real estate in 2005 or early 2006.

These conclusions are obvious with the benefit of perfect hindsight. To get *close* to obtaining these outcomes requires market timing, which we discuss next.

FIGURE 9.4   Monthly Chart 30-Year Treasury Bond
Source: Chart courtesy of StockCharts.com.

MARKET TIMING MYTHS AND REALITIES

A mythical mutual fund market timing scandal dominated headlines and investor attention from 2002–2004. The term was misapplied and you can blame the media. Their desire to seize an easy and catchy phrase to give the scandal was an insult to true timing techniques. The scandal should have carried a more descriptive phrase, but there's little to be done about that

FIGURE 9.5   Monthly Chart REIT ETF
Source: Chart courtesy of StockCharts.com.

now. It involved illegal late trading of mutual funds, which involved no true
analytical market forecasting techniques. Blame the media for latching onto
an easy catchphrase that was an insult to true timing techniques.

Another myth is that passive index investment isn't "timing." That
would be wrong. While as an investor, you may not be timing your
investments, those that control the makeup of each index are making some
changes to the index components. In fact, all indexes are changing according
to their own rules that govern index constituent eligibility. For example, the

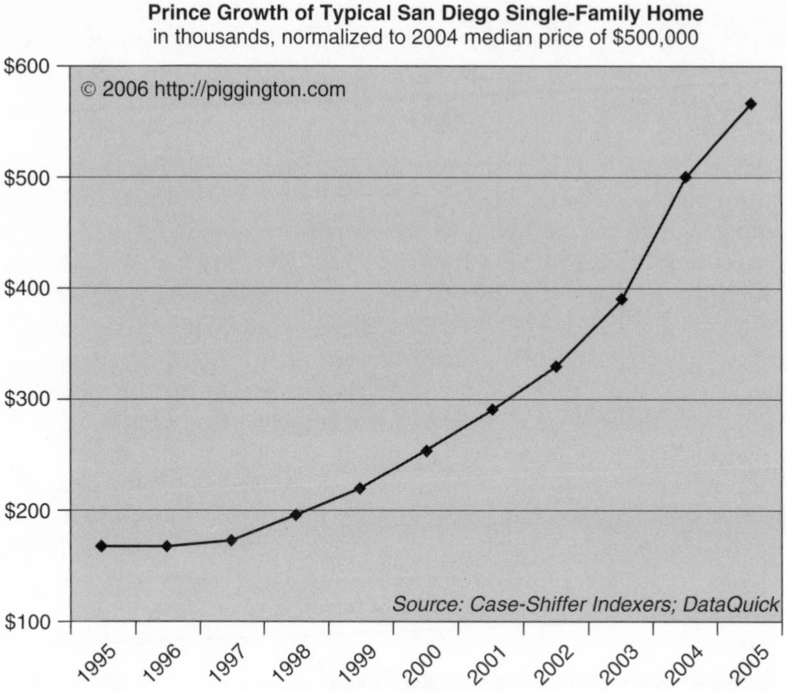
Prince Growth of Typical San Diego Single-Family Home
in thousands, normalized to 2004 median price of $500,000
© 2006 http://piggington.com
$600
$500
$400
$300
$200
$100
Source: Case-Shiffer Indexers; DataQuick
1995
1996
1997
1998
1999
2000
2001
2002
2003
2004
2005

FIGURE 9.6 San Diego Single-Family Home Price
Sources: Courtesy of www.piggington.com. Data: Case–Shiller Indexes; DataQuick.

[DJIA] Dow Jones Industrial Average has made changes just over the past eight years.

On November 1, 1999, Chevron, Goodyear Tire and Rubber, Sears, and Union Carbide were removed from the DJIA and replaced by Intel, Microsoft, Home Depot and SBC Communications. Intel and Microsoft became the first two companies traded on the NASDAQ exchange to be listed in the DJIA. On April 8, 2004, another change occurred as International Paper, AT&T, and Eastman Kodak were replaced by Pfizer, Verizon and AIG. Then on October 1, 2005, AT&T's original T symbol returned to the DJIA as a result of the SBC Communications merger. Now we might wonder if soon Google with its ever-growing presence and market capitalization will become a member of the DJIA as well.

Similar adjustments are made to all indexes and more frequently than just with the stodgy old DJIA since it consists of only 30 stocks where the S&P is greater at 500 and the NASDAQ Composite has 5,000. Each index has criteria for companies to maintain their listings within the index:

the more stocks available to the index, the greater the turnover. If you're invested in an actively managed mutual fund that is part of your portfolio, you can rest assured that the fund manager will be actively engaged in trading the portfolio, even though you're just a passive investor.

Another myth promoted by market timing critics is that timers will "miss the first move." This reflects one reality that much of the gains when stocks turn higher after a protracted downturn are made in the early stages of a rally. Since most timers wait to see if the new rising trend is real they would tend to miss that move, naturally, which would vary among timers. But this criticism assumes one important thing: the next move is up. I often respond to these critics when they say you'll miss the first move by replying, "Which way?" After all, the opposite situation can exist where stocks are declining. Most timers will miss that first move, too. But since these critics never sell or for that matter short, which technique works best?

The reality is that most market timing techniques are intended to produce profits in excess of passive investing. From Figures 9.1 through 9.6, which show bull and bear markets in different market sectors and obvious outlined conclusions, who wouldn't want to optimize returns by timing?

How to do this is the $64 million question.

THE LAZY OR PASSIVE INVESTOR: NO SINGLE STRATEGY ALWAYS PERFORMS BEST

We'll begin with this current popular and well-promoted investment style, since it's theoretically the antithesis of market timing. Also, you can't run a hedge fund lazily.

Passive investing or a "buy and hold" approach works well in the stock market for sharp analytical professionals like Warren Buffett. However, most individuals don't have the time to analyze companies fundamentally and make these types of decisions that are successful. You could just piggyback on what Buffett buys and sells from news articles, but often his style is to buy or sell quietly at prices superior to what's available to you subsequently. Alternatively, you could buy his two funds, the flagship Berkshire Hathaway [BRK.A] which cost more than $100,000 per share and the nonvoting rights [BRK.B] at more th an $3,500 per share as of April 2007. (And by the way, these shares are a hedge fund of sorts—without the massive fees, since Buffett has been known to speculate in commodities long or short and private equity basically doing his own thing.)

Given the high per share costs, will the average individual buy just one or two shares? Probably not. But then why not? The common factor is per share price but all stocks or investments should be judged by percentage returns rather than just price. The bottom line is that while there's a tremendous reservoir of respect and admiration for Buffett there are two considerations: (1) he's getting old so succession is an issue and (2) you can't get retail investors to pay high share prices even though that's an incorrectly viewed obstacle.

Passive strategies work best with indexes and ETFs since there is less risk from individual stocks. For example, while in the charts presented earlier in this chapter (Figures 9.1–9.6) stock indexes experienced both bull and bear market periods, during the same period some individual stocks rose then fell but never came back. A good example is a company like IDEMC, which during the 1990s was extremely well regarded since they dealt with data storage. With the Internet and electronic computer age data storage was becoming more widely needed. EMC's share price hit nearly $100 at its peak, but today continues to linger in the mid-teens. There are many individual tech companies in this condition and some that no longer exist as functioning businesses. So indexes are more vital to the passive investment strategy.

Currently, with markets running higher the popular view is to just allocate a fixed percentage [say 60 percent] of your portfolio to an ETF like SPY [S&P 500 ETF] and the balance to a bond ETF like [AGG] iShares Lehman Aggregate Bond Fund. Then perhaps once per year you would rebalance the portfolio to keep the percentage allocations the same. So it's not a completely passive strategy.

The underlying premise to this strategy assumes that bonds and stocks remain "uncorrelated." That is, if stock prices are rising bond prices will be falling and vice versa. They may not be rising and falling by similar amounts but you should be hedged. As you can see by the previous charts, as stocks rallied in the 1990s, bonds were tamer and as stocks fell subsequently, bond prices increased offsetting stock price declines. So here, too, you were theoretically hedged.

But is this always so? No. Over the past 10 years the strategy has been a success *if* you confined yourself primarily to the model outlined using SPY and AGG. With the NASDAQ utilizing the QQQQ, you'd be much less successful given the poor relative performance to SPY for example. And there are many historical periods during the 1970s and 1980s where both markets have moved in unproductive or "correlated" trends defeating the strategy. Will these patterns repeat in the future? There is no way of knowing.

And today proponents of this theme are branching out to include other asset categories to the passive theme. These may include a wider array of index mutual funds or ETFs to include more than just U.S. stocks and bonds. This might include commodities like gold and energy, global markets and a variety of dividend and value styles. Some passive investment styles are becoming so complex that they require more and more active management. This defeats the lazy style. Further, there is no guarantee [let's throw out the obligatory, "past performance is no guarantee of future results" phrase] that the lazy style, even modified by contemporary additions, will succeed in the future.

The lazy approach is compelling since in its original form it doesn't require much effort. When it works it allows many investors the opportunity to profit while still being able to do other things. After all, many individuals are busy with other aspects of their lives and don't wish to spend time with investment management. If individuals wish to pursue this type of investing they most likely will open an inexpensive online brokerage account buying and rebalancing a couple of ETFs. Or they might instruct their financial advisor to do it for them even though it will be more costly. The latter may be a desire to have a professional implement the investments for them since they're either uninterested, feel inadequate, or are too busy or just plain lazy. There's nothing wrong with any of that, either.

THE LAZY HEDGE FUND INVESTOR: THE DO-NOTHING CROWD

Earlier in the book, I argued that a convergence story is unfolding whereby mutual funds, ETFs, and hedge funds begin offering products that mimic each other. In Chapter 6 we listed several mutual funds that copy hedge fund strategies, most typically using Market Neutral techniques. In fact a *BusinessWeek* article ("Hedging without a Hedge Fund," August 31, 2006) listed five selective mutual funds that are available to retail investors without having to discover or implement any strategies on their own:

- *Market Neutral.* Hussman Strategic Growth [HSGFX] is a no-load fund and has a fee of only 1.1 percent and posted average annual returns of 10.6 percent thru August 2006. The fund uses hedging tactics to reduce risks when certain proprietary conditions are present. It has become a favorite for FAs [Financial Advisors] since they can offer it to clients and overlay their own fee.
- *Arbitrage.* Arbitrage [ARBFX] generally buys a merger target and sells short the acquiring company. Its performance has been 5.04 percent over the same five-year period compared to the S&P 500 of 4.38 percent. The fund's no-load fee structure is 1.7 percent.
- *Convertible Arbitrage.* Calamos Market Neutral Income Fund [CVSIX] has been around for 15 years and carries a front-end load of 4.75

percent and an annual fee of 1.57 percent. Its basic strategy is to buy convertible bonds [convertible to stock] and short the shares of the underlying company's stock. Again returns over five years have been 5.04 percent.

- *Long/Short.* Diamond Hill Long/Short Fund [DIAMX] also carries a front-end load of 5 percent and a 1.55 percent annual fee. The three-year performance of 19.75 percent substantially beat the S&P 500 10.95 percent over the same period. The strategy simply stated is the managers buy stocks they think will rise and short those they believe will fall based heavily on valuations and other proprietary methods.
- *Long/Short.* The Quaker Strategic Growth Fund [QUAGX] similarly buys stocks from all investment sectors and shorts stocks based on proprietary methods. Its annualized return over a five-year period ending August 2006 was 7.54 percent beating the S&P 500. However the front-end load of 5.5 percent and annual fee of 2.04 percent are relatively high.

Paying a high front-end load tends to lock you in to those funds, so you're more captive. FAs may like the heavy initial fee but charging an annual fee with fees already high would be hard to justify. For example, adding a 1 percent fee to QUAGX would push the fee to more than 3 percent per annum, which would be pretty difficult to justify. Further the FA wouldn't have the same incentive to monitor the fund on your behalf since there is no continuing stream of revenue. From the fund's perspective, they like the secondary benefit of the high initial fee that tends to lock investors in.

MERRILL AND GOLDMAN TRY TO SHAKE THINGS UP: CAN PASSIVE INDEXES DESTROY FEES?

To add to the convergence and passive investing stories recently both Merrill Lynch and Goldman Sachs have created indexes that attempt to copy typical hedge fund performance. According to a *BusinessWeek* article ("Hedge Funds: Attack of the Clones," December 4, 2006) the intent is to fashion indexes that should match hedge fund returns at a fraction of the cost.

Merrill Lynch launched its Merrill Lynch Factor Index while on the same day Goldman Sachs unveiled its Absolute Return Tracker Index [ART].

Such hedge fund trackers bring to the hedge fund industry the indexing trend that has already shaken up the mutual fund business.

The products could be a hit with institutional and high-net-worth investors seeking the diversification of hedge funds without some of the drawbacks, analysts say. However, reports suggesting these hedge fund clones are about to crowd out their traditional hedge fund rivals appear premature.

The Merrill Lynch index utilizes "six underlying components: The S&P 500 Index MSCI's EAFE Index, MSCI's Emerging Market Free Index, the U.S. Dollar Index, the Russell 2000 Index, and the London Interbank offered rate. Merrill Lynch uses an algorithm, reweighted monthly, to replicate the performance of several hedge fund benchmarks."

Merrill Lynch believes that the high costs of hedge funds, with typical annual fees of 2 percent and 20 percent of profits, are a turn-off. Merrill Lynch will be charging only 1 percent with daily liquidity. Additionally ease of entry and redemption is easier with the indexes they've created versus the often cumbersome features for hedge funds.

Retail investors won't be able to participate initially but Merrill Lynch "executives are considering wider distribution." That can mean only one thing: Expect in-house product offerings coming to a Merrill Lynch office near you soon and perhaps even an ETF or mutual fund to boot!

Goldman Sachs' ART program will offer similar features [1 percent fee and daily liquidity] but won't be rolled out to later in 2007, and the same *BusinessWeek* article observes:

Indexing may not appeal to current hedge fund investors, though, some analysts observe. "The typical hedge fund investor may not wish to effectively trade in their Ferrari for a potentially more reliable—and arguably boring—Buick," says Jeff Keil, principal at fund consultancy Keil Fiduciary Strategies.

Oh, really? Don't try telling that to Heiko Ebens, head of equity derivatives strategy for Merrill Lynch who stated at a hedge fund conference in San Francisco May 17, 2007, per MarketWatch: "Hedge funds have lost alpha!" That's a pretty impressive statement to make in front of a hedge fund crowd of managers. What's "alpha" again, please? Alpha is the term the industry has given to determine manager out-performance of a given benchmark. In laymen's terms one could say, "What value do you add to justify your high fee?"

Ebens crowed on promoting Merrill Lynch's new Factor Indexes, "We don't have a superstar manager who we have to pay millions of dollars a year to keep." And "... by letting Merrill Lynch take care of the returns that are generated by the market, hedge fund managers can in theory focus on trying to generate gains above and beyond that—the apparently elusive 'alpha,' he explained."

I wasn't at the conference but I can imagine an audience with folded arms in stony silence during this speech.

Beyond the noise and opinion, what's the upshot of these new products? I would concur with Jeff Keil, hedge fund investors aren't going to abandon successful hedge fund managers no matter the fee for a passive Merrill Lynch or Goldman Sachs product. Those investors want alpha and will always be willing to pay for it. Managers who post pedestrian returns may see their clients move to these products or seek out superstar performers. Institutions that find many aspects of conventional hedge funds to be a turn-off may find the Merrill Lynch and Goldman Sachs products an attractive alternative. For retail investors you might well expect an ETF, mutual fund, or in-house products created for your benefit.

DAY TRADING: FRENETIC AND INTENSE

Putting together a hedge fund for an individual investor definitely doesn't mean you have to become a rabid day trader. Many of those trading in this manner crashed and burned with the ensuing bear market beginning in 2000. It's now said that since the market has made a comeback, day traders are making a comeback.

Why engage in this activity? If you know what you're doing it can be an enjoyable way to make money. One advantage I always liked about it is the freedom it affords. Most day traders end each day with flat positions. They don't need to worry about the news or other factors negatively affecting their positions. Each morning they start with a clean slate and hopefully make some money that accumulates over time. Even better they can just quit for weeks at a time and go off tramping in Patagonia or some such place free from the shackles and worries common to conventional portfolio management. Sounds seductive, right? Just remember, you better know what you're doing and be skillful at it.

Nevertheless, this is not a strategy we'd be advocating as a trading regime for most individuals. Those who can do it profitably and enjoyably will continue to do so profitably. But this is not a strategy for typical investors interested in creating their own hedge fund.

However, day trading is a prominent activity among many hedge funds and a focus of brokerage firm trading desks. There it's primarily known as program trading. The definition of program trading has taken a variety of forms over the past 20 years. It began as primarily a stock index arbitrage affair. When the difference between stock futures contract and cash market reached certain spreads, computer programs would automatically sell one and buy another in large baskets to make the perceived differences.

During the market crash of 1987, program trading was identified as a major cause of exacerbating that decline. Subsequent rule changes created "circuit breakers" to minimize unrelenting selling even forcing markets to close briefly to allow spreads to narrow.

While index arbitrage still exists today, many program trades take place for other reasons. With the advent of popular and highly liquid ETFs combined with matching futures contracts and rapid electronic trading platforms, opportunities for trading programs to be utilized increased. With the click of a mouse large baskets of stocks can be purchased using ETFs or even customized indexes with transactions taking only a few seconds to complete.

New York Stock Exchange data indicated the enormity of this type of trading as a percentage of ongoing trading data (see Figures 9.7 and 9.8). Over the past few years program trading has accounted for nearly one-third of all trading volume.

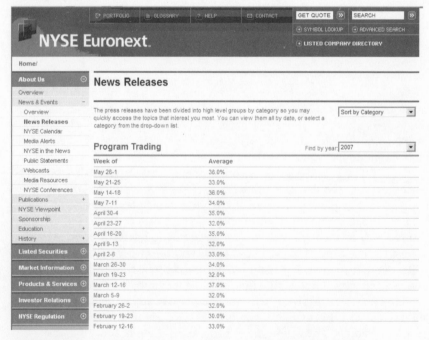

FIGURE 9.7 Program Trading as a Percent of Total Trading on NYSE
Source: New York Stock Exchange.

September 4-September 7, 2007
PROGRAM TRADING PURCHASES AND SALES

Trading on NYSE (Average Daily - Millions)	Current Week	Previous 52 Week Average*
Buy Programs	475.3	544.1
Sell Programs	496.4	548.2
Total Programs	971.7	1,092.3
Total NYSE Volume+	2,830.5	3,334.2

Program Trading as % of Total NYSE Buy + Sell Volume	Current	Previous 52
	34.3%	32.8%

Trading By Executing Market (Percent)	Current Week	Previous 52 Week Average*
NYSE	42.9%	46.7%
Other Domestic	56.6%	48.6%
Non-U.S. Markets #	0.5%	4.7%

#Does not include program trading activity by non-U.S. subsidiaries of NYSE memberfirms.

Total: Average Daily - Millions of Shares	Current Week	Previous 52 Week Average*
	2,267.5	2,344.7

NYSE Program Trading - 15 Most Active Members Firms
(Millions of Shares)

	Index Arbitrage	Other Strategies Subject to Rule 80A(c)**	All Other Strategies	Total	Principal	Customer Facilitation	Agency
Lehman Brothers, Inc.	12.2	-	779.8	792.0	113.1	68.8	610.0
Goldman, Sachs & Co.	1.0	-	469.1	470.1	261.6	15.5	193.1
Morgan Stanley & Co. Inc.	3.9	-	431.6	435.5	132.7	-	302.8
Merrill Lynch, Pierce, Fenner, & Smith, Inc.	-	-	378.1	378.1	190.7	40.6	146.8
UBS Securities, LLC.	-	-	280.7	280.7	256.8	-	23.9
Credit Suisse Securities (USA) LLC.	15.6	-	257.4	273.0	131.5	5.9	135.6
Deutsche Bank Securities	18.3	-	182.7	201.0	32.8	9.0	159.2
Bear Stearns	6.9	-	181.7	188.6	12.6	-	176.0
RBC Capital Markets Corp.	38.5	-	127.7	166.2	-	-	166.2
BNP Paribas Brokerage Services Corp	-	-	142.0	142.0	-	-	142.0
Banc of America Securities LLC	2.8	-	134.2	137.0	51.6	14.6	70.7
Interactive Brokers LLC	-	-	86.0	86.0	-	-	86.0
SG Americas Securities, LLC	15.9	-	27.2	43.1	40.0	-	3.2
JP Morgan Securities, Inc.	-	-	39.3	39.3	22.4	1.6	15.3
Citigroup Global Markets	-	-	38.1	38.1	5.8	9.6	22.7
Total for 15 Member Firms	115.1	0.0	3,555.6	3,670.7	1,251.6	165.6	2,253.5
Tota lfor All Firms Reporting	146.5	-	3,740.6	3,887.1	1,282.3	165.6	2,439.2
% of Total	3.8%	-	96.2%	100.0%	33.0%	4.3%	62.7%
% - Average (Previous 52 Weeks)*	4.8%	0.0%	95.2%	100.0%	32.9%	6.6%	60.5%

+ Total NYSE volume is the sum of shares bought, sold and sold short on the NYSE, including its crossing sessions.
*Average is previous 52 week rolling average. For non-expiration weeks this includes 40 non-expiration weeks; for monthly expirations this includes 8 monthly-expiration weeks; for quarterly expirations this includes only 4 quarterly expiration weeks. Totals may not sum exactly due to rounding.
**See Appendix

Note 1: NYSE program trading to tals include purchases and sales during regular trading hours as well as during Crossing Sessions II and IV.
Note 2: Program Trading Totals in this report were compiled from member submissions through September 13. Subsequent changes to these data may occur.

NYSE Research
September 2007

FIGURE 9.8 The Major Program Trading Participants
Source: New York Stock Exchange.

When I suggest that program trading is an important activity for a Wall Street brokerage firm, I wasn't kidding. Figure 9.8 reflects who dominates these activities. Further, over the past few years the dominant earnings source for these firms is sourced to "proprietary trading."

SHORTING EXPLAINED: TO GO NORTH, HEAD SOUTH

Prior to the introduction and proliferation of ETFs, shorting was seen as a high-risk strategy reserved for professionals only. To the average investor, this technique looked like gambling. However, this view was largely based on a fundamental misperception of the level of risk that shorting entails.

A routine question on brokerage qualifying exams used to be: "Is it riskier to be 'long' or 'short' stocks?" The correct answer *was* short. Why was that? The reason given was that a stock had an unlimited upside if you were "long," whereas if you were "short" your opportunity was confined between the short price and zero and your risk was unlimited. This answer does make mathematical sense, but it doesn't make common sense. Who on earth would short a stock at, say, $20 and maintain a short position if it went to $100 or more? No one. If the value of the stock you shorted were rising, your broker would have to request more collateral from you. The only way for you to stay in under these circumstances would be to continue advancing more money on the losing short sale. Only a fool would do that.

In the recent bear market, many people rode stocks or corrupt mutual funds from $100 to $20, which was just as foolish as shorting a stock at $20 and riding it to $100. If these investors had known how to use shorting they could have protected themselves from much of this loss.

Of course, shorting individual stocks can be risky. First, you have to be able to borrow a stock on margin. Each brokerage firm carries different margin requirements for each stock, and some stocks are more liquid (more easily borrowed) than others. The "uptick rule," which requires each short transaction to be preceded by an uptick, also makes shorting more difficult to accomplish. Finally, there is the "single stock risk." Good news on an individual stock can be the ruin of most short sellers, while with an index or ETF, good and bad news are spread over many stocks.

Most short sellers over the past two decades have found that the options market has offered more opportunity to prosper from both long and short positions. Options eliminated many of the drawbacks of actually shorting an individual stock, but they introduced even more risks. Option premiums and expirations have become too complex for average investors, and most individuals dealing in options have lost money, and continue to lose.

As ETFs have expanded in scope to include many major global indices and sub-indices, they have eliminated many of the risks associated with earlier shorting techniques. First, there are no borrowing or margin difficulties for most ETFs. Second, for most ETFs, the uptick rule has been eliminated, so selling the [QQQQ] NASDAQ 100 ETF or [SPY] S&P 500 ETF is as simple as saying "long" or "short." And most importantly, shorting an index is less risky than shorting an individual stock.

Even though I believe most stock indices go up over the long term, there are serious bear markets that can devastate traditional "long only" portfolios. Protracted bear markets, like those of 1974–1982 and 2000–2003, may last for years. And it may take many more years for investors to get back to their previous portfolio high-water marks.

It is crucial that investors evaluate shorting unemotionally as an investment tool. In my opinion, when you are following a disciplined trading method, being long an index is just as risky as being short an index in an unleveraged manner. Rejecting the shorting technique is like choosing to fight with one arm tied behind your back, especially now that ETFs have made shorting a risk reduction tool for traditional investors, when used judiciously.

QUANTITATIVE TRADING: RESERVED FOR THE LEFT BRAIN CROWD

Quantitative trading is just a fancy term for technically-based trading systems. The current master appears to be James Simons (Renaissance Technologies). His firm has hired many bright mathematically inclined and skilled PhDs, AKA "quants." The quants are engaged in extensive research to lead their fund to new trading regimes as market conditions change. Generally they develop systems based on mathematical algorithms that are improvements over or complement current methods.

Renaissance has been successful earning high double-digit returns for investors net of all fees. And fees are high ranging over 40 percent of capital appreciation. Clearly if returns are great investors are happy to pay the fee. Ultimately investors seek performance or alpha beyond passive index investing. That's the name of the game no matter the novel terms applied.

As for my own experience, I prefer investing by technically-based methods. Investors are always asking me really good fundamental questions about the economy; my projection for earnings at XYZ Corporation; whether current market valuations are too high or too low; if the Fed will raise or lower interest rates soon; why would I buy or short XYZ when everyone knows the price is too high or too low? And so forth.

Like anyone else, I have my own opinions when it comes to the markets. However, I've learned to let the markets take me in the direction it wants no matter what my inner voice is telling me. The markets know more than me almost every time.

No one can predict the market's future—at least not with any consistency. Anyone with any market experience has seen Wall Street pundits and stars come and go. They get hot and their every utterance is widely quoted. When they're real hot, their predictions can be self-fulfilling given their influence. They become sages because they're paid to do and become that. Yet their predictions are as reliable and consistent as old railroad trains. With a bad prediction, they're history. And at one time or another, all of them are just that—forgotten seers and sages.

What has become clear over the years is that there are people who know what's going to happen in different markets at different times. They are a changing group of insiders who may know something about a security that they shouldn't, something about a market impacting news event about to happen, or any important information not generally available to the public or pundits alike. They act on their information in the markets. This activity can manifest itself by simply studying the charts, and looking for unusual activity or trends that are developing without supporting news.

A good example of this occurred in 1990 when Iraq invaded Kuwait. Oil prices were in a steady trading range between $16 to $19 per barrel prior to June. In early July, oil prices inexplicably broke higher. There were no fundamental reasons anyone could cite why prices were suddenly $20 and then two weeks later $22. Of course by August 2, 1990, we all knew about Saddam Hussein's troops in Iraq and oil prices exploded higher. Who was buying oil prior to the invasion to drive prices higher without any "fundamental" news? Knowledgable insiders. It's an extreme example of course, but this type of activity has occurred in other markets where something is going on with prices that are unsupported by current fundamental research.

These are the kinds of circumstances and opportunities technically oriented and disciplined trend followers look to exploit. "The news follows the trend" is an old market maxim worn close to the heart of every technically based trend follower. They identify a budding trend and act on it. If the technician is successful and the trend continues, trend supportive news will reinforce that movement. If not, then a disciplined trader will be stopped-out with small losses.

A skilled and systematic trend-follower will act on every trend. If you pardon my saying so, it's a more humble approach. Good technicians know little beyond their ability to read, identify, and act on what their charts tell them. They don't question themselves or the reasons why their charts are telling them to act. They just act. Utter humility, discipline, and inner emotional strength is the technician's primary requisite.

Another reason to invest following a technically based system is because you want to be on the right side of the market when major moves occur. You don't want to be "in" the stock market [or any market] when it crashes as it did in 1974, 1987, 1990, or 2000. A skilled and disciplined system would be out or short those markets before or as they collapsed. Even a good technician can get blindsided by unexpected developments they were not able to identify. But a good technician can and should minimize these occurrences.

As stated previously the complaint of missing the first market move when trading technically is a consequence that a good trader readily accepts. You can't make every dime on any trade and it's foolish to expect that. More likely you'll just look back over markets, your activity, and accept some losers along with some winners. Naturally the latter should exceed the former by a respectable amount.

We discussed the so-called bullish bias previously and it is a dominant factor always pushing markets higher. But no one has yet successfully eliminated business cycles. Many argued about how "things were different this time" in the late 1990s to justify ever increasing stock prices. That proved to be just a rationalization for the dot-com bubble. Even as authorities cut interest rates to almost zero stock prices still declined for three years and the NASDAQ still remains at half its prior peak. In those circumstances investors have an opportunity to profit by shorting or sitting in cash with their nest egg intact until the dust settles.

Finally, things do change and investors need to adapt. The current global market rally is being driven by hyper-growth in some emerging markets [China, India, Emerging Europe, Latin America, and so forth] and enormous amounts of liquidity courtesy of generous central banks. Favorable demographics within the United States primarily from Baby Boomers and excellent retirement vehicles [IRAs, 401(k)s, etc.] also stimulate investing.

Modern technology that includes sophisticated computer systems and data communications allows markets to become more efficient. Speaking from 35 years of trading experience, I infer that modern trading systems must either shorten dramatically their trading views or lengthen them considerably. Intermediately oriented trading systems become less effective as these efficiencies expand. We discuss this further in the next chapter but frankly, this is a topic for an entire book.

MULTISTRATEGY: ALL THINGS TO ALL PEOPLE

One of the most popular hedge fund structures was a *fund of funds*. That mouthful simply means that a knowledgeable and experienced industry advisor as general partner will put together a fund incorporating a variety of hedge fund managers employing different strategies. This had been the most popular way for most investors to participate in hedge funds. For the same investment amount required for each manager you could acquire them all in one fund.

A new trend has been to use a multistrategy approach developed by one hedge fund advisor. As we described in Chapter 8 the most successful money managers have been those who have spent the most money on research to refine current methodologies or develop new systems. Good examples include Paul Tudor Jones and Louis Bacon, who have done their research and moved far beyond their original core competencies.

Both originally were [CTAs] Commodity Trading Advisors, which was most lucrative in the 1970s–1980s. They were able to expand their core trading activities in the early 1990s to financial markets [currency, equity, and bond futures] and to overseas markets where they could expand to 24-hour trading operations. These moves allowed them to expand their menu of markets and more importantly their trading capacity since some typical commodity markets were more liquidity constrained.

When performance in markets they followed started trailing off, these smart operators started to spend heavily on research geared to diversifying their trading to other sectors and styles. They moved beyond simple trend-following techniques to new opportunities in different areas to include strategies: arbitrage, event driven, fundamental global equity, private equity, and so forth. In so doing they were able to grow their assets under management and diversify their revenue stream. They also became multistrategy managers. CTAs who didn't evolve with the times like Bacon and Jones became less relevant with some even disappearing from the scene. To survive in the modern financial world, research is the key. Damian Handzy, CEO of Investor Analytics LLC stated to *Investment News* on April 16, 2007, "As a hedge fund strategy you need to be nimble. Therefore, the right thing to do is be discretionary and be opportunistic and be multistrategy."

From a cost perspective, the overlay of additional fees from fund of funds management is another attraction to multistrategy. Charles Gradante, managing principal at Hennessee Hedge Fund Advisory Group LLC stated from the same article, "Institutions like the multistrategy funds because they're cheaper than fund of funds. The extra layer of fees is pretty significant and I would imagine multistrategy funds should outperform over the long term, but the jury is still out on that."

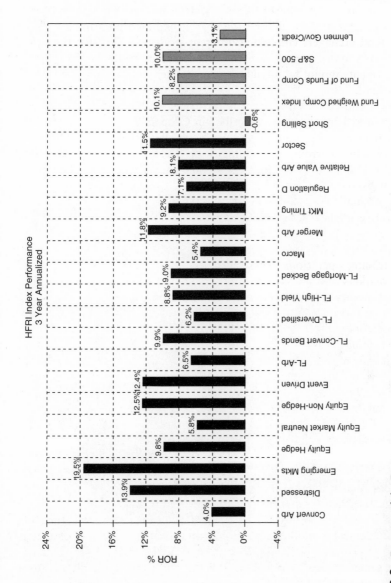

FIGURE 9.9 Returns of the Day

Source: Chicago-based Hedge Fund Research, Inc.

Naturally, fund of funds managers see things differently and are defending their turf. Virginia Parker, president of Parker Global Strategies, a fund of funds manager stated in the same *Investment News* article, "We believe most multistrategy funds are mediocre, because it is very rare for a firm to have the best management team in each area. We don't believe you can get from a multistrategy manager the same things you can get from a fund of funds. And that's how you end up with a lot of manager risk."

Sometimes the proof is in the results. According to Chicago-based Hedge Fund Research [HFRI] in 2006 Fund of Funds Composite returned 10.40 percent while HFRI Relative Value Arbitrage [Hedge Fund Research catchall title for Multistrategy] was 12.37 percent. Further, let's just examine the three-year annualized performance as outlined by HFRI in Figure 9.9.

To this I would add that the available pool of competent multistrategy managers is more limited than for funds of hedge funds. It seems logical to assume that expansion of talent in the former will be much more difficult to come by. All investors want an all-weather strategy; it's only natural. But to find excellent management for every style under one roof is perhaps more than one should expect.

CONCLUSION

There's more than one way to get to heaven, an old friend once told me many years ago. That's no doubt true. It's important for any investor to respect the successful methods of others whether they choose to adopt that styleor not. Some strategies are impossible for individual investors to replicate and that may be a good thing.

Hedge fund strategies are ever changing and some managers are quick to move to "whatever" strategy will make money for themselves and their clients. Some styles become hot fast and grow cold just as quickly. In 2006 to mid-2007, "private equity" was en vogue as cheap money allowed for LBO [Leveraged Buyout] activity. That strategy abruptly ended as financing deals became almost impossible due to the subprime mortgage induced credit crunch. It goes without saying that the collapse of the leveraged mortgage market and associated CDO [Collateralized Debt Obligations] derivatives caused significant hedge fund losses and even forced funds to close halting redemptions.

From here we can now move on to assembling reasonable hedge fund strategies that individual investors and FAs can utilize to get in the hedge fund game.

Hedge Funds for the Rest of Us

Lower-Risk Global Macro Long/Short Strategies

The ETF Digest Methodology

The highly complex and enigmatic hedge fund choices are overwhelming and often intimidating. Most investors just want something relatively simple, without using extensive leverage, that's performance driven. How to get there is another matter.

The ETF Digest is an investment newsletter focusing on using ETFs to assemble custom hedge funds for individual investors. Any good newsletter is just a tool and guide to help investors meet their unique goals and objectives. This chapter reviews how we developed and utilized this strategy. No one newsletter by itself is the Holy Grail for investing; rather, it [or they] should be utilized and combined with other input. We discuss this further in the next chapter.

OVERWHELMED

In 1979 I was fortunate to be introduced to a gentleman who was managing an aggressive stock portfolio for two of my best clients [who were brothers[. One of the two brothers also served as a mentor to me and had taken me under his wing several years previously. He wanted me to gain exposure to and learn highly stylized stock investment theories. Since 1975 I was almost exclusively engaged in dealing with bonds, and the opportunity to expand to other sectors was compelling. How to do that was the challenge.

My client/mentor was the senior partner of a top law firm in Honolulu. He was extremely bright and also had vast investment experience. He had attended the Wharton School and also had graduated with honors from the Penn Law School in the 1920s. His brother had a similar background, and both had made their way to the Hawaiian Islands joining the previously mentioned law firm. One brother was a tax attorney and the other a corporate attorney both representing major Hawaii companies. They were a dynamite team and I was lucky to have their business and friendship. Both, now deceased, lived long and successful lives. They taught me more about the investment business than any brokerage firm ever could. Despite their senior citizen status when I met them, both were forward-looking renaissance men.

At the time they had retained an equity advisor from San Francisco who specialized in technology stocks, which definitely fit the forward-looking mold. My mentor wanted me to meet the advisor in order to expand my knowledge and I think also to watch over what the advisor was doing. The advisor and I struck up a friendship and after some time I started referring clients to him. Our business arrangement was that I would refer clients to him and he would pay me commissions from transactions. Thus began a "managed money" business, which from what I know was one of the first such efforts nationally. After a time of outstanding performance results the advisor suggested that he wanted to form an investment partnership. The reason was to put all the clients in a pool making the trading and accounting easier and more efficient. He thought with one pool he could be more aggressive and even improve what was already excellent performance. Oh, and of course, he could start charging an incentive fee.

After about six months the hedge fund was launched. Why call it a hedge fund? Did he short stocks? Not generally. The manager was skilled at the new issue market and made excellent returns when that market was hot. "Skilled" meant he had good relationships with firms bringing deals to market. But primarily his specialty was fast growing tech stocks since he had a background as an analyst in that field. I guess in the modern vernacular the strategy employed was Global Macro, as he was making bets on selective stocks. At the time, I just considered the vehicle a performance partnership. Further clients wanted what today is considered "alpha" or out-performance from their conventional equity investments. Neither they nor I cared what pigeonhole this partnership belonged in technically. They just wanted to make money, period.

This all worked well and just a short time later I became interested in commodity markets and sought out advisors in that area. Why would this be compelling? Primarily because I was convinced by the recently released Lintner Study cited previously that adding uncorrelated managed futures to a conventional portfolio of stocks and bonds reduced risk and increased returns. This was primarily a factor that commodity asset trends were uncorrelated to those of stocks and bonds.

After doing my research about the subject, I investigated in several different Commodity Trading Advisors [CTAs], trying to find the best fit for my clients. I went through a few before settling on one I trusted and who could produce the overall portfolio diversification results we were seeking, not to mention producing additional alpha as well. So, for those clients willing to engage in this activity it was added as a component to their overall investment structure.

Now clients had bond management through me, a stock investment partnership, and commodity management. What else was there? Real estate? There were plenty of real estate opportunities in Hawaii in those days and no one needed my help since then back you could buy just about any property and make money.

Emerging Markets? Well, no one considered those then other than my forward-looking mentor. He and his brother astutely and with great foresight opened brokerage accounts with Japanese broker Nomura in the late 1960s. [Nomura had opened a small office in Honolulu to serve the large Japanese-American population there.] They purchased many Japanese stocks and made extraordinary profits as growth in Japan was in its early stages of fabulous growth. I tried to start some relationships with Nomura and other Japanese firms in the early 1980s but it was futile since structuring deals with them was too difficult.

But with these three investment components [stocks, bonds, and commodities] we were operating what one would describe as the rough equivalent of today's Fund of Funds. I controlled, with the clients' consent, the allocations from sector to sector and everyone seemed happy as the overall performance continued to be excellent, achieving the intended results.

But then things changed, at least for me. Commissions fell apart, and I was left with ever diminishing returns. So I started my own firm, which was well discussed in Chapter 1.

The bottom line is that during this period I gained exposure to trading systems and asset allocation strategies from very smart and successful practitioners. It didn't hurt that my mentor and his brother offered experienced and wise guidance along the way.

FAST-FORWARD 35 YEARS

So now it's 2007 and how time flies! Designing investment models hasn't really changed very much, but the names given to the tools and strategies used have been given a makeover. Emerging Markets, Distressed Securities, Private Equity and so forth are all old strategies that have been dressed up and modernized to fit the twenty-first century.

Another thing that hasn't changed much is what mainstream investors want—out-performance or the contemporary term alpha. That sounds obvious enough but how to achieve this? You can achieve this based on two approaches: fundamental or technical analysis. Some people think you can blend the two successfully but I've never really seen that accomplished successfully since one method often constrains the other, resulting in no performance at all.

No, you must make a choice.

The Fundamental Approach

There's a lot to be said for smart people trained as financial analysts [CFAs] who can rip apart financial statements and see where a company or industry stands financially and look for clues about its future prospects. Some experienced intuition is also a necessary ingredient to know what new products or services any company might be developing that either would be a drag or a benefit to future performance. Knowledge of competitive pressures and overall industry trends is vital. In addition being able to assess the quality of senior management is also a key level of inquiry and a Warren Buffet specialty.

To this must be added an ability to understand and forecast macroeconomic conditions and prospects. A successful fundamental strategist needs a good grasp of current economic conditions and of future economic developments from interest rate policy to overall employment trends.

Current market trends that include competitive data such as price to earnings ratios, price to book, price to sales, and so forth are also a vital component to establish how a particular company and even how the overall sector is performing compared to its peers.

All this is a pretty tall order and can't really be left to one person. Generally it requires a team with specialists competent in all facets of analytical considerations.

Lumped into this category are hundreds of pundits ranging from economists to so-called market strategists. You read their opinions daily. They present all manner of things from stock market targets to this week's economic data. How often have you read a financial news item that read something like, "Employment report misses analysts' forecast"?

These market mavens provide the content the media seek. They're also the "face" large brokerage and investment advisory firms present to the public. They exist to calm investor anxieties when nervousness is present and publish all manner of projections and recommendations. When I was a broker my in-box was stuffed with their well-intentioned junk mail. For them it was a "publish or perish" affair.

There are hundreds of these analysts on Wall Street providing commentary and forecasts. Occasionally one or two are right with their calls, but more often than not correct calls shift from one to another. Consistent and accurate results from one to another are difficult to find. Some financial news publications have features like "forecaster of the month," which just confirms this ever-changing cast of characters.

Peter Lynch was the successful portfolio manager of the largest growth mutual fund in the world, Fidelity Magellan Fund. He achieved great returns and admittedly plied his craft during the bull market of the 1970s to 1980s. He then turned to writing books promoting some common sense investing methods. One was for individuals to make stock selections by their own observation. That is, if you liked shopping at Costco and you intuitively believed this was a great company, just buy the stock. Well, it's more complex than that even he would admit. But when markets are moving higher as they were then in long-term bullish trends you can buy such a strategy and do well. Ultimately it's a reckless approach since other factors affect a company's stock performance beyond your own personal tastes and observation.

There are some excellent practitioners of fundamental forecasting and investing. The most successful are running hedge funds and making big money. The rest, in my opinion, are just jabbering away.

The Technical Approach

In the previous chapter we extolled the use of technical analysis to achieve the results or the alpha most investors seek. We use this method over all others because we first admit to one perhaps embarrassing reality: We know absolutely nothing about the future. Some people do know things that will affect future market or stock price movements. But there is also one other reality: Whether based on inside information or other circumstances, the cast of characters with market moving knowledge is always changing. Given those facts how does one proceed if not technically?

An astute technician studies charts and develops mathematical algorithms combined perhaps with other commonly available indicators for one reason: to find and follow the footprints of knowledgeable insiders. It's like a Sherlock Holmes study of forensic evidence to tell you what insiders are doing. Sometimes you misread the data and lose money while at other times you win. Sounds simple enough, right? Well, not really.

Over the years having dealt with so many investors and investment managers I find there is always a desire among clients to want to know the future. It's just human nature. It's also the single most dissatisfying aspect of technically based systems from a client's perspective. A case in point is that many years ago I had two investment managers with offices on the opposite side of Fashion Island in Newport Beach, California. One manager used a fundamental approach to markets and could always present a good story about why he was buying certain securities and what his optimistic expectations were for the results. The other manager was a [CTA] Commodity Trading Advisor who, like most practitioners in his field, used only technical methods for investing in the fast changing commodity and futures markets.

One of my Hawaii clients using both managers happened to be in Newport Beach and wanted to meet with them. I arranged that meeting naturally uncomfortable that I wouldn't be present for their discussions. When the client returned to the islands I asked him how the meetings went. With the manager focused on fundamentals he was thrilled by the presentation he received. Then when I asked him about his time with the CTA he was negative. He replied, "He didn't tell me a damn thing that I didn't know already. And he couldn't tell me anything about his expectations for any of the positions we currently maintained." I was taken aback since the CTA was putting up some great returns while the fundamental manager's returns were unimpressive. Over the long-term the performance and trend continued.

Ultimately the lesser-performing manager with all the chatter was fired and the market technician retained.

It just goes to show you that investors are really curious about the future and value well-thought-out predictions that may be ultimately proven wrong. But as economist Edgar Fiedler was fond of saying, "If you have to forecast, forecast often." This is oddly what investors both crave and accept. Some investors find technical trading unsatisfying and generally uninformative despite making better overall returns. It may be entertainment they seek as well as excellent results.

TREND FOLLOWING

Most market technicians have developed their own proprietary systems for dealing with markets. These systems are referred to commonly as "black boxes." They contain highly automated procedures or flow charts for dealing with most market conditions. If A happens, then you do B, and so forth.

Most successful trading systems beyond day trading or program trading schemes revolve around "trend following." When price moves consistently in one direction a trend occurs. This seems obvious. Market moves higher, the trend is bullish and lower, the trend is bearish.

A trend follower attempts to identify emerging trends before they become mature whether the pattern is bullish or bearish. These identifications are often done using a variety of algorithms and other mathematical methods. Trend followers believe that most fundamental market pundits and forecasters are often wrong since few can consistently predict future directions. Trend followers believe their systematic approach, if they remain disciplined, is a humble less subjective method. Trend followers believe that an ever-changing cast of insiders have information that they act on. They leave their footprints in patterns a gifted market technician can frequently spot. When price trends become unusual, whether moving higher or lower, trend-following methods can act on them even though these price movements are unexplained fundamentally or by news.

A powerful case is the example born of the Iraqi invasion of Kuwait in 1990. Prior to this event in August, crude oil prices were rising inexplicably in late June and all through July. No one could explain this movement, yet it was happening. Then came the invasion and the news bore out the trend. Someone knew what was about to happen and the effect it would have on prices and made major bets in that direction. The old market maxim, "the news follows the trend" was apt. If the market is on the move in one direction, supportive news will have to follow.

Managing risk is an important aspect of using trend-following methods. Know when you're wrong and exiting a position is a fundamental component of effective technically based trend-following methods.

There are different time measurement periods and techniques that tend to separate one practitioner's system from another. The shorter the time periods analyzed, the more active or frenetic the system becomes, while longer time views tend to slow everything down.

Trend-Following Approach Applied

After studying and using many different strategies for many years, the trend-following system seemed to suit my tastes best. Further with so many years of experience in dealing with individual investors it was easier to design and tailor a trend-following system to satisfy their tastes and needs.

Three basic conditions needed to be satisfied for both myself and clients: a long-term approach, low, and the right tools.

Most trend followers use chart analysis to identify budding trends, identify risk parameters, manage an open position, and know when a successful trend ends. A simple way to tailor this process to individual investors interested in less frenetic activity and trading is to use longer-term chart views. There are three basic chart views: daily, weekly, and monthly. [We eliminate for practical purposes charts in minutes and those in quarters or years.] The following are some typical charts selected using QQQ [NASDAQ 100 ETF] from the volatile 1999–2000 period. First, we feature a "daily" chart of the overall period [Figure 10.1]. Shortening the time period from two years to six months yields a much different perspective [Figure 10.2].

Figure 10.3 shows viewing conditions using a "weekly" chart perspective. Finally, viewing markets from a "monthly" chart [Figure 10.4] seems even smoother. It seems obvious that most investors would want to follow

FIGURE 10.1   Daily QQQ Chart—Two Years
Source: Chart courtesy of StockCharts.com.

FIGURE 10.2 Daily QQQ Chart—Six Months
Source: Chart courtesy of StockCharts.com.

the longer-term "monthly" chart analysis. In reality that wouldn't be the most effective for one reason: "it's too slow causing huge equity give-backs or drawdowns." For example, from the QQQ top around $108 in March 2000 most systems would require you to wait a month to identify a turn. This means that your next action wouldn't occur until May at the low $83 price. This is a decline of roughly 23 percent. Most investors would find this unacceptable.

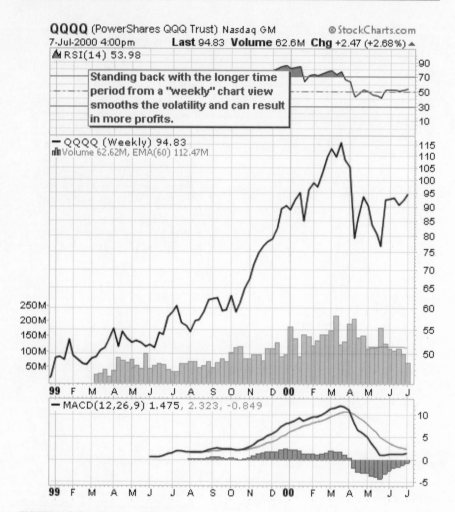

FIGURE 10.3   Weekly QQQ Chart
Source: Chart courtesy of StockCharts.com.

What to do?

The ETF Digest blends all three chart analytical approaches into one. First, we try to identify emerging trends using "monthly" charts. If we elect to take a position based on our internal and proprietary analytical methods, we will do so based on what the "monthly" charts dictate.

We then monitor our position from that perspective until our analysis indicates from that view the market is overextended, whether we're long [overbought] or short [oversold].

FIGURE 10.4 Monthly QQQ Chart
Source: Chart courtesy of StockCharts.com.

If that's the case we switch to "weekly" chart analysis to determine our next move [Figure 10.5], combining these leads to capturing most of the move whether up or down while finding a satisfying level of trading activity—not frenetic and not too slow.

Are "daily" charts ever used? Yes. We use them in times of unusual market stress like the crash of 1987; Iraq's invasion of Kuwait in 1990; the Asian Financial Crisis in 1997; the Long-Term Capital crisis in 1998; and, of course, 9/11. We also employ them if there is an abrupt change in Fed policy that runs counter to our positions.

FIGURE 10.5 Weekly QQQ Chart
Source: Chart courtesy of StockCharts.com.

The overall goal is to make two-thirds of any major market move whether up or down.

RISK MANAGEMENT

I'm often asked an important question. "Dave, how do you use 'stops,' and how are they communicated in your newsletter?" The answer is more complex than you might think.

What Are Stops?

I should first describe what "stops" are and how they are generally used. [More experienced investors can skip to the next section.] Used to both protect gains and limit losses, a stop is the price at which an investor orders an exit from a long or short position for a security he or she has been holding. Stops are seen as a means of reducing risk, but they can be misunderstood and poorly applied.

Most investors use an "intra-day" stop, which means that a stop order is left with a broker, requiring that a "sell" or "buy" market order be executed if the market price for a security reaches a certain level. With this type of stop, the investor is entitled to "the next best price," which can sometimes be disappointingly far from the requested stop price due to fast-moving markets driven by unexpected events. Some investors use "closing stops" or "end-of-day stops," which means that if a security's closing price is below the stop price (for long positions) or above it (for short positions), then the investor will exit the position through a market order when trading opens the next day. There are a number of other types of stop orders (such as "market on close" and "good until canceled").

Stops are most commonly used in the following manner. Let's say that an investor has decided to risk no more than 3 percent on a fresh long position for security XYZ, entered at $20. This investor would place a stop order to exit XYZ at $19.40 or 3 percent. However, with any stop, it is impossible to guarantee that the investor will not lose more than the specified amount, because markets can suffer significant price swings or "gaps." For instance, XYZ could have something negative happen to it during a trading day, or a negative announcement affecting it could be made after the close of trading. When trading resumes, XYZ would then gap open significantly lower, at $18.00, and our investor would automatically get stopped-out at $18.00 or lower. Despite the use of a stop, the investor's 3 percent risk would become a 10 percent loss. This investor would have to either accept this loss or, abandoning good trading discipline, gamble that the price of XYZ will recover in the future.

The use of stops can vary from position to position. We usually try to limit losses to 3 percent to 5 percent on fresh positions, but there may be occasions when we are willing to assume a larger risk of up to 5 percent to 8 percent, or when we do not want to risk more than 1 percent. And while we may exit a position because our stop price has been reached, we can also decide to exit because of other indicators.

Because the Digest methodology identifies developing long-term trends and uses monthly and weekly as opposed to daily charts, our approach to stops is unusual. Our system requires us to wait out the entire week or month and allow the market to establish whether a stop should be executed.

This is why Action Alerts are issued only once a week or month, unless a significant disaster occurs.

Waiting a week for stops to become effective may seem risky; however, empirical evidence shows that waiting works best, more often than not. While intra-week prices may dip below or rise above our stop prices, by the week's end such movements usually prove to be nonevents. The patient discipline required by our long-term approach contributes a great deal to the success of our methods.

Many subscribers have asked me why the Digest stop prices are not communicated to them beforehand. There are two reasons: Stops are proprietary information and broadcasting stops may allow market professionals the opportunity to "front-run."

"Front running" occurs when market professionals [floor traders, specialists, scalpers, etc.] become aware of other investors' stops and drive prices to where they know stops exist, through their buying or selling activity. By positioning themselves in front, front runners gamble that many stops will be reached, causing prices to rise or fall in a direction favorable to their positions. They profit at others' expense. In the current environment of corruption and scandal, this is something we wish to avoid for the benefit of our subscribers.

THE TWO-THIRDS OBJECTIVE

Our investment objective is to capture two-thirds of major market moves. What does this mean?

A "major market move" or "long-term trend" is a period when markets persistently go up or down, and such a period can last many months to several years. The trend-following methodology entails entering a market when trend signals are strong [through either a long or short sale] and selling when the trend weakens or changes direction. We can tell whether we have achieved our two-thirds goal after a major trend has ended and a new trend has become apparent. We measure the gains allowed by our entrance and exit against the total profit that could have been made by a hypothetical, omniscient trader who bought exactly when the market began to move in one direction and sold just before the market changed direction. If our gains are at least two-thirds of this ideal amount of profit, then the goal for an individual trade has been realized.

Why do we aim for only two-thirds of the theoretically possible gain? While it would be desirable to always buy at the bottom and sell at the top, there is no trading system that can do this with any consistency. This approach accepts the wisdom of the old Wall Street maxim "you can't make every dime." What we can do is offer a stable, rational way to achieve superior overall performance.

Generally, ETF Digest methods result in entering markets long when prices break out above the trading range and entering markets short when the opposite occurs. As one example of this typical outcome, Figure 10.6 shows the QQQQ from the market period between early May 2003 and November 2003. On May 5, 2003, a Digest position was established outside the trading range, at roughly $28.50. Nearly seven months later, the position was closed at approximately $34.50.

If the QQQQ moves to roughly $37 and then drops lower, establishing a new trend in a different direction, our trade will have met the two-thirds objective. If the QQQQ rises above $37 and appears to be in a continuing upward trend, the Digest will reestablish a long position for this ETF. Reentering a market at a price higher than the one you exited with can feel frustrating, but this is what the system requires and it should be accepted as part of the longer-term process of accruing good overall returns.

My methods seek to avoid the pitfalls of "trading-range" markets. When a market does not trend, it usually remains caught in a trading range, which may last as long as a major market movement. Trading ranges can be difficult to identify at their onset, and while they last, they can create small losses for trend followers who enter long or short positions. See Figure 10.7 for an example of trading range environments or Figure 10.8 for an example from a broader index.

An important note is that when you're dealing with unleveraged index-based ETFs you can never "beat" index performance, you can only match it. If market indexes are screaming higher, a system such as ours will

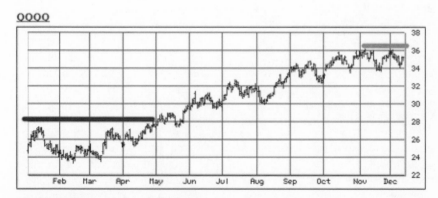

FIGURE 10.6 QQQQ Chart Displays Two-Thirds Objective
Source: Chart Courtesy of StockCharts.com.

FIGURE 10.7 Trading-Range Environment
Source: Chart courtesy of StockCharts.com.

theoretically be somewhat late to each position and therefore underperform. The same thing is true when you are viewing short position trades.

Various reporters [Barron's, MarketWatch and so forth] featured and complimented us on our results from 2000 to 2003 since we spent a great deal of time short with no long positions until spring 2003. Many investors remained in now losing technology stock positions with many down more than 70 percent at various points. In the meantime, our unleveraged short positions in QQQQ were prospering by roughly 5070 percent. Did we beat

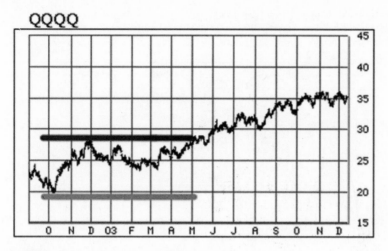

FIGURE 10.8 Broader Index Example
Source: Chart courtesy of StockCharts.com.

the market on the downside? No, because we were late to short in the same manner as we are customarily late to a long position. See Figure 10.9.

To understand this process better "flip" any chart over [Figure 10.10]. While the data and other information are backwards, just pay attention to the chart with annotations. Did we beat the market on the downside? No. Did we make our two-thirds objective? Sure.

The superior performance of the ETF Digest methodology is created through the steady accumulation of successful trades. Since it's impossible to develop a perfect trading system, small losses must be tolerated along the way. However, with a disciplined unleveraged approach like ours, losses are contained and counterbalanced by profitable transactions. If individual trades meet our two-thirds goal, we consider them successful trades. And if our successful trades significantly outweigh our losses over months and years, then our main objectives are being met.

FINDING YOUR SACRED COWS

Every systematic or disciplined trader needs to have a set of rules and principles to guide them. I have developed my own 10 guidelines, which I choose to call my Sacred Cows.

1. *Make Every Indicated Trade Every Time.* How many times have I kicked myself because I thought I could outsmart my own system? When

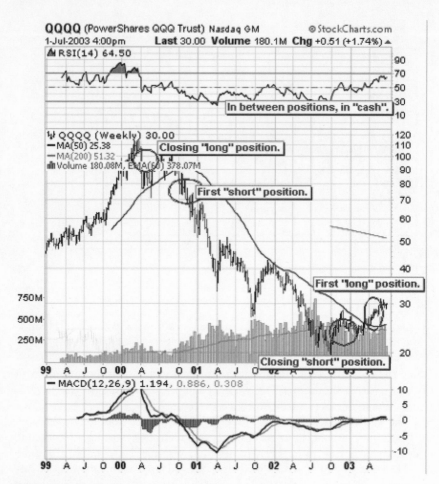

FIGURE 10.9   QQQQ Chart with Trade Annotations
Source: Chart courtesy of StockCharts.com.

I first started trading, it seemed perfectly natural to do things like put off placing an order because I was waiting for current news stories to develop favorably, thinking that I, rather than some system, knew more about current market conditions. I thought it was prudent to err on the side of caution, and, in short, I was not pulling the trigger when I was supposed to. This is a recipe for certain failure for any trader, whether you trade off the signals generated by The ETF Digest or by any other system. A wise trader once said, "An inferior system consistently implemented, is superior to a great system inconsistently implemented."

FIGURE 10.10 Upside-Down Chart—QQQQ
Source: Chart courtesy of StockCharts.com.

2. *Turn Off the TV During Market Hours.* Mad Money or The Money Honey may have their following, but watching TV is a major distraction to a systemized trader following a technical system. Most people are shocked to learn that I don't watch the market during the day unless I'm placing an order. But it's true. One needs to be disciplined and tune out distractions. I work on my system after the market closes and work my orders at the opening of the market the next day if I have a signal. If there is some market-rocking news during a particular day, I'll miss

it. But, in all my studies, it seems to balance out that waiting until the next day is just as profitable, or more so, as acting on some intra-day news event.

3. *Market Sector Rotation Is a Fact of Life, So Diversify.* It makes sense for investors to spread their portfolio over a wide asset class. The ETF Digest offers effective trading signals on a wide variety of market sectors, and subscribers can benefit by placing themselves in the strongest sectors and out of the weakest sectors at the best time. A key risk-reducing strategy that will optimize overall portfolio return has been the advent of ETFs that cover an ever-expanding universe of fixed-income, international, commodity, and currency-based issues for maximum uncorrelated diversification. These low-expense securities allow investors broad market exposure, flexibility (including the ability to short via "inverse" issues), and little individual stock risk.

4. *Accept Your Trading Losses as a Cost of Doing Business.* I hate losing money. Everyone does. Yet, if you were operating a newsstand on a street corner, you'd lose money from time to time. It happens. Accept trading losses as a cost of doing business and move forward. It's the only path to success

5. *To Avoid Severe Losses, Stocks Must Be Traded.* A "buy and hold" approach is a prescription for ultimate failure. Even the "averaging down" principles touted by many experts have proven to be a disaster. Just ask investors involved in the 1973 to 1975 and more recent bear markets how well their stocks recovered when at last bull markets resumed. Many of the hottest stocks from those markets had disappeared from the scene and never returned. Bull market maxims such as "buy and hold," "invest for the long term," and "average down" can be hurtful to investors. Fee-conflicted firms want investors to stay in the market for the long term so they can earn long-term fees. I remember Dysan, a high flyer in the early 1980s. They made floppy disks for early PCs. Everyone used Dysan disks at the time, but Dysan was essentially producing a commodity. The stock price was in the high $30s at one point, and then it started to fade. I remember a friend calling the institution covering the stock and asking them what was going on. They told him that earnings might be a little light this next quarter. That was the beginning of the end. From there it was a death spiral downward. That bull market in techs ended in 1983. When the next bull market returned in 1986, Dysan no longer existed, as people were using hard drives and not floppy disks.

That's why you must remain vigilant and willing to switch your port-folio holdings. The Chinese have a saying, "Even the monkey can fall from the tree." This is true for Dysan, Polaroid, Kmart, UAL, Lucent, Hewlett-Packard, and even IBM.

6. *Have Respect for the Successful Methods of Others.* One of my favorite people once said, "There are many ways to get to heaven." That maxim may also apply to investing or trading the markets. Warren Buffett, Peter Lynch, Bill Gross, and Barton Biggs are just a few of the more famous names on Wall Street. Each has different methods, but do share some things in common. They are successful because they are disciplined and consistent in their methods. I respect that in them. They would not necessarily agree with my style of investing, but they would respect the discipline and the results.

7. *You Don't Need a PhD to Make Money in the Market, But You Do Need a Good Feel for the Trigger.* Years ago, when I was running my own brokerage firm, an opportunity was presented for me to hire a gentleman who possessed a PhD. He was a great guy whom I liked very much, but unfortunately, the relationship didn't work out for either of us.

Shortly after I had retained his services, I excitedly told my mentor and best client of what I thought was a hiring coup for my company. His silence let me know he wasn't impressed. About two weeks later, I received a plain manila envelope from him containing a photocopy of an essay entitled, "From the Garden." It was written in the 1930s about the great economist, John Maynard Keynes. In London during this period a group of very smart and well-connected financiers had convinced Keynes to manage a public fund that they would market. His stellar reputation and credentials would surely bring in many clients, and high fees would flow to these organizers and Keynes. It never occurred to them that Keynes couldn't manage money. During a short period of time, the value of the assets garnered by these individuals and entrusted to Keynes dwindled away. He was quietly removed from the management of the portfolio and returned to his proper role as an economist.

The bottom line was that Keynes didn't have the stomach for trading and wasn't able to pull the trigger.

More recently, investors will remember the collapse and demise of Long-Term Capital in 1998. They had hired 1997 Nobel prize winning economists Robert C. Merton and Myron Scholes to be on their team. It ended in failure as well. Recently, Wisdom Tree Investments brought in respected economist Jeremy Siegel from the Wharton School to help oversee a variety of dividend-based ETFs. With his face on the packaging and his reputation, the many new ETFs they have issued are too new to rate now.

8. *At Any Given Time, the Market Can Make Anyone Look like an Idiot—Always.* All forecasters or traders have experienced being wrong and have felt dumb as a consequence. Unless you made a mechanical or systematic error, you must put poor results behind you and move forward.

9. *"If You Have to Forecast, Forecast Often."*—*economist Edgar R. Fiedler.* Forecasting markets and economic data is a tough business and most who do it are often wrong. This is a reason not to do it since being systematic is a more humble approach. The quotable economist Fiedler makes the point well for punditry. After all, weatherpersons get to forecast every day.

10. *Things Change.* Always.

ETFs PROVIDE THE TOOLS FOR IMPLEMENTING GLOBAL MACRO LONG/SHORT STRATEGIES

By now, individual investors have all the tools they've ever needed for creating and managing their own Global Macro Long/Short [GMLS] hedge fund. ETF sponsors have been working overtime pushing new ETF products out the door. And more are on the way.

I'm asked frequently by financial media reporters: "Are there too many ETFs?" My response is always the same: "No." Breaking down the answer further I tell them: "The more ETFs the better. What I think are needed issues don't necessarily agree with what Wall Street new product engineers and sponsors are issuing. But the more that are issued the more likely it is we'll find what we need, like a miner finds a gem in the rubble or tailings of his efforts."

But as of this writing most of the ETFs we feel are needed have either been issued or are in registration to be released soon.

Just contemplate all these new straightforward products that now allow individual investors the opportunity to participate in markets previously closed to them completely or available only via expensive and illiquid products:

- *Commodity trading or investing.* For example, previous to extensive commodity-based ETF issues were available only through high-cost Managed Futures funds that engaged in speculative and leveraged trading.
- *Currency investing.* Also confined previously to options and futures markets and/or similar Managed Futures products. But now there exist a wide variety of currency ETFs whether for just the Dollar Index or individual currencies where investors at the retail level can use to hedge or speculate.

- *Inverse ETF issues.* Allow most tax-exempt accounts [foundations, IRAs, 401(k)s and so forth] for the first time to hedge their portfolios or speculate in bear market conditions using unleveraged and liquid ETFs.
- *Leveraged ETFs.* Also exist to add both more risk and possible return to portfolios just using ETFs.

For financial advisors, it's just a question of time before your firm will create in-house products that will mirror many hedge fund strategies. These may take the form of conventional mutual funds using ETFs that will pay a trailer commission to you that your clients may want to use. These products will change your business model, and mutual funds that don't join the party will be quickly outmoded.

For DIY investors let's outline just some of the ETF issues that can change your investment focus and thinking for many years to come. The ETF Digest roster of ETFs is outlined in Table 10.1.

Table 10.2 lists the top ETFs by assets. It reflects global diversity through SPY [S&P 500], EFA [Europe Asia & Far East], EEM [MSCI Emerging Markets] and EWJ [Japan ETF] among others. You'll also find a commodity ETF in streetTRACKS Gold [GLD].

TABLE 10.1 ETF Roster

Major US Market ETFs Name	Symbol
Nasdaq 100 Index	QQQQ
Russell 2000 Index	IWM
S&P 500 Barra Value ETF	IVE
S&P 500 Index	SPY
S&P Mid-Cap Index ETF	MDY
Vanguard Total Market Viper ETF	VTI

US Tech ETFs Name	Symbol
Biotech Index	IBB
First Trust Dow Jones Internet Index	FDN
Goldman Sachs Networking	IGN
iShares Goldman Sachs Software	IGV
iShares Goldman Sachs Technology	IGM

(continued)

TABLE 10.1 *(Continued)*

US Income ETFs Name	Symbol
Dow Jones Dividend Select	DVY
Dow Jones US Real Estate	IYR
iShares Lehman 1–3 Year Treasury Bond	SHY
Lehman 20+ Year T-Bonds	TLT
Lehman 7–10 Year T-Bond	IEF
PowerShares Intl Dividend Achievers	PID
Utility Index ETF	XLU

US Equal Weight Sector ETFs Name	Symbol
Rydex S&P Equal Weight Consumer Discretionary Index	RCD
Rydex S&P Equal Weight Consumer Staples	RHS
Rydex S&P Equal Weight Energy	RYE
Rydex S&P Equal Weight ETF	RSP
Rydex S&P Equal Weight Financial	RYF
Rydex S&P Equal Weight Health Care	RYH
Rydex S&P Equal Weight Industrials	RGI
Rydex S&P Equal Weight Materials	RTM
Rydex S&P Equal Weight Technology	RYT
Rydex S&P Equal Weight Utilities	RYU

Commodity ETFs Name	Symbol
AMEX Market Vectors—Gold Miners ETF New	GDX
DB Commodity Index Tracking Fund ETF	DBC
PowerShares DB Agriculture	DBA
PowerShares DB Base Metals Fund	DBB
PowerShares DB Energy Fund	DBE
PowerShares DB Oil New	DBO
PowerShares DB Precious Metals	DBP
PowerShares DB Silver New	DBS
streetTRACKS Gold Shares	GLD
US Oil	USO

Currency ETFs Name	Symbol
CurrencyShares Australian Dollar Trust	FXA
CurrencyShares British Pound Sterling Trust	FXB
CurrencyShares Canadian Dollar Trust	FXC

TABLE 10.1 (*Continued*)

Currency ETFs

Name	Symbol
CurrencyShares Euro Trust	FXE
CurrencyShares Japanese Yen Trust	FXY
CurrencyShares Swiss Franc Trust	FXF
PowerShares DB G10 Currency Harvest	DBV
PowerShares DB US Dollar Index Bearish	UDN
PowerShares DB US Dollar Index Bullish	UUP

Inverse & Leveraged ETFs

Name	Symbol
Short MC400 ProShares	MYY
Short QQQ ProShares	PSQ
Short S&P 500 ProShares	SH
Ultra MidCap400 ProShares	MVV
Ultra QQQ ProShares	QLD
Ultra S&P500 ProShares	SSO

Multinational Programs

Name	Symbol
Europe Asia&Far East	EFA
Morgan Stanley Emerging Markets	EEM
MS Pacific Ex-Japan	EPP
S&P Europe ETF	IEV
S&P Latin American	ILF
SPDR S&P Emerging Markets	GMM

International ETFs & Funds

Name	Symbol
Brazil	EWZ
Canada	EWC
China Xinhua 25 Index	FXI
iPath MSCI India Index ETN	INP
iShares MSCI Australia Index	EWA
Japan	EWJ
Mexico	EWW
South Korea	EWY
SPDR S&P China	GXC
Van Eck Russia	RSX

TABLE 10.2 Top ETFs by Assets

Fund	Ticker	Assets ($US Millions)
SPDR S&P 500	SPY	$60,378
iShares MSCI EAFE	EFA	$44,140
iShares S&P 500	IVV	$19,586
Nasdaq 100 Trading Stock	QQQQ	$17,717
iShares MSCI EM	EEM	$16,294
iShares MSCI Japan	EWJ	$14,562
iShares Russell 2000	IWM	$12,869
streetTRACKS Gold	GLD	$10,950
iShares Russell 1000 Value	IWD	$10,110
MidCap SPDR	MDY	$ 9,414

THE TRICK IS PUTTING THEM TOGETHER

The list of ETFs in Table 10.1 is extensive, and clearly no one investor is going to use all these issues at once. The ETF Digest menu is like playing a game of 52 Card Pick-Up where for fun someone drops a deck of cards on the floor for a victim of the ruse to collect.

Investing isn't for fun but for profit. So we need to put these ETFs together in some sensible fashion to create that GMLS portfolio. Doing that is for the next chapter.

CHAPTER 11

Constructing Your Own
ETF Hedge Fund

Before you can even begin putting a portfolio of ETFs together, you first need to define your goals and investment personality.

- Are you older, when you need to lessen risk taking?
- Do you consider yourself or want to be more aggressive?
- Do you just want basic growth with low volatility?
- How would you best describe your profile to match your goals and objectives?

These are the basic issues that need addressing and can be done only by you if you're a DIY. But you must be honest with yourself. If you're using an FA the third-party help can be especially useful with the right person. Why should you seek out help? Because one thing I learned over the past 35 years when dealing with individual investors is what they say they want versus what they really mean can often be two different things. The discovery process requires the assistance of an experienced and highly skilled FA.

Much of this miscommunication and/or misconception can be due to inexperience by both FA and client. This has always made comprehensive interviews that much more vital in helping investors achieve success financially. Discovering your emotional quotient is an equally important consideration that a competent FA will help you determine. Sometimes you can achieve success in performance but are nevertheless unhappy with the route you're taking. This sounds odd, nevertheless good results using mismatched methods is often a cause of dissatisfaction.

Will computer driven questionnaires help? Possibly since many an FA's firm has gone through extensive research tailoring questions that reveal inconsistencies and has helped develop the right investor profile. Also firms use the questionnaire for their own protection. That may sound cynical but sometimes it's just the case.

With the high-volume demands placed on FAs, a "get 'em in and get 'em out" routine can often hurt small investors. Sometimes computer generated questionnaires fulfill only the most superficial requirements. And investment models built on old market performance data can be misleading. A charming but fast-talking FA may leave you completely frustrated over the long run. Worse yet, as we've discussed in previous chapters, you'll be stuck with high-cost products with heavy redemption and exit fees. A Hobson's choice investment fate.

Frankly, with all due respect to my FA friends and colleagues, the less experience they have the more they'll rely on computer generated once-overs. The old maxim, "there's no substitute for experience" comes into play. So if you're lucky you'll know or find an FA with plenty of investment gray hair who is beyond just pushing product out the door. It's becoming more difficult to find competent FAs since their world has been dumbed-down to product marketing knowledge versus investment expertise and experience with stocks, bonds, and commodities.

TYPICAL QUESTIONNAIRE

So let's try a few representative questions that might appear on typical questionnaires.

1. If one of your investments lost 25 percent of its value how would you react?
   A. Hold steady.
   B. Buy more.
   C. Sell.
2. How old are you?
   A. Above 75 or below 18.
   B. Between 66 and 75.
   C. Between 56 and 65.
   D. Between 46 and 55.
   E. Between 18 and 45.
3. How much of your monthly income are you able to devote to investments?
   A. 0 percent.
   B. 0 percent and 10 percent.
   C. 10 percent and 25 percent.
   D. More than 25 percent.
4. How much investment experience do you have with stocks, bonds, mutual funds, or commodities?
   A. No experience.
   B. Less than 3 years.
   C. Between 3 and 6 years.

    D. Between 7 and 10 years.

    E. More than 10 years.

5. Investment risk means to me:

    A. Higher risk in return for potentially superior returns.

    B. Moderate to higher risk in return for potentially greater return.

    C. Moderate risk in return for some growth opportunity.

    D. Low risk in return for a little growth opportunity.

    E. Slight to no risk.

6. If the stock market does poorly over the next few years what would you expect from your investments?

    A. To perform equally poorly.

    B. Not to make much return.

    C. To rise somewhat.

    D. To make gains.

7. I describe myself as:

    A. A novice investor.

    B. Somewhat experienced investor.

    C. Experienced investor.

    D. Very experienced with investments.

8. When will you be retiring?

    A. In 5 years.

    B. 6 to 10 years.

    C. 11 to 14 years.

    D. More than 15 years.

9. What is your annual income?

    A. Over $250,000.

    B. Over $150,000.

    C. Between $75,000 and $150,000.

    D. Between $30,000 and $75,000.

    E. Less than $30,000.

10. How much of your investable assets will this account represent?

    A. Less than 25 percent.

    B. Between 25 percent and 50 percent.

    C. Between 50 percent and 75 percent.

    D. This will be my only investment account.

And so forth.

One question rarely asked and not within the process of most questionnaires is: "How much risk can you take that you can sleep with?" In other words, invest only to the level of risk you can rest easy with and never exceed that no matter how tempting.

As suggested some questionnaires can be highly detailed while others superficial. So our little example is by no means complete but if you've been an investor with any major firm currently, you've no doubt answered similar questions before opening your account. In the old days brokers didn't even bother asking these questions. They just checked a box that noted investment objectives as: "speculative," "growth," "income," or "balanced." Often they didn't even ask the questions and filled out forms later on their own. So these modern inquiries are an improvement. These questions and many others are designed to help your FA pigeonhole you as an investor. They also provide the FA's firm with legal protection arising from investor complaints. If the FA places the investor in investments that don't agree with the conclusions reached by these questionnaires, the firm could be responsible for losses. It does provide the firm and the FA with protection from investor complaints. And speaking as an NASD and NFA Arbitrator, I believe this information is the first level of inquiry. If, when analyzed by an arbitrator, the investment strategy employed varies or agrees with that found in the questionnaire, it will make or break any formal complaint.

But beyond these routine inquiries is the more personal approach each FA brings to the process based on their own experience and reading of each client and prospect. It's a serious business and requires skill from the FA and forthrightness from the client. As to the latter, unfortunately many prospective clients sometimes don't provide the FA with reliable information. This may be due to a lack of understanding of questions asked, inexperience, or just misstatements of correct information. This is where the FA's experience should be highly integrated to the process. Just giving a prospective client a questionnaire to complete on their own without the FA being a part of the process is a mistake. The task should be a joint venture between all parties so that terms and meanings may be defined and questions explained. This is particularly true with inexperienced investors since they may be more eager to get going and too prideful to admit a lack of knowledge or sophistication. A prospective client wishing to rush through this interview and questionnaire process will have trouble waiting to happen in the future. For FAs and DIY investors alike, take your time and to coin an old phase, "know thyself."

Once you have completed this process, you're just beginning to understand portfolio construction.

LONG-TERM INVESTOR OR SHORT-TERM TRADER

In terms of personal style, do you consider yourself someone who can stay with markets through good times and bad? How many wiggles in market trends can you tolerate? Ten percent, fifteen percent, or more? Do you dislike trading? Answers to these questions may be the single most factors in determining your hedge fund investment suitability.

Generally speaking hedge funds do a lot of trading. One advantage to managing or investing in a hedge or actively managed mutual fund is investors don't have to do anything but note the [NAV] net asset value. They don't see the transactions taking place with their money which might be more rapid than by their own philosophy if it were slower-paced. But as long as the NAV is rising, who's to complain? However, if you're an investor with a longer-term focus and a partner/investor in a fast-moving fund you may get a nasty tax bill at the end of the year due to many short-term gains. This is another example of mismatched investing caused by poorly communicated profiles.

But if you're a hands-on DIY investor you'll have to make some decisions about the level of trading activity you're willing to undertake. Most people don't want to be bothered with a lot of trading activity. Perhaps using an FA to do the day-to-day trading work is more your style. Obviously you'll need then an FA knowledgeable and experienced with disciplined trading systems. Perhaps your FA subscribes to newsletters that assist them with these activities.

But if you're a DIY investor you will either need some help or have developed your own methodologies. These may feature a longer-term focus with just some occasional tweaking and rebalancing. If the methodology has a shorter-term focus and is more intense, hopefully you'll know what you're doing. As to the latter, for most investors you'll need some help either through your FA or independent sources such as subscription-based investment newsletters.

AWASH IN ETF CHOICES

As an investor, you've heard it a million times: Diversify, diversify, and diversify. I couldn't agree more. But exactly what is appropriate diversification? With several hundred ETFs available to consider as portfolio components, where do you begin?

First, it's important to know that many ETFs being issued today are repetitive. They're just some sponsor's or issuer's creation or twist on an existing index that allows them to get in the game and earn fees. Competition among issuers is intense and sectors are limited, making many ETFs just so many "me too" creations. For example, there are at present four different biotechnology ETFs:

1. FBT: First Trust Biotechnology ETF.
2. PBE: PowerShares Dynamic Biotech & Genome ETF.
3. IBB: iShares NASDAQ Biotechnology ETF.
4. BBH: Merrill Lynch Biotech Holders.

Do investors need so many? No. Why would you choose one over another? The only major difference between those listed for example is with Holders, which is an archaic structured product. Holders were created a long time ago by Merrill Lynch before the ETF boom. They are trusts, and as such, can't add new issues to their holdings. As time has passed since these were issued some components within the trust have been bought out by or consolidated with other firms. When this happens, the proceeds are distributed to the holders of the trust. This can work both for and against the investor.

As an example, let's look at another previously popular Holder, [HHH] ML Internet Holders. It sounds pretty sexy but since it was issued before Google went public it can't be added to the trust. Given the dominance of Google in the Internet space you're not really getting the true exposure you need for that sector. On the other hand, as time has passed and many consolidations have taken place within the Internet space, Holdings in the remaining companies have increased. Therefore, Holdings in Yahoo!, Amazon, and eBAY dominate HHH. If there are positive developments for any or all those three companies HHH could perform quite well. Of course, the opposite circumstances can cause negative performance since there exists an undue concentration in just a few names. Theoretically an investor could just buy those three companies' stock and mimic the performance of HHH. Why use it, then? [In fact, as this is being written there is a move for MSFT to buy YHOO.]

With current tax policy favoring dividends, it didn't take long for ETF issuers to jump into the fray with new issues centered on that feature. Wisdom Tree Investments was created by a partnership that included Jeremy Siegel a well-known economist with the Wharton School. His research and theories demonstrated that common stocks that paid ever-increasing dividends outperformed those that didn't. Armed with this evidence he set about to create indexes based on his research. Together with some Wall Street notables they created Wisdom Tree Investments and launched ETF products based on this research.

Following is a list of sectors to which Siegel's dividend model was applied to ETF issues.

Domestic Dividend Funds
WisdomTree Total Dividend Fund [DTD].
WisdomTree LargeCap Dividend Fund [DLN].
WisdomTree MidCap Dividend Fund [DON].
WisdomTree SmallCap Dividend Fund [DES].
WisdomTree High-Yielding Equity Fund [DHS].
WisdomTree Dividend Top 100 Fund [DTN].

Not satisfied with just those issues, the company set about to apply the same methodology to overseas markets and came up with even more ETF structured products.

International Dividend Funds
WisdomTree DEFA Fund [DWM].
WisdomTree DEFA High-Yielding Equity Fund [DTH].
WisdomTree International LargeCap Dividend Fund [DOL].
WisdomTree International MidCap Dividend Fund [DIM].
WisdomTree International SmallCap Dividend Fund [DLS].
WisdomTree International Dividend Top 100 Fund [DOO].
WisdomTree Europe Total Dividend Fund [DEB].
WisdomTree Europe SmallCap Dividend Fund [DFE].
WisdomTree Europe High-Yielding Equity Fund [DEW].
WisdomTree Pacific ex-Japan Total Dividend Fund [DND].
WisdomTree Pacific ex-Japan High-Yielding Equity Fund [DNH].
WisdomTree Japan Total Dividend Fund [DXJ].
WisdomTree Japan High-Yielding Equity Fund [DNL].
WisdomTree Japan SmallCap Dividend Fund [DFJ].

International Sector Dividend Funds
WisdomTree International Basic Materials Sector Fund [DBN].
WisdomTree International Communications Sector Fund [DGG].
WisdomTree International Consumer Cyclical Sector Fund [DPC].
WisdomTree International Consumer Non-Cyclical Sector Fund [DPN].
WisdomTree International Energy Sector Fund [DKA].
WisdomTree International Financial Sector Fund [DRF].
WisdomTree International Health Care Sector Fund [DBR].
WisdomTree International Industrial Sector [DDI].
WisdomTree International Technology Sector Fund [DBT].
WisdomTree International Utilities Sector Fund [DBU].

Slicing and dicing this index strategy even further, why not apply it to as many sectors as possible?

International Sector Dividend Funds
WisdomTree International Basic Materials Sector Fund [DBN].
WisdomTree International Communications Sector Fund [DGG].
WisdomTree International Consumer Cyclical Sector Fund [DPC].
WisdomTree International Consumer Non-Cyclical Sector Fund [DPN].
WisdomTree International Energy Sector Fund [DKA].
WisdomTree International Financial Sector Fund [DRF].

WisdomTree International Health Care Sector Fund [DBR].
WisdomTree International Industrial Sector [DDI].
WisdomTree International Technology Sector Fund [DBT].
WisdomTree International Utilities Sector Fund [DBU].

International Dividend Funds
WisdomTree DEFA Fund [DWM].
WisdomTree DEFA High-Yielding Equity Fund [DTH].
WisdomTree International LargeCap Dividend Fund [DOL].
WisdomTree International MidCap Dividend Fund [DIM].
WisdomTree International SmallCap Dividend Fund [DLS].
WisdomTree International Dividend Top 100 Fund [DOO].
WisdomTree Europe Total Dividend Fund [DEB].
WisdomTree Europe SmallCap Dividend Fund [DFE].
WisdomTree Europe High-Yielding Equity Fund [DEW].
WisdomTree Pacific ex-Japan Total Dividend Fund [DND].
WisdomTree Pacific ex-Japan High-Yielding Equity Fund [DNH].
WisdomTree Japan Total Dividend Fund [DXJ].
WisdomTree Japan High-Yielding Equity Fund [DNL].
WisdomTree Japan SmallCap Dividend Fund [DFJ].

International Sector Dividend Funds
WisdomTree International Basic Materials Sector Fund [DBN].
WisdomTree International Communications Sector Fund [DGG].
WisdomTree International Consumer Cyclical Sector Fund [DPC].
WisdomTree International Consumer Non-Cyclical Sector Fund [DPN].
WisdomTree International Energy Sector Fund [DKA].
WisdomTree International Financial Sector Fund [DRF].
WisdomTree International Health Care Sector Fund [DBR].
WisdomTree International Industrial Sector [DDI].
WisdomTree International Technology Sector Fund [DBT].
WisdomTree International Utilities Sector Fund [DBU].

Not satisfied with just dividend models, Wisdom Tree expanded its menu to include an earnings growth series of ETFs.

Domestic Earnings Funds
WisdomTree Total Earnings Fund [EXT].
WisdomTree Earnings Top 100 Fund [EEZ].
WisdomTree MidCap Earnings Fund [EZM].
WisdomTree Low P/E Fund [EZY].
WisdomTree SmallCap Earnings Fund [EES].
WisdomTree Earnings 500 Fund [EPS].

These issues seem unsupported by Siegel's original studies and themes. But remember, the founders of this firm are in the game to make more money on fees and see their stock price rise accordingly. You can't fault them that, but you have to know how it affects your strategy as well.

In a one-year period Wisdom Tree's menu of offerings went from 0 to 36. And as of this writing the roster may continue to grow. Are all these new ETFs necessary to structuring a portfolio? How would you go about choosing from this menu? You're right, it's virtually impossible. So we can now eliminate another group from the selection menu.

There are other active ETF issuers with PowerShares being the most prolific. PowerShares is a relatively new company issuing its first ETF as recently as 2003. It was a relative upstart compared to established and dominant players like State Street Global Advisors [streetTRACKS ETFs] and Barclays [iShares ETFs].

I interviewed Bruce Bond, CEO of PowerShares in 2005. Even by then the firm had become a prolific issuer of ETFs. In the course of the interview I had the temerity to offer a few new ETF suggestions that I thought the market needed. Bruce candidly responded: "We aren't in the business of filling needs. We are just trying to build a business." I walked out the door from that meeting with the very clear impression that his business was being dressed up to sell and reported that impression to our subscribers the following week. Sure enough just a few months later in early 2006 PowerShares was purchased by AIM Investments, a subsidiary of London's AMVESCAP. This allowed this huge mutual fund company an entrée into the ETF world.

PowerShares, like Wisdom Tree Investments, had created their own proprietary indexes [Intellidexes] based on quantitative analysis and elements from research. Armed with this index they believe its methodology could be applied to any market sector which caused the number of issues currently available from PowerShares to rapidly expand now exceeding 70.

Can you use 70 ETFs from PowerShares plus 36 from Wisdom Tree not to mention the many dozens offered by Barclay's and State Street among others? Of course not.

PERFORMANCE MYTHS AND REALITIES OF STYLE

Growth versus value styles of investing have generated many arguments and research among investors as to which is the better approach.

Value investing as defined by Wikipedia is "a style of investment strategy from the so-called Graham & Dodd School. Followers of this style generally buy companies whose shares appear underpriced by some forms of fundamental analysis; these may include shares that are trading at, for example, high dividend yields or low price-to-earnings or price-to-book ratios." Warren Buffet is a disciple but has used variations of this approach when making contemporary acquisitions.

Growth investing, also from Wikipedia, is "a style to invest in companies that exhibit signs of above average growth, even if the share price appears expensive in terms of metrics such as price-to-earnings or price-to-book ratios." Wikipedia continues, "Warren Buffett also has stated there is no theoretical difference between the concepts of value and growth ['Growth and Value Investing are joined at the hip'], in consideration of the concept of an asset's intrinsic value".

Moneychimp.com offers a more amusing and perhaps also more accurate and straightforward explanation.

	Value	Growth
Large Cap	Well-known boring businesses.	Well-known exciting businesses.
Small Cap	Unknown boring businesses.	The next Microsoft is in here somewhere!

Former Vanguard CEO John Bogle in his book *Common Sense of Mutual Funds* studied performance data from mutual funds using both styles from 1937–1997 and concluded that: "For the full 60-year period, the compound total returns were: growth, 11.7 percent; value, 11.5 percent—a tiny difference." Bogle concluded that over long periods there was a "reversion to the mean" which eliminated many of the differences. And in an updated op-ed piece in the *Wall Street Journal* ["Turn on a Paradigm?" June 27, 2006] Bogle updated the data through May 2006 and reported a performance differential of just .03 percent.

So why bother?

TABLE 11.1 Total Returns (3/24/00–12/31/06)

	Value	Growth
Large	Russell 1000 Value 69.45%	Russell 1000 Growth <36.31%>
Small	Russell 2000 Value 172.96%	Russell 2000 Growth <18.41%>

Source: Russell 1000 Value Index and Russell 1000 Growth Index.

Within such long periods there are periods of roughly one to even six years when one style will outperform the other and sometimes by a wide margin. And if you're nimble you can make a difference. Table 11.1 reveals a dramatic difference from the bull market top in 2000 through the end of 2006.

From this table the performance differential was breathtaking. However, this period was quite unique and making calculations perhaps misleading. But they are based on the actual indexes.

FIGURE 11.1 Russell 2000 Small-Cap Value ETF [IWN]
Source: Chart courtesy of StockCharts.com.

FIGURE 11.2   Russell 2000 Small-Cap Growth ETF [IWM]
Source: Chart courtesy of StockCharts.com.

Let's look at how ETFs linked to these indexes performed graphically using just [IWN] Russell 2000 Small Cap Value ETF in Figure 11.1 and [IWM] Russell 2000 Small Cap Growth ETF in Figure 11.2.

It would appear that IWM outperformed the data from Table 11.1. But the way performance is calculated factors in highly cumulative negative performance data from 2000–2003 around a negative 45 percent. But, from the low of 2003 to the end of the period, IWM gained 166 percent. What this means is you can fool around with numbers all you want and come to various conclusions based on selective dates you choose for your study.

Therefore when sales literature or advisors try to sell you one style versus another based on cherry-picked historical data, beware. It may not be what it seems.

Why not just blend the two? Sure you can do that but remember one thing. If you just bought [SPY] S&P 500 ETF, [VTI] Vanguard Total Market ETF, or [MDY] Mid-Cap ETF you would be getting a blend of growth and value since companies categorized in that manner are included in the component mix.

ONE WORLD MARKET

It used to be considered pretty radical to start investing overseas. After all the U.S. market was dominant for most of the twentieth century having overtaken London. That started to change in the 1970s with the emergence of Japan. And, as mentioned in the previous chapter, my mentor and his brother made fortunes buying Japanese common stocks from the 1960s forward.

In the early to mid-1980s I was convinced that China would be emerging and that the best way to participate there was through selective Hong Kong-based companies. This was a pretty radical notion then. I remember being interviewed about the subject by the local Honolulu newspaper. When the article appeared something amazing happened. As I arrived at work the next morning there were a handful of Chinese nationals standing outside my office door waiting for me to come in. They were excited and wanted to know how to invest in Chinese stocks. I was truly impressed. However, the next thing to happen was equally impressive but from a negative perspective—a call from the State of Hawaii chief securities regulator. He was pretty steamed. "No one's gonna be selling Hong Kong securities in this town as long as I'm in charge!" he roared. Well, you can't fight city hall or a regulator with unlimited discretionary power. Who needs that?

But over time we were able to build positions carefully. Naturally during the 1990s as the bull market took off in the United States most investors were more interested in investing at home since that's where the action was, given the explosive growth in technology and a friendly Fed chief.

The "U.S. only" sentiment shifted after the bear market of 2000–2003. When markets started to perform better in the spring of 2003 through early 2007, all global markets started to climb. And outpacing U.S. market gains were indexes and ETFs linked to overseas markets. This was noted in detail in Chapter 7 as we demonstrated the clear outperformance of global ETFs compared with those with only a U.S. focus.

Why was this happening? A major reason overlooked by most pundits is the end of the Cold War in 1990. Once this happened many countries that had been locked in to the Soviet Bloc were now free to pursue freedom and economic growth. Countries didn't need to be in one camp [East or West] or the other. Further, just as they didn't need to focus on these old alliances neither was protecting archaic state-run enterprises. In China, Deng Xiao Ping was telling his people to "get rich" and instead of referring to capitalism as evil just said, "It's a good cat that catches mice" meaning whatever breeds prosperity to the country is just fine, so state-run companies were transitioned gradually to public companies.

Global economic growth exploded in this new environment as Latin America became free of dictatorships; India had no Soviet Union to please; and Eastern Europe was no longer a part of the Iron Curtain. Previously lowly regarded stock exchanges became more accepted and mainstream, and where there had been no stock exchange previously, new exchanges were formed and launched.

ETFs were launched to take advantage of these opportunities. It may surprise investors to know that the second most popular ETF trading in the United States, as measured by assets, is [EFA] MSCI Europe, Asia & the Far East. This convenient ETF gives investors the opportunity to gain exposure to developed or mature global markets from London to Japan. But this popularity just isn't reserved to the largest and most familiar markets, as other themes have emerged to include the now popular [BRIC] Brazil, Russia, India, and China theme. There are ETFs available for just this theme or each individual country.

Nevertheless, it's not all peaches and cream investing overseas since some markets are extraordinarily volatile and corporate governance oversight is more undeveloped, to put it charitably. In 1993 I was with a small group visiting the Shanghai Stock Exchange and listened to a brief presentation by the exchange chief executive. One questioner asked, "How will you be able to verify company financial disclosure?" Answer: "We'll just adopt American rules." Question: "How will you enforce these rules?" Answer: "We'll just adopt American rules." You can see in that brief exchange why a developed and contemporary Hong Kong market remained more attractive from a corporate governance view.

But as a contemporary investor you can't afford not to be invested globally. In fact investment king Warren Buffett announced to his investors during his annual 2007 shareholder meeting that Berkshire Hathaway would be investing a considerable portion of its $40 billion in cash holdings overseas.

If your portfolio is not exposed to these areas or not globally focused, then you're "so last century" to quote a modern catchphrase.

TRUE DIVERSIFICATION

The father of [MPT] Modern Portfolio Theory, Professor Harry Markowitz articulated in the article "Portfolio Selection" [*Journal of Finance*, March 1952], that holding securities that tend to move mathematically in concert with each other [correlated in trend] increases risks. Further, a less-risky portfolio is one featuring noncorrelated asset classes. For his research Markowitz received the Nobel prize.

A survey by USA Futures found that when investors were asked if they had any portfolio asset outside their home that would perform well in a stock market decline, most answered no.

Our intent is not to get involved in complicated mathematical calculations or demonstrations of "efficient frontiers" or their associated "sharp ratios," [CAPM] Capital Asset Pricing Model and other complex tools that would only overwhelm you. By way of example, CAPM is:

$$r = R_f + \beta \times (K_m - R_f)$$

where:
  r is the expected return rate on a security
  R_f is the rate of a risk-free investment, i.e. cash
  K_m is the return rate of the appropriate asset class

Should I continue? I thought not.

Beyond the "know thyself" dictate, assembling an efficiently diversified portfolio is typically a four-step process: asset allocation, understanding correlation coefficients, returns, and risk.

Asset Allocation

A typical mistake that most investors make is to allocate among a variety of stock market sectors and think they've diversified. But in a general market downturn most markets will trend more or less downward as well. This includes value versus growth as well. With some sectors it's just a matter of degree in the downturn that spells the difference.

The traditional method of asset allocation relies on a balance between stocks and bonds. But there are periods when bonds [Figure 11.3] and stocks [Figure 11.4] will trend in the same direction especially when inflationary

FIGURE 11.3 Lehman Bros. 20-Year U.S. Bond ETF [TLT]
Source: Chart courtesy of StockCharts.com.

pressures are evident. For example bond and stock prices fell in the late 1970s. And both stocks and bonds rose from 2003–2006 yielding no uncorrelated advantage.

Correlation Coefficient

This is the measure that multiple assets move together. Correlation coefficients range generally from −1 to +1. A negative number means two different assets are uncorrelated. And a correlation coefficient of 0 means there is no relationship.

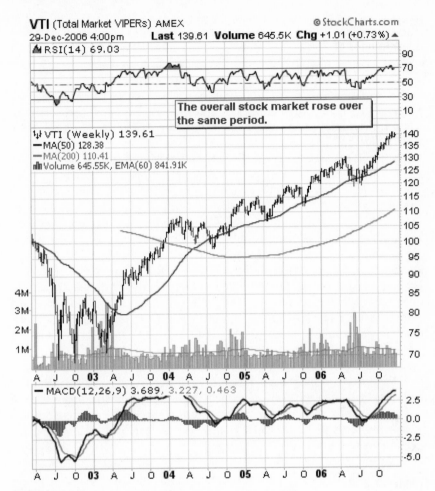

FIGURE 11.4 Vanguard Total Stock Market ETF [VTI]
Source: Chart courtesy of StockCharts.com.

By way of example, gold moves historically inversely to movements in the dollar making them uncorrelated. Over long periods, growth and value investment styles are highly correlated but possess lower correlations over shorter time periods.

Returns

These are the historical returns that generally are easily understood by investors.

Risk

One measure of risk is the standard deviation of historical data of each selected asset or index. The wider the deviation, the greater the risk. Beta is a measure of volatility that is related to standard deviation. The overall market as expressed by the S&P 500 has a beta of 1. The more volatile the asset, the higher the beta. ETFs and indexes can carry high or lower betas. Emerging Market and many tech-related ETFs carry higher betas while Utility and Dividend ETFs lower.

Index Funds and associated ETFs reduce risk even further by spreading it over a wide variety of components eliminating single-stock risk.

Most investors typically wouldn't consider adding commodities or currencies to their overall investment portfolios. However, based on the Lintner studies featured in Chapter 4 combined with MPT argue strongly that these are risk-reducing tools. For example, during the same period [2003–2006] the value of the U.S. dollar declined [Figure 11.5]. This was an uncorrelated event to conventional investments. The major effect was that stocks and bonds priced in U.S. dollars actually declined over the same period! And beginning in 2007, [UDN] PowerShares/Deutsche Bank Bearish Dollar ETF existed for you to incorporate to hedge your U.S. dollar portfolio or speculate.

And beginning in late 2002 gold ETFs [Figure 11.6] began trading, allowing investors to hedge against inflation or to speculate as they chose.

Many investors moved from the stock market to real estate [Figure 11.7] as the collapse in equity prices turned them away and low interest rates attracted them to real estate. Typically, [REITs] Real Estate Investment Trusts are securities and ETFs that investors can use as uncorrelated investments to stocks. Here's the proof!

Investors need to be forward looking. Historical data can be just so much rearview window information and can be quite misleading. Let's say for example you were building a portfolio and developing asset allocation strategies in 2000. You'd be plowing back typically through 5 or 10 years of data. Where would it lead you? Directly to the NASDAQ, U.S. stocks in general, and big-time trouble.

So despite all the computer power and historical data at your fingertips, you still have to use your brain. Nowhere is this truer than with computer-generated financial plans.

How do you avoid this pitfall? There is only one way I know: *market timing!*

FIGURE 11.5 U.S. Dollar Index
Source: Chart courtesy of StockCharts.com.

FIGURE 11.6 Spot Gold Prices
Source: Chart courtesy of StockCharts.com.

FIGURE 11.7   DJ U.S. Real Estate Index [REITs]
Source: Chart courtesy of StockCharts.com.

SHORTING ESSENTIALS

No matter the strategy, to run your own hedge fund optimally and successfully it is necessary to take short positions from time to time. This was well outlined in Chapter 6 [Trading]. If you're not willing to engage occasionally in this practice you're missing out on potentially large performance results.

Investors have short memories unless they're still sitting on some losers from the bear market of 2000–2003. When a bull market starts running, who would possibly be interested in shorting? But as ETF Digest Sacred Cow 10 advises, "Things change."

If you had shorted the markets as we did in late 2000 and had stayed mostly short through the bottom in 2002, you would have made substantial profits. This meant that when you repurchased stocks, also as we did in the spring 2003, your asset base was larger and buying power greater than even if you had just remained in cash during that period. And, of course, if you had just ridden out the down market, you're only now possibly returning to prior portfolio highs.

And market tools for shorting are rapidly being created that retail investors can use to take advantage of both speculative shorting opportunities as well as hedging. Shorting ETFs can be difficult to accomplish within some sectors as we've outlined previously. Inverse ETFs are being issued to accommodate retail investor demands. Further, most IRA and 401[k] plans are unable to short at all. But now with inverse issues entering the markets these retail investors will now be able to short by going long. This is a development of epic proportion.

PORTFOLIO REALLOCATION

How often should you be doing this? Many large indexes rebalance their holdings quarterly. You don't have to do this that often. If you're smart and invested in ETFs, let them do this part for you.

But overall portfolios should be rebalanced once per year. If through various market timing techniques you're out of a market for a period, there's nothing wrong with that. Sitting on the sidelines gaining some perspective free from risk is just fine at times. But at the same time you're ever alert to getting back in a position.

Too much rebalancing leads to the pitfall of selling your winners and reinvesting in losers. The old market maxim of riding your winners and selling your losers is apt in this circumstance.

ACTIVELY MANAGED ETFS AND MUTUAL FUND POSERS

Because of the popularity of the ETF structure there will be sponsors and even mutual fund companies issuing so-called "actively managed" ETFs.

These types of ETFs basically defeat the indexing feature as there will be no index to link these to. What will no doubt occur is that firms and their new product engineers will develop strategies that they can market to the public through their in-house network [Merrill Lynch, Smith Barney, Morgan Stanley and so forth] of FAs or directly to the public through their impressive marketing operations.

These products structured either as an ETF or mutual fund may have hedge fundlike characteristics, but I strongly advise caution despite what no doubt will be seductive presentations and literature.

If you're using an FA who is recommending this product to you, try to ascertain if the FA understands how the trading and asset allocation strategies within the product work. Is this something the FA really knows anything about beyond sales promotion talking points?

Just remember, hedge fund managers are a very well-paid lot and the best won't be dealing in lower fee products that dilute their time and skills. So posers will no doubt enter the scene appealing to average investors who feel they've found a cheap way to get invested in hedge funds. They could be dead wrong.

CONCLUSION

This completes the basic information and necessary steps to prepare you to assemble your own hedge fund. In the next chapter we put it all together with some representative ETF hedge fund portfolios that comport with the guidelines and philosophy we've outlined to this point.

CHAPTER 12

ETF Hedge Fund Portfolios

When we set about constructing various hedge fund structures for our subscribers using ETFs, we wanted to focus on and stay within certain criteria:

- Keep it simple.
- Limit the ETFs to as few as possible while still generating high impact returns.
- *Try* to include only highly liquid ETFs. New and much needed ETF issues may suffer from low liquidity initially and then build over time. If the index to which the ETF is linked is excellent, that feature trumps initial illiquidity.
- Diversify, employing various levels of uncorrelated assets.
- Tailor for several different profiles: Aggressive, Moderate, and Conservative.
- Emphasize that portfolio structures are just starting points or guides. Substitutions are widely available.

While no buy and hold strategy is employed by the ETF Digest, many subscribers have profited just following those allocations. In fact, the "Lazy Investor" is a philosophy dedicated to "not" trading. Rather this widely followed method recommends just an annual portfolio reallocation while remaining fully invested. As suggested by our Sacred Cows in the previous chapter, we respect other methods but choose our own path to investment success. However, if you wish to utilize those methods you wouldn't be following any recognized hedge fund strategy.

Another popular approach is to mimic the results of successful portfolio managers like David Swenson of the Yale Endowment. But total portfolio assets there exceed $20 billion, and replicating Swenson's strategy is extremely difficult for retail investors since nearly 70 percent of the portfolio sectors are private investments. Real Assets constitute 27 percent of the portfolio and would include real estate investments [either direct or through partnerships], commodities, timber, and energy deals. Real estate assets "can" be somewhat replicated by an ETF [IYR] which covers Real Estate Investment Trusts [REITs] and which we utilize. Private Equity is another 17 percent and while a private equity ETF exists [PSP], its construction only allows investors to reap the scraps from successful direct private equity investments. Absolute Return strategies constitute another 25 percent of portfolio allocation and attempts to achieve positive returns with below market volatility regardless of market conditions. Sounds great but confusing. It's also difficult for retail investors to copy since there isn't an ETF available in the category. However, a successful Market Neutral mutual fund may be a substitute.

Swenson suggests that retail investors not try to emulate his approach. After all, a $20 billion asset base allows for more adventuresome investments than are normally available to the average investor. Further, Swenson recommends that retail investors reallocate their portfolios every month—hardly a passive or lazy approach.

No newsletter can satisfy the tastes and needs of diverse investors but it's important to tailor the approach to suit basic requirements. After nearly 37 years of dealing with investors I've learned enough to put together approaches that work for all but the most conservative or most aggressive investors. This chapter lays out the basic framework upon which we build our themes and models.

So let's get to it.

LONG-TERM OR SHORT-TERM APPROACH

No newsletter, FA, or mutual or hedge fund can be all things to all investors. That's a given. However, at the ETF Digest we've developed two separate approaches to our activities that may satisfy both long- and short-term investors.

Our longer-term approach for *some* [emphasis added] ETF market sectors is based on a proprietary technical approach, which we believe is quite unique. What we're willing to share is that in this case we utilize monthly charts [Figure 12.1] to determine our primary positions. If an evaluation of monthly charts based on our analysis determines that a particular market is overbought/oversold, we switch to weekly chart [Figure 12.2] analysis. This process by definition extends the time horizon to longer-term. Why do we do this? Most investors can't abide a market reversal as severe as can occur in some months.

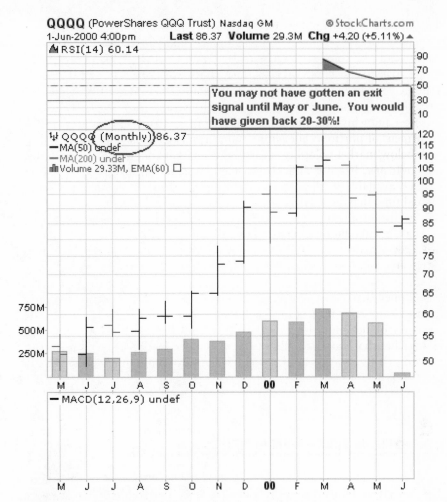

FIGURE 12.1 NASDAQ 100 ETF Monthly Chart [QQQQ]
Source: Chart courtesy of StockCharts.com.

Why don't we use the monthly/weekly approach for all ETF sectors? Because many ETFs and their respective indexes are too new to develop a meaningful history for chart data.

Our shorter-term term strategy follows technical analysis of weekly/daily charts [Figure 12.3 and Figure 12.4]. This by definition then shortens the timing process considerably. We switch to daily chart analysis when weekly charts also become overbought/oversold by our proprietary measurements.

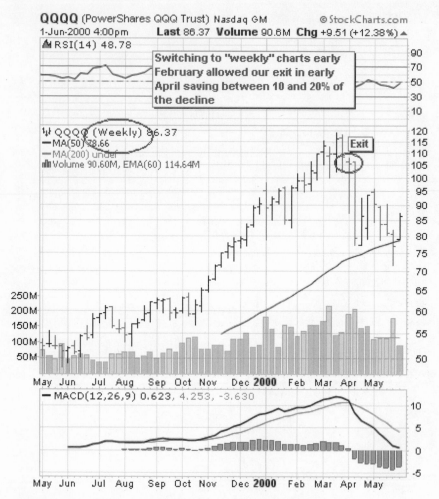

FIGURE 12.2 NASDAQ 100 ETF Weekly Chart [QQQQ]
Source: Chart courtesy of StockCharts.com.

So in evaluating the same market during that time period more trading activity is taking place. Is it productive activity? With hindsight maybe not, but certainly during that volatile period there was considerable investor nervousness and portfolio manager performance anxiety.

So, name your style poison. With more than 60 different ETFs in our roster you're able to pick your own style to deal in them. In 2006 and with

FIGURE 12.3 Weekly Chart Demonstrating Overbought Conditions
Source: Chart courtesy of StockCharts.com.

some alterations in 2007, the following were the three fixed model hedge fund portfolios for various investor profiles.

1. Aggressive Growth
2. Growth
3. Growth and Income

FIGURE 12.4   Daily Chart Demonstrating Trading and Exit Points
Source: Chart courtesy of StockCharts.com.

AGGRESSIVE GROWTH

Aggressive Growth [AG] investors are willing to be speculative with growth-oriented assets. This means that while these individuals fit within the Digest's long-term, nonintensive orientation, they are also comfortable utilizing the most aggressive sectors of the market and are willing to take short, long, and cash positions. See Figure 12.5.

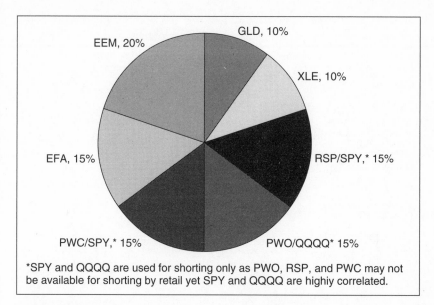

FIGURE 12.5   2006 Aggressive Growth Portfolio Allocations

You'll note in Figure 12.5 an overweight to overseas markets that started the year at 35 percent of assets. Further, only seven ETFs were utilized not including alternating issues used for shorting.

1. *EEM* [iShares MSCI Emerging Markets ETF] allowed exposure to a variety of markets especially weighted to Latin America.
2. *EFA* [iShares MSCI EAFE ETF] offered investors exposure to mature European markets with a heavy weighting in Japan and some lesser weightings in Asia/Pacific markets like Singapore and Australia.
3. *PWC* [PowerShares Dynamic Market ETF] and *PWO* [PowerShares Dynamic OTC ETF] provided exposure to U.S. markets while generally outperforming the S&P 500 and NASDAQ indexes, respectively.
4. *RSP* [Rydex S&P Equal Weight ETF] just takes the S&P 500 and equally weights the components. Further, since its launch, it has out-performed its weighted traditional counterpart.
5. *XLE* [Select Sector SPDR Energy ETF] and *GLD* [streetTracks Gold ETF] gave exposure to commodity markets that also made powerful moves higher in 2006.
6. *DBC* [PowerShares/Deutsche Bank Commodity Tracking ETF] pro-vides exposure to metals, grains, and energy.

7. *GLD* [streetTracks Gold ETF] remains a popular investment given its role as an inflation hedge. The ETF structure makes investing in gold now easier than ever in addition to being both cost-effective and liquid.

Since portfolios are rebalanced only annually and overseas markets dramatically outperformed U.S. markets by year's end, the weighting had increased to more than 50 percent. This is an excellent example of riding your winners and not reallocating too frequently.

In 2007 allocations for AG were changed as representedin Figure 12.6.

2007 Changes and Summary

In 2007 portfolio allocations were shifted in a more targeted manner toward overseas markets where it was felt there was the greatest investor interest. However, the total overseas exposure increased to 50 percent which is roughly the same exposure as where 2006 ended. Further new ETFs such as *INP* [MSCI India ETF] and the bullish/bearish U.S. Dollar Index ETFs

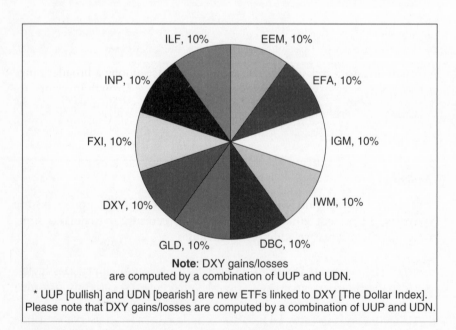

Note: DXY gains/losses are computed by a combination of UUP and UDN.

* UUP [bullish] and UDN [bearish] are new ETFs linked to DXY [The Dollar Index]. Please note that DXY gains/losses are computed by a combination of UUP and UDN.

FIGURE 12.6 New 2007 Aggressive Growth Portfolio Allocations

[*UUP* & *UDN*] had become available and the feeling was these would be popular additions. Further additions to the portfolio include:

- *FXI* [FTSE Xinhua China ETF] is a volatile and popular investment vehicle with its components consisting of 25 former state-owned enterprises.
- *ILF* [iShares Latin America 40 ETF] is heavily weighted by Brazil and Mexico with lesser weightings in Argentina and Chile for example.
- *IGM* [iShares GS Technology ETF] is a pure play U.S. technology holding linked to the Goldman Sachs Technology Index.
- *IWM* [iShares Russell 2000 Small-Cap ETF] we have featured previously and is included, as historically small-cap stocks tend over long periods to outperform large-cap stocks.

As the flood of new ETFs continues there may be opportunities to substitute intra-year if there are superior ETFs issued. For example, a new Russia ETF has just become available as has a new series of emerging market ETFs from State Street. Their structure and characteristics may be more appealing than those we're currently using.

GROWTH

Growth investors seek a more conservative balance among a broader range of investment sectors. For example, while Aggressive Growth investors are more willing to have assets concentrated in volatile tech market sectors, growth investors favor more diversification and less risk. Also, some growth investors may prefer to avoid shorting. See Figure 12.7.

Analysis

The 2006 Growth portfolio is different given a slightly lower exposure overseas, 30 percent initially versus AG's 35 percent, and contains some other more conservative additions to include:

- *DVY* [iShares DJ Dividend ETF], which obviously emphasizes higher dividends versus growth. Given the tax benefits currently afforded dividends it's not surprising that DVY has been popular.
- *IVE* [S&P 500 Value ETF] adds to the mix a more conservative value approach that also generates by definition higher dividends.

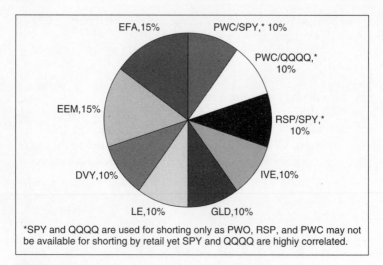

*SPY and QQQQ are used for shorting only as PWO, RSP, and PWC may not be available for shorting by retail yet SPY and QQQQ are highiy correlated.

FIGURE 12.7   2006 Growth Portfolio Allocations

2007 Changes and Summary

Beginning in 2007 alterations to the portfolio were fairly modest, as shown in Figure 12.8.

- *DBC* was substituted for *XLE* and *GLD* given similar components. DBC is a relatively new ETF issue and tracks the price movement of

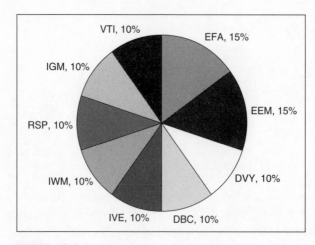

FIGURE 12.8   New 2007 Growth Portfolio Allocations

commodity prices rather than stocks such as contained within XLE. It also features a significant weighting in gold mimicking GLD.

- *IGM* replaced *PWO*. IGM is based on the Goldman Sachs Technology Index, which gave us more exposure to that sector while PWO featured selective OTC [over the counter] stocks based on PowerShares allocations through its Intellidex system analysis.
- *IWM* and *VTI* [Vanguard Total Market ETF] replaced *PWC*. Over long periods small-cap stocks tend to outperform, making IWM an appropriate addition. VTI on the other hand gives exposure to the entire U.S. stock market while PWC was PowerShares Intellidex allocation for large-cap US stocks.

GROWTH AND INCOME

Growth and Income investors generally pursue an equal balance between traditional growth securities and income securities. Figure 12.9 focuses on established domestic and international ETFs to satisfy the growth component of this type of portfolio. Its income component is dominated by bond ETFs including SHY, IEF, and TLT. Within the income component, it may be unsuitable for conservative investors to short ETFs; these investors will prefer a cash position instead.

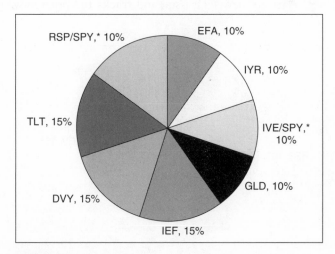

FIGURE 12.9 2006 Growth and Income Portfolio Allocations

Analysis

A common substitute classification for this portfolio approach is "conservative." You'll see within this portfolio many of the same ETFs as previously but with more of an emphasis on income.

- *TLT* [iShares Lehman Bros. 20-Year Treasury Bond ETF] is as it appears, an ETF focused on high quality bonds.
- *IEF* [iShares Lehman Bros. 7-10 Year Treasury Bond ETF] contains shorter maturities.
- *IYR* [iShares DJ Real Estate ETF] was featured in Figure 11.7 and is composed of REITs [Real Estate Investment Trusts], which also produce income.

2007 Changes and Summary

In 2007 only slight changes were made to the portfolios after reallocations were made. See Figure 12.10.

- *PID* [PowerShares International Dividend Achievers Portfolio] was added to produce another aspect of dividend income from overseas markets.
- *SHY* [iShares Lehman Bros. 1-3 Year Treasury Bond ETF], which adds a shorter maturity to the mix, and other bond ETF issue allocations were reduced proportionately.

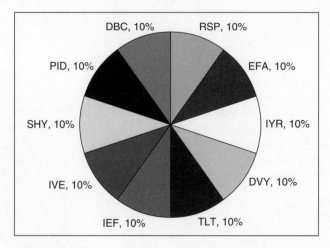

FIGURE 12.10   New 2007 Growth and Income Portfolio Allocations

- *DBC* [PowerShares/Deutsche Bank Commodity Tracking ETF] was substituted for GLD [streetTracks Gold ETF] since the former contained both gold and other commodity market exposure.

DAVE'S SPECIAL PORTFOLIO

Dave's Special Portfolio [DSP] is intended to serve a different subscriber profile—a more active and aggressive investor. We do this while still maintaining our core trend-following competency.

There are four major differences with DSP to the main trading programs: time, activity, open menu, and leverage.

Time

Where the basic program emphasizes a monthly/weekly chart analysis routine, DSP will utilize a weekly/daily approach. The objective is for profits to very much outweigh losses. But there will be losses and more activity. That's the tradeoff. When, trading actively, losses are a necessary cost of doing business to experienced traders.

Activity

Using a shorter time frame to analyze markets means more trading. There may be dozens of trades in the course of a year. For example based on analysis of just trading the NASDAQ from 1982–2006 would have yielded 12 trades per year. If we utilized 10 securities over the course of a year that might mean 120 trades total. If you were paying normal retail commissions, the process would be prohibitively expensive. However, if you are utilizing an online firm and paying $15 commissions, the cost might be $1,800 for the year. Is that a cost you wish to bear? If your firm offers an inclusive "wrap-fee" allowing you unlimited free transactions in exchange for a low annual fee, that might also work for you. Finally, using this method would almost guarantee short-term versus long-term tax consequences.

Do you wish to be this active? Some do, while others may choose a slower approach.

Open Menu

The basic menu of ETFs is, notwithstanding the deluge of new ETF issues, relatively fixed. DSP is free to trade any ETF and security. If as a subscriber, there are issues you wish included or commented on, let us know.

Leverage

Given the proliferation of ULTRA ETFs issued and pending by ProShares and Rydex we employ them using only a smaller portion of the assets. This means highly active trading activity featuring use of daily charts almost exclusively. I call this Power Walking the Tape. For individual investors trading from a taxable account, this means active trading with hopefully an accumulation of short-term taxable gains. Naturally, this type of activity isn't for everyone, so we advise those subscribers not to participate in that portion of DSP activity.

Other Features

DSP may have positions long or short that are contrary to positions in the basic programs. In other words, we could be long a position in DSP and short or in cash in the other programs. This should not be a surprise given the different time perspectives involved.

There are times when the basic program will outperform DSP and vice versa. What are those situations? When markets are in very long protracted and extended (up or down) trends, the basic program will excel, since you can ride the trend longer. On the other hand, if markets are more range-bound and choppy, we believe DSP will offer more opportunities.

For subscribers who choose to follow the basic programs, another use of DSP can help you augment your own gauge of market conditions. If you're a new subscriber, DSP can assist you with entry points to existing trades if both programs are out of sync for one reason or another.

ETF SUBSTITUTES

There are plenty of other ETFs you can plug into the models we've outlined. Don't be afraid to experiment and conduct your own research. At the ETF Digest, we cover more than 60 different ETFs on our fixed roster. Picking what you like from this roster to assemble what best suits your tastes and needs is just fine. However, you should try to remember some of the principles we've outlined regarding portfolio construction.

For example, suppose you didn't want to deal in three separate income ETFs like [SHY], [IEF], and [TLT]. You could substitute [AGG] iShares Lehman Aggregate Bond ETF, which covers the total "investment grade" bond market and not necessarily just Treasury bonds. That would drop the number of ETFs in the Growth & Income hedge fund portfolio from 10 to 8. Perhaps this is more manageable for you. Also there are new bond ETFs available featuring lower expense ratios that may prove more appealing.

Further [VTI] Vanguard Total Market ETF could substitute for many U.S. market subsectors. This could further reduce the number of ETFs you would have to deal with since theoretically different styles and sectors are included within such a broad ETF. Another alternative could be to use an ETF like [VEU] Vanguard FTSE All-World ex-US ETF in lieu of several different overseas ETFs.

You can eliminate having to deal with so many ETFs in a portfolio by gravitating toward broader-based securities. The trade-off is you can't target as well as you might like. Naturally, this can work both for and against you.

The tsunami of new ETFs is an ongoing reality. By the time this book reaches store shelves dozens of new ETFs will have been issued. Some may be useful while others will require careful scrutiny to eliminate repetitive issues.

CONCLUSION

We've wound our way to finally putting together some hedge funds using lower-risk strategies similar to global macro long/short. We've outlined various portfolios to suit different investor profiles as to risk and objective.

The ability of retail investors and their financial advisors to develop customized hedge funds had never been available until now. ETFs have changed the game completely, which put retail investors on a more equal footing with large hedge fund investors.

You're on your way now so let's get in the game. Like any other program, there's NO GUARANTEE any of our programs will be successful or effective.

CHAPTER **13**

Tools and Resources
Where to Get the Help You Need

Now that we've outlined some typical hedge fund strategies and portfolios using ETFs you'll need some resource help to implement and monitor your own portfolio. Following current and new ETF issues and industry trends is important in remaining up-to-date. Further, monitoring your personal hedge fund investment portfolio will require some tools.

The purpose in this chapter is to give you some direction in finding technical resources you can use. Naturally, searching via the Internet can yield results that can direct you to some helpful organizations not mentioned here. But it's strongly recommended that you make your own inquiries to find either complementary or alternative insights to what has been outlined here.

ONLINE TOOLS

Tiburon Strategic Advisors provides consulting, market research, and other related services to senior executives in the brokerage, investment management, banking, and insurance markets. Located in California they publish extensive research publications and host a variety of what they refer to as CEO Summits where the captains of the financial services industry gather several times a year to discuss a variety of issues regarding current industry trends and possible future developments.

Their publications have a broad industry focus and each report may cost in excess of $5,000. Obviously these aren't widely distributed to average investors and are primarily directed to larger industry organizations. Nevertheless, we're fortunate to have access to many of their reports and are able to cull some relevant data that suit our theme.

Their April 28, 2006, report "Back to the Future: The ReEmergence of the Online Financial Services Industry" was rich in content regarding the continued rise in global Internet usage; increased investor and consumer comfort with Internet commerce; and the re-emergence of online investing from the previous bear market collapse of day trading.

Within the report is an abbreviated listing of some tools available to investors. But as you can well imagine, available tools are changing rapidly, which require staying informed through various publications and Internet searching.   [http://www.tiburonadvisors.com/ResearchReports/06.04.28_ Online_Financial_Services.pdf].

Advent

Advent was founded in 1983 and has been public since 1995. It is based in San Francisco, California, with other offices in Boston, Massachusetts, and New York, New York, and an international presence in Australia and Europe.

The firm historically focused on serving mid-tier fee-only financial advisors and smaller institutional managers, and today serves four types of customers: investment managers, broker/dealers, trust companies, and hedge funds.

AXYS is Advent's core portfolio management software product. It is the leading portfolio management provider for mid-tier fee-only financial advisors and includes key functionality for fixed income and derivatives.

It is primarily a tool for professionals to provide and fulfill client ongoing statement needs. As such it may be too expensive for routine use by individuals with upfront costs perhaps exceeding $6,000, and perhaps expensive computer hardware requirements not to mention high annual maintenance fees. But it remains the industry standard for professionals.

Advice America

Advice America is based in Silicon Valley, California. It offers the Wealth Vision modular financial planning system. Advisor Vision is a core modular asset allocation program, part of the overall package or stand-alone.

Advice America's flagship comprehensive planning edition of its Advisor Vision asset program costs $2,000 upfront and $200 monthly.

Advisor Central

Advisor Central is based in Boston, Massachusetts, and provides views of clients' mutual funds and 529 plan holdings across participating companies. It is jointly owned by Fidelity Investments, Franklin Templeton Investor Services, Putnam Investments, and PFPC.

Advisor Software

Advisor Software is based in Lafayette, California. The firm is a market leader in providing solutions that enable financial institutions and advisors to improve the quality and delivery of investment advice. Clients include Barclays Global Investors, M Financial, State Street, and Yodlee.

In 2003 the firm launched Client Acquisition Solution. For example, Barclays Global Investors uses these products to allow advisors to build investment proposals functioning around ETFs. These services include Client Acquisition Solution, Portfolio Rebalancing Solution, and Self-Directed Investor Solution.

Again, Advisor Software is primarily a tool for professionals including FAs.

Advisor Tools

Advisor Tools is based in East Lansing, Michigan and produces Harvest Time modular retirement planning software solutions for advisors. The product comes in both PC and web-based versions. The former costs $300 annually, and PC software costs $795.

Advisory World

Advisory World was formerly known as Wilson Associates. It is based in Van Nuys, California and has 1,000 users of its products. Its main product is the Integrated Capital Engine line, which has numerous modules including retirement planning tools, optimizer, Monte Carlo simulations [technically-based forecasting tool meaning from Investopedia: "A problem solving technique used to approximate the probability of certain outcomes by running multiple trial runs, called simulations, using random variables."], cash flow modeling, mutual fund hypotheticals, and a database of stocks, mutual funds, and variable annuities.

Costs vary since most services are sold a la carte as plug-ins and have upfront costs that may be around $400 per package plus monthly costs less than $100 each.

The Annuity People

The Annuity People is based in Portland, Oregon. It has 2,000 clients with its prime product being TRAK Retirement Analysis Kit. Its upfront cost is $495 plus $150 annually.

The Annuity Price Center

Annuity Price Center is based in Bloomfield Hills, Mchigan and specializes in the retrieval of more than 33,000 funds in 859 products via the Internet. It reportedly is the only variable annuity pricing service with unit values from the previous night's close available each business day.

The desktop software costs $150 upfront plus $60 monthly.

Brentmark Software

Brentmark Software is based in Orlando, Florida. It offers a variety of estate, financial, and retirement software to both advisors and consumers.

It also offers a host of software products to financial services providers including: Pension & Roth Analyzer, Pension Distributions Planner, PFP Notebook, Retirement Income Navigator, Scenario Now Retire Now, Stock Options Risk Analyzer, Estate Planning Tools, Estate Planning Quickview, Kugler Estate Analyzer, Brentmark Asset Transfer System, and Charitable Financial Planner. Most products cost between $200 and $1,000.

Captools

Captools is based in Issaquah, Washington. The company now claims 4,250 licenses [retail and professional], but in 1999, it had more than 14,000 licenses. Its core business is to provide portfolio management solutions to individual investors and smaller advisors.

While Captools attempts to compete with Advent's AXYS program, most reviewers feel it's not on the same playing field, since its service is much more rudimentary.

Captools Professional Investor is the company's core portfolio management software product for advisors. It costs $1,900 for the first year and $1,000 annually thereafter.

Of all Captools' licenses 80 percent are for individual investors, and those products cost $250.

Cheshire Software

Cheshire Software is based in Newton Highlands, Massachusetts and provides the eight-module Cheshire Financial Planning Suite. This product costs $1,800 for the first year and $750 annually thereafter.

Cheshire offers an asset allocation program it calls the Cheshire Asset Allocation planner for a fee of $500 initially and $150 thereafter.

Decisioneering

Decisioneering is based in Denver, Colorado. The primary product is Crystal Ball Professional, a simulation program for measuring risk and maximizing and protecting portfolio value and return. The firm currently is used by more than 85 percent of Fortune 500 companies and all 50 top MBA programs.

There are two versions of its Crystal Ball software suite, with one focused on simple modeling and the other portfolio optimization. The Standard Edition costs $1,795 upfront plus $300 annually. The Professional Edition costs $835 upfront and $140 annually.

EISI [NaviPlan]

EISI is based in Winnipeg, Manitoba, Canada. The NaviPlan flagship is licensed to more than 70,000 financial services professionals.

NaviPlan comes in three versions: Standard Offline with a cost of $625 annually, which provides three levels of goal-based financial planning, Extended Online, which costs $1,250 annually and offers comprehensive cash flow based financial planning, and Central, which costs $995 annually and is a web-based turnkey business solution platform.

Financeware

Financeware is based in Richmond, Virginia and has more than 29,000 users. It offers a wide range of financial planning tools for individual investors and advisors. Its key product is Monte Carlo simulation. Its basic tools are free on its web site. The firm's product is highly rated for serving the high net worth market. The price of its software is $200 per year for all services.

Financial Computer Support [FCSI]

FCSI is based in Oakland, Maryland. Its most popular product is dbCams+ but it also offers Ontra+ and Vestige+ .

dbCams+ provides a wide selection of both client and management reports, including a client presentation report, 12 asset and insurance reports, 9 income reports, 6 allocation reports, and 10 exception reports.

Its primary competition is with AXYS just as is Captools. But most users don't feel they need all the features of AXYS. dbCams+ is available at a fraction of the cost at less than $1,000.

Financial Engines

Financial Engines is based in Palo Alto, California. It was founded by Nobel Prize winning economist Bill Sharpe. It primarily offers its services to individual investors and FAs. Costs vary and may be custom structured based on need.

Financial Planning Consultants
Financial Planning Consultants is based in Middletown, Ohio. It has more than 3,000 advisors. Its main products include Text Library System [Practice Builder] and its Plan Builder software. The former costs $995 upfront and $225 annually thereafter and the latter $1,125 upfront and $611 annually.

Financial Profiles
Financial Profiles is based in Carlsbad, California. It has more than 50,000 users. It primarily caters to financial professionals.

Profiles+ is their flagship product. It offers 14 different planning modules. It seems more focused on presentation of the Financial Plan than a detailed analytical approach. The product seems targeted toward financial planners who have a fee-commission mixed business, as it provides insurance training and sales materials. The software cost is $1,195 upfront and $695 thereafter.

Financial Psychology
Financial Psychology is based in Sarasota, Florida. Their primary product is Money Max profiling system, which is an advanced client profiling management system. It costs $200.

Forefield
Forefield is based in Marlboro, Massachusetts. It is a leading provider of financial content and planning solutions to serve institutional and independent financial advisors and web sites. Forefield Advisor, an advice management software for financial web sites is available as an XML data feed as well as a hosted solution.

Forefield has three core product offerings, Forefield Advisor, Forefield Newsletters, and Forefield Seminars. Forefield Advisor costs $365 per year and offers content for education, sales, and marketing.

iCLUB
iClub [www.iclub.com] is an online firm popular in the United States and the United Kingdom. It offers turnkey solutions for investors seeking to form and manage an investment club.

Informa Investment Solutions

Informa Investment Solutions is based in White Plains, New York. It offers software for financial institutions, investment managers, and independent financial advisors. It offers two basic products, AdvisorDecide and iDecide. Pricing is available upon request at www.finormais.com.

Informa also acquired Effron, which offered a performance reporting tool called Performer. It is a performance measurement engine and reporting tool, which offers multicurrency portfolio accounting. It focuses on analytics, graphics, flexibility, and scalability. The Perform IQ line is an integrated web-based client reporting across multiple portfolio product lines.

Informa also owns NetDecide, which provides advisory tools and services for advisors, brokers, and salespeople. It is not designed for the consumer as it is complex, often lacks explanations, and requires in-depth knowledge.

Intuit

Intuit was founded in 1983 and is based in Mountain View, California. It tried to sell to Microsoft in 1995. The firm has 7,000 employees and generates $2.0 billion in revenues and $381 million in net income. The firm has an $8 billion market cap. Its core product is Quicken, which holds 80 percent market share of the personal finance software market. Its second core product is TurboTax, which holds 70 percent market share.

Intuit produces QuickBooks and Quicken. QuickBooks was launched in 1992. It originally had lots of problems, but quickly passed leader Peachtree. Today the product enjoys 75 percent market share, with 3,000,000 users for all QuickBooks versions. The product retains the ease of use and simplified business processes found in the QuickBooksPro and Basic versions. Quicken was launched in 1984 and is for consumers to use for managing seven key areas of their finances: banking, investing, taxes, planning, spending and saving, loans, and insurance. The software has a rich array of accounting and analysis tools that make it a superior product.

Intuit produces QuickBooks online edition, its web-based accounting product. This software handles all basic accounting functions including payroll. It counts 131 charts of accounts, and 55 customizable reports. The software also has an Expert Analysis tool.

Intuit's Quicken owns an astounding 80 percent share of the personal accounting software market.

Investools

Investools [http://www.investools.com/] is based in Draper, Utah, and owns Prophet Finance. It is an extremely complex and expensive investor education and resource program. It offers extensive online investment courses and various trading software. A visit to the web site will provide more detailed information.

IW Financial

IW Financial [https://www.iwfinancial.com/iwf/] is based in Portland, Maine, and offers comprehensive financial planning software and web solutions. The firm offers six financial products and services: Research workstations, Portfolio management tools, Custom research integration, Investment compliance reporting, Private label solutions, and Training and support. J&L Software

J&L Software [http://www.jlplanner.com/] offers Monte Carlo financial planning software, which Accounting Today called best of breed.

Leimberg & Leclair

Leimberg & Leclair [http://www.leimberg.com/] is an estate and financial planning software company based in Havertown, Pennsylvania, led by CEO Steve Leimberg. The firm offers three core planning products, including Number Cruncher, Estate Planning Quick View, and MRD.

Leimberg Associates is a subsidiary of Leimberg & Leclair. Leimberg Associates offers four core PC based software products without an annual fee, including its Financial Analyzer II, IRS Factors calculator, Long-Term Care Presentation, and Gifts That Give Back.

Leimberg Associates also offers three products for which clients pay an annual fee, all PC based as well. These are a Pension & Roth IRA Calculator, Charitable Financial Planner, and Toward a Zero Estate Tax Presentation.

Lumen Systems

Lumen Systems [http://www.leimberg.com/] was founded in 1982 and is based in San Jose, California. The firm has 3,000 clients. Its software costs $1,995 plus $495 in maintenance fees. Lumen claims to be the first financial planning software package to convert to Windows. It has a specialty in addressing business valuations, and good graphics displays (but is not known to be as accurate as some of the higher end packages).

Lumen systems provides the Financial Planning Professional [FPP] desktop tool and the Northstar Back Office Solution.

Major Technology Resources

Major Technology Resources [http://www.majtech.com/] was founded in 2005 by CEO Rob Major (the former co-founder of ASP PMS system innovator TechFi). The firm makes Asset Book, an ASP portfolio management software solution.

Major Technology Resources intended to add up to a half-dozen new RIA clients per month in 2006, and 5 to 10 a month thereafter.

Major Technology Resources charges more than $20 per account per year for its Asset Book ASP portfolio management software. For most other accounts it charges $24 per year, but accounts with more than 50 securities or funds are charged $36.

Mantic Software

Mantic Software [http://www.manticsoft.com/] is based in Loveland, Colorado. Its products transform the mathematics and behavior of complex financial instruments into interactive, graphical displays.

Master Plan Financial Software

Master Plan Financial Software [http://www.masterplanner.com/] was founded in 1985 and is based in Vacaville, California. It has more than 200 clients and a complete offering and claims to be the only package that analyzes real estate. The system is fully integrated and uses SQL Server technology and database versus client folder technology. The firm's system includes Client management tools, Client data forms, and Customizable graphics for client plans. There are additional charges for support based on number of people.

Master Plan Financial Software offers its core Master Plan, the analyst financial planning software product. The cost of the software is $745 upfront and $500 annually and takes a modular financial planning approach. It is PC based software.

Merit Software Concepts

Merit Software Concepts was founded in 1980 and is based in Houston, Texas. Its core Financial Strategies financial planning software comes pretty cheap, at $100 per year.

Microsoft

Microsoft is based in Redmond, Washington. Microsoft is the world's #1 software company, known primarily for its Windows operating system, Office software (including Word, Excel, and PowerPoint), Outlook e-mail software, and its Access & SQL database systems. Looking at its financial services business, it acquired Great Plains Software in 2001. Excel is the primary tool for customizing spread sheets to import to portfolios.

Money Tree Software

Money Tree Software [http://www.moneytree.com/] was founded in 1981 and is based in Corvallis, Oregon. It is a Top 5 provider of financial planning software, primarily to independent reps.

Money Tree Software has two core products, the Total Planning System and the Silver Financial Planner.

Total Planning System
- Cost: $850 upfront and $850 annually.
- Three-component financial planning software (Easy Money goal-based software, Golden Years cash-based retirement planner, and Strategic Solutions Monte Carlo simulation and report capabilities).
- PC based.

Silver Financial Planner
- Cost: $450 upfront plus $150 annually.
- Interactive retirement planning software.
- PC based.

PIE Technologies [Money Guide Pro]

PIE Technologies was founded in 1985. Its name is derived from Plan-Invest-Enjoy. The firm is based in Midlothian, Virginia and has 21 employees. Money Guide Pro has 50 client institutions, and 17,000 users.

Money Guide Pro is an interactive financial planning program, which is simple enough to appeal to clients, but sophisticated enough to satisfy advisors. The program uniquely allows clients to prioritize goals, though it lacks an estate planning module. It is relatively inexpensive at $995 annually. It reportedly relies solely on randomized historical returns.

The product is highly ranked for financial advisors serving the emerging affluent market. Its output is also very meaningful for clients, telling them their chances of reaching goals.

Portfolio Systems

Portfolio Systems [http://www.scscompany.com/] was founded in 1998. It is focused on developing and supporting best of breed portfolio management systems for individual investors and advisors alike. The firm offers five products: Portfolio Gains, Option Money, End of Day Quote Service, Portfolio Director, and Portfolio Director Web.

Specialty Software

Specialty Software [http://www.proaxis.com/~rwi/finsuite.htm] was founded in 1991 and is based in Corvallis, Oregon. The firm offers two financial planning products: The Financial Suite ($80) and the Financial Manager ($85).

Tools For Money

Tools For Money [http://toolsformoney.com/] develops Excel-based consumer, investor, and financial advisor planning software. Prices range from $158 unsupported to $259 with phone support. Or if you purchase all their products, prices range from $749 to $879.

Unger Software [Methuselah]

Unger Software [http://www.methuselah.com/] was founded in 1994 and is based in New York, New York. The firm has 30 employees and generates $3.5 million in revenues.

Unger Software's Methuselah financial planning platform is a comprehensive financial planning software solution. It costs $129 monthly.

Wealthtec

Wealthtec [http://www.wealthtec.com/] is based in Clarksville, Maryland and is specialized in high-end financial and estate planning software applications. The firm has three products: WealthMaster, Foundations, and Affluence.

Yodlee

Yodlee [http://corporate.yodlee.com/solutions/wealth_management/advisor_view.htm] was founded in 1999, and is based in Redwood City, California. The firm has 4.3 million users, and is known for the fact that it invented aggregation. The firm provides personal finance and bill pay, wealth management, risk management, and market research software solutions. It originally targeted the consumer market; later it moved to serving financial services companies. The firm still serves bank and broker markets, and lays claim to having

32 of the top 50 financial services organizations as clients. The firm has access to 20 million consumers through its clients.

Yodlee is rolling out AdvisorPro for advisors, which it began widely marketing in 2005 again. It is available to Charles Schwab advisors as Correct Net, and also offers services to SunGard clients. The product runs as an ASP.

Quote Vendors

Bloomberg

Bloomberg was founded in 1981 and is based in New York, New York. It counts 8,000 employees and a total of 126 countries served. Bloomberg news has 1,600 reporters who print 4,000 articles daily.

For individual investors quote feeds from Bloomberg are expensive and, depending on the levels of services, can cost thousands of dollars per month.

Bloomberg.com is a source for global index quotes and individual securities prices within the United States. Its site has been revamped recently to make it very usable for news and commentary.

Briefing.com

Briefing.com is a web site that provides up-to-date company financial information, announcements, and live interviews with CEOs. Many of its services are free while there is some premium content and services.

Brill's Mutual Funds Interactive

Brill's Mutual Funds Interactive [www.brill.com/] is a web-based mutual fund data and information service. Much of its information is free but they do sell some premium products from books to special publications.

Data Transmission Network

Data Transmission Network was founded in 1984 and is headquartered in Omaha, Nebraska. The firm has 120,000 subscribers overall. It offers fully integrated information for financial professionals, including real-time quotes on equities, fixed-income securities, and real-time business newswires.

It also offers market data services, client management services, consolidated position statements, online trading systems, and Web content. Its products include ProSource, ProSource Premier, and National Datamax. Its ProSource functionalities include client account information, capable of downloading from Pershing.

Dow Jones
Dow Jones is based in New York, New York, and has 7,100 employees. It generates $1.7 billion in revenues and $100 million in net income. The firm publishes the *Wall Street Journal*, Barron's, SmartMoney, and web-based MarketWatch.com among others.

MarketWatch is a popular source for news and delayed quotes.

Free Real Time
Free Real Time [http://quotes.freerealtime.com/dl/frt/S] is a financial media company that claims to provide sophisticated investors from around the world real-time actionable insight into financial markets.

Interactive Data
Interactive Data [http://www.interactivedata.com/] was founded in 1968 and is based in Bedford, Massachusetts. The firm updates information on 3.5 million securities.

Interactive Data owns four firms, including CMS Bond Edge, Comstock, eSignal, and FT Interactive Data. [eSignal is a product the author has used successfully in the past.]

Interactive Investor International
Interactive Investor International [http://www.iii.co.uk/] was founded in 1995 and has 1.4 million registered clients. It was a speaker at the September 2000 Forrester U.K. Finance Forum and has services investors in the United Kingdom.

Market Access
DTN Market Access [http://www.dtnmarketaccess.com/] provides a variety of premium market data products including: ProphetX, DTN.IQ, ProphetX on the Net, DTN Real Time, PxBrowser, Fin-Win, BullsEye, and Data Feeds.

The McClatchy Company
The McClatchy Company acquired the much larger Knight Ridder in 2006, also a premium quote vendor.

PC Quote
PC Quote is based in New York, New York, and provides direct access to accurate, timely, and complete financial and business information. It offers a variety of premium products that can be accessed on the Web [http://www.pcquote.com/products/index.php].

Quote.com

Quote.com offers a variety of free and premium content covering stocks, world markets, forex, and futures markets.

Reuters

Reuters features a wide variety of data feeds with expensive services in the thousands of dollars per month that provide quotes for practically all the publicly traded securities in the world.

For investors seeking charting services with either end-of-day or real-time quotations Reuters owns Equis [www.equis.com], which combines either in their popular MetaStock format.

Thomson Financial

Thomson Financial is a rapidly growing financial services company that in 2007 acquired Reuters. There are many divisions to this company but for our purposes we can focus on Reuters and its many services and on a variety of public services [http://www.thomson.com/solutions/financial/].

Online News and Research Companies

Edgar Online

Edgar Online was founded in 1996 and has been public since 1999. It is based in Norwalk, Connecticut, and generates $12.9 million in revenues and in $2.2 million in net loss income. Edgar is a leading provider of value-added business and financial information on global companies to financial, corporate, and advisory professionals.

Factset

Factset is based in Norwalk, Connecticut and has 1,000 employees. It generates $313 million in revenues and $72 million in net income. It offers financial information from more than 200 databases focusing on areas such as broker research data, financial information, and newswires. The firm sells applications for presentations, data warehousing, economic analysis, portfolio analysis, and report writing.

McGraw-Hill

McGraw-Hill's financial services business line operates under the Standard & Poor's brand. It was formed in 1941 and acquired by McGraw-Hill in 1966. It is based in New York, New York.

Its services include widely recognized credit ratings, independent investment information, analytical services, and corporate valuations. It provides the largest network of credit ratings analysts in the world.

Moody's

Moody's is based in New York, New York and is a famous credit rating system developed in 1909 by John Moody. The firm is particularly highly regarded in municipal bond research.

Morningstar

Morningstar was founded in 1984 and is based in Chicago, Illinois. The firm reports that it covers more than 125,000 investment offerings. It has operations in 16 countries and 18 offices worldwide. Morningstar has 1,120 employees, 300 of which are located outside the United States. Morningstar's client list includes 4 million individuals, 140,000 advisors, and 500 institutional clients. It also had $225 million AUIDM in managed retirement accounts, a figure that is set to jump up with its acquisition of Ibbotson Associates.

Morningstar earned its reputation by covering mutual funds primarily, which has been its primary revenue source. It isn't surprising therefore that they are not as positive on the growing ETF market since it cuts into their revenues.

Motley Fool

Motley Fool [Fool.com] is based in Alexandria, Virginia and generates $50 million in revenues. The firm is a broad portal site that aggregates financial content or educational material. It does not offer advice beyond articles and simple single-topic calculations, though some day it could expand to offer personal financial advice to their user base. Motley Fool sends a weekly e-mail called Notes from a Fool, and is led by Co-Chairmen David and Tom Gardner.

Value Line

Value Line was founded in 1931 and is based in New York. The firm has 250 employees and reports 500,000 users of its products. It generates $85 million in revenues and $21 million in net income. Value Line Publishing provides stock and mutual fund information through packaged databases (on more than 170 data items on over 7,000 mutual funds). This product provides asset allocation and hypothetical client scenarios, fund manager bios and pictures, and fund lists for major supermarkets. The firm has four subsidiaries [Value Line Publishing, Value Line Securities, Value Line Distribution Center, and Vanderbilt Advertising].

Online Brokers

This chapter describes the current state of the online brokerage industry, with a particular focus on the emergence of, and consolidation of share by, the Big Five online brokerage firms. Those firms are:

1. Charles Schwab & Company
2. Fidelity Investments
3. TD Ameritrade
4. E*Trade
5. Scottrade

This chapter of the report compares these firms' successes, failures, and corresponding strategies in comparison with one another, the other 45 or so smaller online brokerage firms, and the online offerings of the traditional full-service brokerage channel.

Dominance of the Big-Five Online Brokerage Firms

The core business of the Big Five online brokerage firms is, intuitively, online investing. Over time, these five firms have cleaned up between 75 percent and 90 percent of market share of the entire industry's accounts, assets, trades per day, revenues, and net income. This section of the report discusses in detail that dominance as a broad context of how to view the entire industry.

The number of online brokerage firms has now slipped to the 50 mark, down 30 percent from the peak of 77 in 2002. The number of online brokerage firms began in 1996 with 20 in total, a number that increased to 33 in 1997 and exploded to 52 in 1998. The figure continued to climb fast, reaching 72 firms in 1999 and 76 in 2000. From there, the industry flattened out for a few years (76 in 2000, 75 in 2001, and 77 in 2002). With the stock market's tech bubble bursting, the number of firms then proceeded to drop to 62 firms in 2003, 54 firms in 2004, 52 firms in 2005, and began 2006 at 50 firms.

There are less than 50 online brokerage firms, but this figure still makes for an impressive looking list. A comprehensive list of firms is as follows:

■ AB Watley Direct
■ Accutrade

- America First Trader
- Bank of America
- Interactive Brokers
- InvestIN Securities
- Investrade Discount Securities
- Securities Research
- ShareBuilder
- Sherry Bruce's
- Sloan Securities
- Barry Murphy & Company.
- Cambridge Discount Brokerage
- Charles Schwab & Company
- Cutter & Company
- Cyber Trader
- Downstate Securities Group
- E*Trade
- Fidelity Investments
- Fimat Preferred
- First Discount Brokerage
- First Financial Equity
- FirsTrade Securities
- Freedom Investments
- JH Darbie & Company
- MB Trading
- Mercantile Brokerage Services
- MTDirect
- Muriel Siebert & Company.
- myTrack
- NetVest
- Online Brokerage Services
- optionsXpress
- Regal Discount
- Saturna Brokerage Services
- Scottrade
- Seaport Securities
- StockCross Financial Services
- T Rowe Price
- TD Ameritrade
- Terra Nova Trading
- Think or Swim
- TradeKing
- Trading Direct

- Vanguard Brokerage Services
- Wall Street Electronica
- Wang Investments
- Wells Fargo Investments
- WR Hambrecht + Company
- York Securities

However, to paint the most accurate picture, there are really only the Big Five, and everybody else. The leading five online brokerage firms impressively have a stranglehold on the online brokerage business, across industry accounts, trades, assets, revenues, and net income. For the clearest analysis of the online brokerage industry, one must first take a look at the leading firms' total businesses, and then online retail services only. Total businesses includes all other businesses apart from traditional online retail accounts, which slant the numbers to Charles Schwab & Company and Fidelity Investments significantly. The first has a dominant institutional custody business that represents roughly 30 percent of its assets, whereas the latter was built on its leading mutual fund business, and is also a dominant player in both clearing and 401[k]. Conversely, online retail services only includes online financial services aimed at retail customers, namely online investing, online banking and bill pay, online mortgages, and online insurance.

Online Retail Businesses Analysis

When cutting out all other businesses, such as Fidelity Investments' dominant 401[k] and clearing businesses, the picture of online retail assets and trades comes closer together among the Big Five.

Charles Schwab & Company emerges as the top online brokerage firm when one does not include clearing, custody, or asset management businesses. When one does not include clearing or 401[k] businesses, Charles Schwab & Company and Fidelity Investments' dominant hold on assets is greatly reduced. When cutting out those businesses other than online investing, online banking, and bill pay, online mortgages, and online insurance, Charles Schwab & Company winds up controlling 35 percent of the asset pie. Fidelity Investments controls 30 percent of assets, reduced from 57 percent when one is including their other businesses. The big boosts in share come to TD Ameritrade (15 percent of assets), E*Trade (11 percent), and to a lesser degree Scottrade (3 percent). However, the insignificance of the other firms is still apparent, with their controlling 6 percent of the assets.

Charles Schwab & Company leads in assets when only online retail services are counted. Specifically, it has $582 billion, while Fidelity Investments has $500 billion. TD Ameritrade has $256 billion, E*Trade $187 billion, and Scottrade $44 billion.

The average number of daily trades placed at online brokerage firms has amazingly rebounded back to pre-bubble levels. As was mentioned in the Context Setting chapter of this report, during the Internet boom years of the late 1990s and into 2000, the peak average number of daily trades was 1.20 million per day, reached in the second quarter of 2000. In the first part of 2006, however, that number was actually eclipsed. When one adds up the average number of daily trades of the Big Five, and a conservative estimate for the other 45 firms, there has been an amazing average of 1.27 million trades placed per day this year.

Online brokerage firm trades are less dominated by the Big Five firms, with each of the top firms and all the rest having about equal share. Charles Schwab & Company controls 23 percent of online retail trades, while Fidelity controls only 9 percent when one is cutting out its National Financial and other ancillary businesses. TD Ameritrade controls 22 percent, E*Trade 14 percent, and Scottrade 9 percent. When one is cutting out the other businesses, the other firms now control an estimated 23 percent of trades.

The dominance of the Big Five over the online brokerage industry has certainly not come about by happenstance. These firms tend to spend much more money than their competitors (not only in the online market, but across the financial services industry) on advertising. Impressively, four of the Big Five online brokerage firms are in the top 10 of industry advertisement spending, meaning those firms pay for their dominant position.

Scottrade and Fidelity Investments' highest overall satisfaction scores are nothing new to those firms, while TD Ameritrade's scores have come up fast since 2001. Since being followed in these ratings in 2002, Scottrade amazingly has led the online brokerage industry in satisfaction twice (tied for #1 in 2005 and won outright in 2004), and came in second place in other years (2003 and 2002). Likewise Fidelity Investments has led the overall satisfaction ratings an even more amazing six years since 1999 (tied for #1 in 2005, 2001, and 1999, and won outright in 2003, 2002, and 2000), and placed #2 the other year (2004). Charles Schwab & Company, on the other hand, placed a consistent third place in overall satisfaction for three years (2005, 2003, 2002), placed second once (2000), and won twice (tied for #1 in 2001 and 1999). Of note, TD Ameritrade posted very poor scores in overall satisfaction early but has made consistent progress year after year [scores of 2.4 out of 4.0 in 1999 and 2000, 2.7 in 2001, 2.9 in 2002, 3.1 in 2003, 3.2 in 2004, and 3.3 in 2005].

Traditional Product Offers

Perhaps surprisingly, there is a significant amount of variability in the traditional products offered by online brokerage firms across the industry. Many firms target only niche clients, while others have tried to appeal to everyone by offering a comprehensive product menu. However, when it comes to comparing the Big Five, the variability across the 50 or so firms in the industry disappears, and uniformity ensues.

The traditional products offered by the online brokerage industry include stocks, bonds, mutual funds, options, futures, and cash management accounts. There is a great deal of product variability across the online brokerage industry, but among the Big Five things are rather uniform in these categories.

Obviously, 100 percent of online brokerage firms offer stocks, which has been consistent for many years running. Surprisingly, only half of online brokerage firms now offer online bond trading, which has remained consistent three years running. In 2004, only 52 percent of all online brokerage firms offered the online trading of bonds. And that share has actually fallen the past couple of years, to 51 percent in 2005, and to 48 percent in 2006.

Commissions and Fees

Much like that described in the historical context of this report, there has been an aggressive price war in the online brokerage industry over the past three years. This has affected everyone, from the small players to the Big Five.

Industry Segmentation on Price

Firms continue to be segmented based on price, with expensive online brokerage firms, moderately priced firms, and deep discounters. For this segmentation, deep discounters are those that offer a standard online market order equity trade for $10 or less. Moderately priced firms are those that offer the same trade for between $10 and $30. Finally, expensive firms are those that offer that same online trade for $30 and above [amazingly, there are evidently enough clients out there to keep five such firms in existence today].

The Continuing Price War

While the price war that dominated the online brokerage industry before 1998 has certainly slowed, there is still increasing competition along the lines of price affecting the top firms. Looking across the past 10 years, the average market order commission across the online brokerage industry in

1995 was $40 a trade. That price plummeted quickly the next three years, to $36 in 1996, $33 in 1997, and to a much cheaper $20 in 1998. In 1999 and 2000, the average commission was $18, before jumping back up to $20 in 2001, then back down to $18 in 2002 and 2003. In 2004, the average commission was $19, and in 2005 and 2006, it was $18 again.

Anybody thinking the price war hasn't affected the Big Five firms is sorely misguided, as the standard commission charged across them has dipped 25 percent since 2004. In 2004, an online market or limit order cost clients of the Big Five an average of $19.58 apiece. In 2005 that figure dropped nearly 20 percent, to $15.58. In 2006 it dropped another 5 percent or so, to $14.80 apiece.

Free equity trades have even become a reality again, and they are coming from an unlikely source—the banking channel. Banks by and large had stayed out of the price war until Wells Fargo's move to free trades in 2005. The new strategy seems to be to treat stock trade commissions as loss leader. They intend to attract clients on price, then cross sell them on banking and other products.

Among the Big Five firms, Scottrade offers the lowest flat market order commission to clients at $7, 30 percent lower than its nearest competitor. In second place is TD Ameritrade at $10.99. From there, it goes E*Trade at $12.99, then Charles Schwab & Company and Fidelity Investments at $19.95 each.

TD Ameritrade offers the cheapest options market order commission for a 10 contract order, just a hair cheaper than Scottrade, which would win out on smaller orders. For a 10 contract order, it would cost a TD Ameritrade client $18.49 for the trade. At Scottrade, it would cost $19.50. At Charles Schwab & Company, it would cost $23.95, which beats both E*Trade [$25.49] and Fidelity Investments [$27.45].

Scottrade offers the cheapest online purchases of no-load funds not in a no-transaction fee program, with Fidelity Investments using high prices to shoo clients into their home funds. Specifically, Scottrade charges clients $17.00, TD Ameritrade charges $17.99, E*Trade charges $19.99, and Charles Schwab & Company charges $35. Finally, for funds not in its Fidelity mutual funds loaded no-transaction fee program, Fidelity Investments charges $75.

The Blurring of the Line Between Online and Full-Service Brokerage Firms

In the past, there was a clear dividing line between what was offered by online and full-service brokerage firms, forcing investors to make a fundamental choice on what range of service they desired.

In the future, there will be a blurring of that line as online firms add capabilities to make them look more and more like their full-service competitors. As a matter of fact the online brokers, discounters, and full-service firms are beginning to aim for the same clientele. The ideal client for all three of these groups today is the older investor with more than $1 million in investable assets. While today the full-service brokers are the closest to these clients, the discounters and the online brokers are moving aggressively up-stream trying to reach these investors, and they are experiencing some success.

Both Charles Schwab & Company and E*Trade have been proactively reaching out to clients with $250,000 in assets or more. Charles Schwab & Company sent a letter and made follow-up calls with clients more than $250,000, saying they had been assigned a personal financial consultant to meet with in branch and review portfolio. Further, it cleverly advertised to "hundred thousandollaraires" in its Talk to Chuck ad campaign, promising value to higher net worth prospects.

Charles Schwab & Company has gone as far as to declare itself a new breed of full-service firm in the past. Former CEO Dave Pottruck once declared, "We are not a discount firm anymore.... Our mission now is to create a new model of full-service brokerage firm, and I mean a new kind of full-service firm—not the kind that sells its own load funds and gives free trips to Hawaii."

IMPORTANT TOOLS I LIKE

Some of the tracking resources that I use almost every day are as follows:

- *Yahoo/Finance* [http://finance.yahoo.com/]: May be the single most important service that allows users to monitor a portfolio from most performance aspects through the use of an Excel-like spreadsheet. It's very user friendly.
- *Google* [http://finance.google.com/finance?tab=we]: A new entrant to compete with Yahoo!, Google's services are growing rapidly and given their creative bent the quality of their offerings may eventually equal or exceed their competitor's.
- *StockCharts* [http://stockcharts.com/]: Offers charting and delayed quote services [featured frequently throughout this book] much of it free. More detailed services cost approximately $100 per year.
- *Big Charts* [http://bigcharts.marketwatch.com/default.asp?siteid=& avatar=seen&dist=ctbc]: Is a service of MarketWatch.com, which is a part of Dow Jones. Like *StockCharts* they provide charting tools of good quality and also offer a premium service.

- *MetaStock* [http://www.equis.com/] *and* Super Charts [http://www
.tradestation.com/strategy_testing/charting.shtm]: Are premium charting services that offer more comprehensive and customized services
at higher fees than either Big Charts or StockCharts. We're users of
MetaStock currently.
- *eSignal* [http://www.esignal.com/], Reuters [http://about.reuters.com/
productinfo/salesandtrading/?seg=26], *Bloomberg* [http://www.bloom
berg.com/index.html?Intro=intro3], and Quote.com [http://new.quote
.com/]: Are either providers of end-of-day or real-time quote data.
We use Reuters end-of-day since it's economical and we're not day
trading.

MARKET INFORMATION RESOURCES

I'm not going to list all the obvious information vendors from the *Wall Street
Journal*, *Barrons*, *Investors Business Daily* and all the other publications
you're already familiar with. What follows are Internet web sites and blogs
that I frequent almost daily.

ETF Resources
- *Index Universe* [http://www.indexuniverse.com/]: Is published by Jim
Wiandt and its premium service is inexpensive at roughly $25 per
year. We interchange information and interviews frequently. Their ETF
reporter Matt Hougan is first-rate.
- *ETF Connect* [http://www.etfconnect.com/]: Is a free service of Thomson Financial and provides users with profiles of ETFs and closed-end
funds. My only gripe with them is that they can't seem to differenti-
ate between closed-end funds and ETFs. Users should be cautious to
understand what each security they're viewing really is.
- *Morningstar* [http://www.morningstar.com/]: Their primary mission
has been mutual funds. Since our theme is a "convergence story"
between mutual funds, ETFs, and hedge funds they currently cover some
mutual funds structured as long/short, market neutral funds. They're
quite negative about ETFs, however, since I believe their core business
strength and revenues come from the previously popular mutual fund
sector. It's a bit of sour grapes on their part, in my opinion.
- *Seeking Alpha* [http://usmarket.seekingalpha.com/article/35801]: Is a
rapidly growing blog aggregator where commentators get to showcase
their opinions. A recent coup for them is their linkage to Yahoo!/Finance,
which has given them very broad exposure. Our web site and daily
commentaries are posted there.

- *Barclay's* [www.ishares.com]: They remain the leading issuer of ETFs and no doubt will not give up that lead.
- *State Street Global Advisors* [https://www.ssgafunds.com/]: Also is a large provider/sponsor of ETFs having created the famous SPDR products.
- *PowerShares* [www.powershares.com]: Is a relatively new company that despite its newbie status has been perhaps the most prolific ETF issuer over the past few years. In 2006 the company was purchased by mutual fund titan AMVESCAP, which also operated AIM Funds. Their claim to fame is their Intellidex Indexes, which modify conventional indexes by quantitative methods. In plain English—they're more actively managed indexes.
- *DB Commodity Services* [http://www.dbfunds.db.com/]: A part of Deutsche Bank this division has created highly useful commodity-based ETFs, which are managed by them but marketed by PowerShares. As mentioned in earlier chapters these ETFs have truly completed the menu for hedge fund portfolio construction. Further, as with ETFs the world of commodity investing is now available to retail and institutional investors alike in a highly liquid and unleveraged manner.

    Important note. A free podcast interview with product investment manager Kevin Rich is available on our public homepage [www.etfdigest .com] *which explains more about these products.*
- *Rydex* [www.rydexinvestments.com]: Offers both mutual funds and ETF issues focused on currencies, equal weight sectors of the S&P 500 Index, and, as soon as the SEC has completed their review, will have dozens of inverse and leveraged issues.
- *ProShares* [www.proshares.com]: ProShares is a subsidiary of mutual funds sponsor Profunds. It often seems that Rydex and Profunds/Pro-Shares are joined at the hip in product offerings. Both are located in Maryland. We're grateful for their offerings since they fill a real need for either adding leverage or allowing investors to hedge/speculate with their inverse issues. *Important note: Free podcast interviews are available on our public homepage* [www.etfdigest.com] *with both Rydex and ProShares executives.*
- *First Trust Securities* [http://www.ftportfolios.com/Retail/etf/etflist .aspx]: Is a relative newcomer in issuing new ETF issues. Of the dozens of issues they've brought to market, we've used only one: *FDN* [DJ Internet Index ETF]. They're becoming very active in the market but their issues have yet to catch on.
- *Claymore Securities* [http://www.claymore.com/etf/public/etf/etfhome .aspx]: There must be something in the water in the suburbs of western Chicago since Claymore, First Trust, and PowerShares are all within a

stone's throw of each other. Their style of ETF issues seems similar in many ways. We're not using any of their issues at this time.

General Market Information

- *MarketWatch.com* [http://www.marketwatch.com/]: Is a part of Dow Jones and has good information despite a bullish bent for the most part. Just remember who their advertisers are and you'll better understand their focus. We have been past commentary contributors.
- *The Street.com* [http://www.thestreet.com/]: Jim Cramer—say no more.
- *Briefing.com* [http://www.briefing.com/]: Provides some commentaries as well as being a good source for earnings and economic data.
- *CNN* [http://money.cnn.com/]: While they've given up on their business TV channel, their business web site is still active and contains useful stories.
- *Bloomberg*: Beyond just a quote vendor and TV channel, Bloomberg has upgraded its web site with many interesting stories and features.
- *CNBC* [http://moneycentral.msn.com/investor/home.asp]: Always bullish with an occasional bearish guest that hosts use as a piñata to bang away at any bearish sentiment. Again, remember their sponsorship comes mainly from companies with financial services to sell.
- *Emerging Markets Monitor [London]*, [http://www.emergingmarkets monitor.com/]: A part of Business Monitor, this publication is expensive for most retail investors. They publish research on the state of emerging markets and cover the world in that regard.

   Important note: Free podcast interviews with Emerging Markets Monitor executives are available on our public homepage [www.etf digest.com].

Hedge Fund Resources

- *Hedge Fund Alert* [www.hfalert.com]: Is an expensive resource [$2,297 per year for weekly newsletter] for individuals but may possess the best industry news.
- *HedgeWorld* [www.hedgeworld.com]: Is a part of Reuter's Lipper subsidiary and provides research on more than 4,000 hedge funds. It publishes limited free basic information and some of its more detailed publications are nearly $700 per year.
- *HedgeFund.net* [www.hedgefund.net]: Also publishes research and performance data for a variety of hedge funds with different levels of services from $195 per year on up. Hosting conferences is another chief revenue source for organizations like this.

- *HedgeCo.net* [www.hedgeco.net]: Unlike other similar sites HedgeCo .net offers a lot of free information [registration required] and sponsors many seminars and conferences.
- *MARHedge/Institutional Investor* [http://marhedge.com/about.asp]: Was the leading provider of hedge fund research and information before being purchased by Institutional Investor. Now it seems they're focusing on conferences but have a free daily e-mail [registration required] that contains some information as well as promotional material.
- *Naked Shorts* [http://nakedshorts.typepad.com/]: Colleague Greg Newton, formerly president of MARHedge, writes a colorful and humorous blog regarding issues affecting the hedge fund community. I never let a day pass without reading it.

CONCLUSION

The Internet remains the best tool for finding the resources and tools you need to organize your ETF hedge fund. Whether it's discovering more about strategies, analyzing investment advice from newsletters and blogs, finding tools to monitor your portfolio, and so forth everything currently exists that you can use.

If you want more control over your financial portfolio, you'll have to make some effort to do so. But the help you need is there.

CHAPTER 14

Eight Steps to Building Your ETF Hedge Fund

Now that we've covered current trends in the industry, the booming ETF industry, hedge funds and hedge fund strategies, and the tools you'll need to get started, let's outline the simple steps to put your own hedge fund together.

STEP 1: DEFINE YOURSELF

- Goals and objectives will require you to complete a typical investment questionnaire similar to those we outlined in Chapter 11.
- Determine your investment style. Are you a trader? Or do you only think of yourself as one? If you're a long-term investor, what does that really mean to you? Is long-term a month? A year? Many years?
- What is your emotional investment IQ? Can you manage your emotions when investing or do you easily get rattled? Some like to say, invest only to the risk level you can sleep to.

STEP 2: DEVELOP YOUR HEDGE FUND STRATEGY

- We've outlined all the popular hedge fund strategies including even the more eclectic.
- From my perspective what most individual investors want is a Global Macro Long/Short strategy. But this is just a fancy term for a "performance-based" strategy. As a contemporary twenty-first century investor you must "think and invest globally."
- A performance hedge fund inevitably involves some degree of market timing.

- A performance hedge fund usually involves a willingness to short. And as we've outlined shorting index-based ETFs possesses from a practical viewpoint, the same low risks on the short side as long.
- Review the portfolios outlined in Chapter 10 and use them as a starting point in assembling your own hedge fund strategy.

STEP 3: USE ETFS AS THE PRIMARY TOOL

- Since I publish an all-ETF focused newsletter, clearly I'm biased toward these as the best hedge fund tool for individual investors.
- Clearly wide-ranging ETF product development [commodities, currencies, and inverse issues among others] have made it possible to construct portfolios that mimic desirable hedge fund strategies.
- While ETF issuance will continue to flood markets, most of the ETFs needed are already issued and available. Investors can ignore the vast majority of new ETFs issued going forward.
- To stay abreast of valuable issues you'll need to subscribe to and/or search publications that can help you identify suitable products.

STEP 4: USING MUTUAL FUNDS AS AN ALTERNATIVE VEHICLE

- For many investors there now exist mutual funds employing some of the strategies we've outlined. These will grow only in number and style. Many investors will prefer using those in lieu of either subscribing to advisory newsletters and going through the effort of implementing the transactions necessary. For those investors perhaps the mutual fund format will prove more satisfying.
- I've had many subscribers just say, "Dave, why don't you just start a mutual fund so we can invest in it without having to do all this work?" Well, that's easier said than done. Starting a mutual fund is a very costly and time-consuming enterprise. Further its people intensive and requires a vast marketing structure.
- There are mutual funds that are currently available, mostly following a market neutral strategy. Some have done quite well.
- There will be mutual funds issued that follow the global macro long/short strategy using ETFs and/or conventional securities. It's just a question of time before they start flooding the market.
- Will they be any good? Maybe. Just remember the best talent for hedge fund performance will stick with the existing hedge fund structure since it remains the most lucrative for them.

STEP 5: GET HELP, EVEN IF YOU'RE A DIY

Validators

From the same previously cited April 28, 2006 Tiburon Strategic Advisors report from Chapter 13 is the following important gem:

> ### Rise of Validators
>
> *The parallel rising of online financial services activity and continued demand for access to branches and advice will result in a swelling population of vali}dators. Traditionally, investors can be categorized somewhere between being self-directors, and delegators. Validators stand right in between those two polar opposites, wanting to have involvement in their affairs, but admittedly needing help with their affairs. This continuing movement is exceptional news for the online financial services business, which has increasingly armed its traditionally do it yourself investors with both branches and advice, and will continue to do so.*
>
> *Half of the high net worth investor market is validators, up 10% since 1999 to half. This share will likely continue to grow, to as high as 60% by the end of the decade.*
>
> *The ranks of validators will be coming from those that waffle on the economy; in 2000, when the market was strong, as many as 20% of high net worth investors were self-directors. As the markets receded, more and more investors realized that they needed the help of financial advisors and other advice channels.*
>
> *Younger investors are even more likely to be validators; nearly two-thirds of generation x investors consider themselves as such.*
>
> *Many consumers interviewed by Tiburon in a telephone survey consider themselves validators. These consumers interviewed report taking a more active role in their investments:*
>
> *"For most of my investing years, I was a delegator, but more recently, I got more involved with the process ... I don't go gung ho over my investments, but I enjoy being a bit more proactive."*
>
> *"I want to be involved in the process of investing my money, but I realize I can't go it alone."*
>
> *"I can't imagine turning my money over to someone and allowing them to make all the decisions without my involvement."*
>
> *Future movement in the investment market will continue to swell the ranks of the validators segment.*
>
> *Based on recent efforts, online brokers have made serious progress in attracting validators, who now make up nearly half*

of their clients. Specifically, it is estimated that 43% of online brokerage clients are considered validators, with the other 57% self-directors.

Future movement in the investment market will continue to swell the ranks of the validators segment. To take advantage of the validator movement, having multi-channel offers with a strong branch network and offering advice will prove critical to capturing consumers' wallet share.

Importance of Multi-Channel Offers

There are several non-financial services industries that have succeeded using a multi-channel approach. Some examples include retail stores (Wal Mart, Barnes & Noble), personal computer providers (Gateway, Apple), automobile companies (Ford, Chevrolet, Honda, Volkswagen, Porsche, et al), and airlines (American Airlines, United Airlines, Jet Blue, Southwest, et al). In each of these examples, the company offered its prospective clients both an opportunity to do business over the web, or step into a branch to do it there.

Many may wish to avoid the headaches of the innumerable semantics & hype phrases surrounding the idea of providing a product or service across a number of different channels. Some catch phrases regarding the idea of providing several channels include Bricks & Clicks, Multiple Channels, Multi-Channel, and Clicks & Mortar.

However, hype & semantics aside, industry participants must draw a hard line between multi-channel, and multiple channel offers—both of which exist, and one of which is a business disaster waiting to happen. There are some fundamental differences to use in describing each. A multi-channel offer is characterized by highly integrated data across channels, client transition between the channels being seamless, and the long term cost of maintenance being relatively low. A multi-channel offer is designed with efficiency in mind, and is a highly profitable strategy. Without proper planning, other firms may wind up with multiple channels, but this can be poor for business. A multiple channel offer can be characterized as disparate data between channels, a painful transition process for clients to use one channel and then another, and a relatively high cost of maintenance.

Firms must define the core role each channel will play in the client experience to avoid the 3E trap—trying to provide everything to everyone everywhere. This leads only to overinvesting.

Half of customers—and typically the highest valued customers at that—use multiple channels for shopping and purchasing, a good watermark for the financial services industry as well.

Further, multi-channel customers in the banking industry are between 25% and 50% more profitable than single channel customers. This is explainable to the facts that they buy more products & services than traditional one-channel customers, and their use of internet & telephone channels keeps costs lower.

Delivering clients an optimal multi-channel experience provides them improved convenience in three ways, including faster access to information, the avoidance of salespeople, and a richer service experience. First, web & telephone channels provide clients quick & easy updates on information. Second, the web channel allows for clients to research products without pressure from salespeople. Third, clients with multiple channels in which to do business benefit from the overall richer service experience.

A robust multi-channel offer can be graded on the substitutability of channels, and frequency of client contact; banking & investing multi-channel offers must provide both. Specifically, both the banking & investing channels must offer high customer substitutability, with clients able to access the same data and information from every channel. Further, each requires capabilities to handle frequent client contact, due to the often day to day transaction nature of both businesses.

Investment Newsletters as Validators

From the excellent research provided by Tiburon you can see the need for a "validator" bridge even for most DIY investors. If you think we're going to recommend alternative premium investment newsletters to what we publish, you would be mistaken. Since we don't subscribe to other newsletters we're not in a position to recommend them. Some you can find by reputation while others can be found via a typical Internet search.

While it's common to think that investment newsletters are primarily directed to individual DIY investors, many FAs [Financial Advisors] use them as well to assist them with managing their clients' affairs. Many of our subscribers are FAs.

The most important thing to remember about investment newsletters is that they're just a tool or guide. They are best used along with other input that may be personal and unique to you. You may, in fact, subscribe to a number of newsletters that may be complementary. For example, you may wish to follow one that focuses exclusively on fundamental market analysis while combining with another that provides a technical approach. It's good to have a diverse source of information and guidance. No newsletter should turn you into an automaton.

STEP 6: IF YOU WANT TO USE A FINANCIAL ADVISOR, FIND THE RIGHT ONE

- All investors should check with the NASD to discover if their FA is a registered representative/broker or has a history of complaints that might prove unacceptable to you. [http://brokercheck.nasd.com/Search/Search.aspx?PageID=1]
- Look for a broker who is stable and employed with a firm for a long period. Many FAs jump around as they get better commission structures or some upfront money. If a registered representative has made a recent move they may be conflicted by a high initial commission structure where payouts to them cause them to push certain products.
- An FA with a few gray hairs wouldn't hurt, either.
- Find an FA that has some independent views apart from his firm without being too reckless. After all, an FA's firm is just one source of information and not always the best. Is the FA going to just push firm product? Is that acceptable to you?
- As an investor you may wish to use an FA that can arrange to find you outside advisors in SMAs [Separately Managed Accounts] or in the hot new area of Unified Accounts. Assembling a variety of registered investment advisors with different styles may allow investors with substantial assets [perhaps over $1 million] to construct hedge fund portfolios in that manner. But beware; always try to have multiple managers whose style is uncorrelated one from another. This will reduce risk in the long run.
- A message to FAs is to stay current with ever-changing industry trends. Sometimes you get satisfied and even smug with your position in the industry much like I was in the late 1980s. When you need to change course you may find it like trying to power-turn the Titanic. The only way to avoid this is to stay flexible and humble.

STEP 7: DIYS NEED AN ONLINE BROKER

The Big Five online firms remain:

- Charles Schwab & Company
- Fidelity Investments

- T.D. Ameritrade
- E*Trade
- Scottrade

These firms may consolidate further. In fact, other than transaction commissions, many online firms are starting to mirror the major wire-house firms in terms of their business models to include advice and validator services.

New entrants to the field where price is an issue include:

- Zecco.com—a new firm offering zero commissions.
- Bank of America—also offering zero commissions.
- Wells Fargo—offering zero commissions with high minimum account balances.

There are dozens more including some you've never heard of. Does that make them unsuitable? Certainly not. It depends on the services you're looking for. Some are new up and coming firms with a lot of excellent services. If price and execution are singularly important to you, then you should make your choice on that basis. You can use other sources to cobble together services you might need. Most investors view the whole picture and see if the firm they're choosing satisfies their needs.

STEP 8: FIND THE SUPPORT TOOLS YOU NEED

- Review and use the tools outlined in Chapter 13, which include: quote vendors, research organizations, and thorough listing of online brokers.
- To repeat, I use a simple a Yahoo!/Finance spreadsheet to monitor my own portfolio. [http://edit.finance.yahoo.com/e61?.done=pf&.intl=us &.exchange=us&.list_portf=1&.create=1&.src=quote&.sym=].
- Some online brokerage firms now offer many of their own support tools.

CONCLUSION

Let's return to my friend's situation featured so prominently in Chapter One, "Hobson's Choice." Here was a person who wanted assistance with her investments but also more control. But she was stymied by her captive investment situation and the reality of how her FA/validator had refused to make any adjustments owing to both arrogance and costs. This is an FA who will not make it as a validator and may require a "terminator."

Structuring your own hedge fund using ETFs has never been easier and the longer you wait to do so the further you'll be left behind. The convergence story mixing hedge fund strategies with ETF tools is now a reality. Mutual funds will need to compete and no doubt will be offering more hedge fundlike product with many employing the use of ETFs as vehicles.

Is "the bloom off the rose" for hedge funds in 2007? Given trading losses stemming from real estate and mortgage issues, not to mention fraud, concerned investors started pulling money out for the first time in seven years. On the other hand, it always seems that investors have short memories and in no time will be chasing performance once again. They'll find that in a variety of seductive hedge fund strategies.

For us, we just want to keep things simple using the most straightforward strategy combined with the most effective ETF issues.

Finally, remember that the choices and industry conditions are rapidly evolving. Many new products will be introduced sooner rather than later making for more choices and requiring even greater scrutiny by investors.